D1567810

# Romance Reader's Handbook

Romantic Times Inc.
Brooklyn Heights, New York

# ROMANCE READER'S HANDBOOK

*Dedicated to all the women
who have read romantic
novels and found friends,
adventures, and
escape therein.*

*Special thanks to Kay Garteiser,
co-compiler of* The Romantic Spirit, *
for her expert eye and assistance
with the pseudonyms.*

## *Romantic Times Books*

**163 Joralemon St., Brooklyn Heights, NY 11201
718/237-1097**

*An original Romantic Times Books edition,
published for the first time anywhere.*

**First printing, JUNE 1989**

ISBN: 0-940338-25-4
Printed by Atelier Unlimited, New York, N.Y.

# *The Compilers*

*Kathryn Falk ❤ Melinda Helfer ❤ Kathe Robin*

*Dear Romance Reader,*

*We hope you enjoy this handbook.
It was truly a labor of love. We
plan to update it every three years
and find more good reads to add to
your passion for books.
Write anytime—we'd love to hear
from you.*

**Kathryn Falk,** %RT
163 Joralemon St.
Brooklyn Heights
NY 11201

**Melinda Helfer**
P.O. Box 1428
Lewisville
TX 75067-1428

**Kathe Robin**
P.O. Box 289
Denville
NJ 07834

# *Contents*

*Sherryl Woods*

## *PSEUDONYMS*

*JoAnn Algermissen*

## *RECOMMENDED READS*

*Jan McGowan*

*Irene Saunders*

*Glenda Sands*

# BOOKSTORES THAT CARE

# CORRESPONDING WITH AUTHORS

# SOURCE SECTION

*Linda Barlow*

*Patricia Rosemoor*

*Julia Fitzgerald*

*Jeanne Montague*

*Sydney Clary*

OVER 2 MILLION COPIES IN PRINT!

"A BIG HISTORICAL EPIC...
LEAVES THE READER LIMP...
A FIERY AND RESILIENT
HERO AND HEROINE"
Publishers Weekly

AVON
38869
$2.25

# SWEET SAVAGE LOVE

## ROSEMARY ROGERS

A TEMPESTUOUS ROMANCE
ABLAZE WITH THE FIRES OF
LOVE AND ADVENTURE!

HISTORICAL ROMANCE
POOL1
45474-9
$3.95

Their wildfire passion blazed
across the years... and
the proud Texas land
they loved

## LINDA SHAW
# Songbird

By the author of
Ballad in Blue

Silhouette Desire

437

## LASS SMALL
### Goldilocks
### and the Behr

J
JOVE BOOK

# BARBARA CARTLAND

## FOR ALL ETERNITY

# Hello, Booklovers!

*R*omantic fiction has a long and rich history in America. Most women who read historical romances today grew up reading Nancy Drew mysteries, *Gone With the Wind, Forever Amber, Katherine*, and that all-time great escape, *Angelique*. These novels were more than books. They were adventures into another, more exciting world through the magic of the imagination.

In the 1970s, when Avon editor Nancy Coffey discovered authors **Kathleen Woodiwiss** and **Rosemary Rogers,** she "opened the bedroom door" for readers and started the historical romance genre that we know today. *The Flame and the Flower* (1972) and *Sweet Savage Love* (1974) turned millions of women into passionate, dedicated readers.

Soon other novelists with now familiar names began writing similar types of historical romance: **Jennifer Wilde, Bertrice Small, Johanna Lindsey, Jude Deveraux, Laurie McBain, Patricia Matthews, Rebecca Brandewyne, Dorothy Garlock, Sylvie Sommerfield, Karen Robards, Karen Harper,** and more....

The most vivid personality on the scene in these years was **Barbara Cartland** in her flamboyant pink outfits and exotic hats, quipping quotable quotes, and turning the eye of the media upon the romance genre. Although she had been published in England since the 1920s, her popularity exploded in the United States in the 1960s and 70s, and she was soon writing one or more books a month, appearing on every bestseller list, and creating a large and loyal following.

In England, during this exciting time of romance literature, an entirely different kind of romantic fiction phenomenon was being produced. English women writers for Mills & Boon, a London hardcover publisher, were creating a sensation with their sweet contemporary romances, reprinted in paperback and distributed in America and overseas by a Canadian company called Harlequin.

Few authors in the world had a following comparable to **Charlotte**

Lamb, **Anne Hampson, Violet Winspear, Roberta Leigh, Mary Burchell,** or **Penny Jordan.**

In 1976, a young American writer, **Janet Dailey,** joined this hallowed company of English writers and established her reputation by writing a romance set in every state in America.

The American publisher Simon & Schuster recognized Harlequin's success and created a similar type of short contemporary books in the early 80s called Silhouette Romances.

They selected an electrifying new group of writers to launch unique plots and romances reflective of modern American readers. Their stable of stars through the years included **Stephanie James, Diana Palmer, Nora Roberts, Dixie Browning, Linda Howard, Linda Shaw, Lindsay McKenna, Sherryl Woods, Terri Herrington, Sara Chance, Kathleen Korbel,** and **Lass Small,**

Other American publishers developed new lines—Berkley's Second Chance at Love and Bantam's Loveswept—and discovered yet more unusual contemporary romance novelists for the genre. Arriving on the scene with their special brand of romance were **Jayne Castle, Amii Lorin, Heather Graham, Alice Morgan, Iris Johansen, Sara Orwig, Kay Hooper** and **Billie Green.**

The period of rapid expansion came to an end when too many romances had flooded the market by the mid '80s. Harlequin bought Silhouette Romances and the two publishing houses now exist quite amicably, with offices in New York and Canada. Between them, they publish nearly 60 contemporary romances a month, and several historicals and Regencies. In 1989, Harlequin celebrated their 40th anniversary.

In June 1981, at the beginning of this blossoming of romantic fiction, *Romantic Times* arrived in the bookstores.

Created by **Kathryn Falk,** an avid historical romance reader, the magazine immediately filled a need for a publication to cover the genre. Although millions of romances were being read, there was no publication that reviewed and rated romance novels, profiled the authors, or offered how-to-write information.

*RT's* first base of operations was a walk-in closet in a carriage house, and the first issue was a 24-page tabloid newspaper designed by Barbara Hackney, who still acts as *RT's* art director.

It was an immediate hit with readers. Within a few months, stacks of letters arrived from women who wanted to join the staff. Two readers' letters stood out from the others, as the story goes— **Kathe Robin,** former bookseller and school teacher from New Jersey, and **Melinda Helfer,** a computer expert, residing in Texas.

These women, while raising their families, went on to become authorities of their respective categories and their cover quotes are now seen every month on paperback titles. Each reviews approximately

25-40 books a month and can remembers most of the titles and authors' names—a feat in itself.

The early 1980s was also the golden period of American romantic fiction in the minds of the media. Reporters became enamored of the hundreds of newly published novelists and the thousands more who wanted to become one. Articles about "women turning their fantasies to fiction" appeared in publications as diverse as *New York Magazine, Playgirl, The New York Times, The Wall Street Journal, Life, Self, Newsweek,* and *People.*

When *Romantic Times* sponsored an Amtrak Love Train and brought readers and writers across the country to New York to the 2nd Booklovers Convention in 1983, it garnered even more extraordinary publicity for the genre. Nearly every national and local news program covered the event.

As a result, **George Csicsey**, who brought a documentary camera crew on board the Love Train, produced "Where The Heart Roams" which became an award-winning film and is still shown on PBS.

Kathryn Falk also wrote two nonfiction books during this period, *Love's Leading Ladies,* (1982) and *How To Write a Romance and Get It Published* (1983), which became widely read reference books for both readers and aspiring romance writers. The first update of the paperback version of the *How To Write* book (from NAL) was scheduled in January, 1990.

Statistics concerning romance readers were astounding then, and now, and they haven't radically changed.

Publishers bring out approximately 100-120 romantic novels each month, with print runs from 50,000 to 700,000 per book, which accounts for 25% of paperback sales.

The average reader is a cross between a devoteé and a fanatic. She reads 12 to 30 books a month, or more, and treats reading as a passionate hobby.

Now that bookmarks are in vogue, many readers match them with the books to further enhance their enjoyment, or collect them like trading cards or stamps.

The typical readers usually have large areas to hold their books. The designs range from a spare bedroom with floor to ceiling shelving, to elaborate set-ups in garages and attics created by considerate husbands. Most avid fans keep voluminous cross-indexed notebooks in which they rate their books and indicate which have been bought but not read, or read and not liked.

The avid reader always makes regular visits to her local bookstore as part of her weekly routine. The friendly bookstore owners encourge readers to sit awhile and "chat," treating readers with TLC.

Often coffee or other beverages are available, and part of the discussion centers around the forthcoming new books and new covers that have arrived in promotional packets or in the latest shipment of *Romantic Times*. Such a store is known far and wide as part of the Bookstores That Care network.

Each year on the first Saturday of November, the BTC stores make elaborate plans to celebrate **BOOKLOVERS DAY.** There are speakers to talk about the hobby and local authors to explain how they write their romances as well as furnish tips to aspiring writers.

An interesting spin-off of the romance genre is the great number of readers who have turned their hobby into a business by opening specialized new and used bookstores. Although they sell a large volume of used paperbacks, they also have considerable sales in new paperbacks because their customers plan their future "buys" from the reviews and publishers' previews in *Romantic Times*.

This Handbook is the first in a series of readers guides that *Romantic Times* will be publishing. In 1990, the second handbook, THE STORY CONTINUES, will contain a comprehensive listing of series, sequels and trilogies through the years.

The ROMANCE READER'S HANDBOOK was a labor of love. We hope you find it helpful for your reading hobby. Enjoy!❤

# *Love from the*
# *Brooklyn Booklovers!*

## The Staff of Romantic Times...

KATHRYN FALK, **publisher**       CAROL STACY, **production**

MELINDA HELFER, **reviewer**       KATHE ROBIN, **reviewer**

JERRY JOHNSON, **store sales**       SUSAN PERRY, **proof reader**

BARBARA HACKNEY, **cover design**

# The Story Behind Pseudonyms

### by Kathryn Falk

Why do so many romance authors use pseudonyms, you ask? It's so confusing, you sigh? Well, the answers are as varied as the books the authors write. In fact, *variety* is one of the reasons.

Some writers are so prolific that years ago they preferred a name for each genre in which they wrote. The most famous example is bestselling **Victoria Holt**, one of the many pen names of Eleanor Hibbert.

While Victoria Holt is her romantic suspense/Gothic name, **Jean Plaidy** is on the titles of her historical biographies—the Norman trilogy, Plantagenet saga, Tudor novel, Stuart saga, and Georgian saga to name a few. She went on to choose the name **Philippa Carr** for her historical romantic mysteries.

Born in 1901, Mrs. Hibbert, an English writer, is still going strong, writing under all three names with her usual energy.

Sometimes a pseudonym results for euphonious reasons— the pure *sound* (and look) of a name on a book. Many romance writers choose a romantic name on their covers out of choice or command.

For a romantic tone, Rhoda Cohen prefers to use **Eleanora Brownleigh** for her Edwardian novels, while Donna Meyer came up with **Megan Daniel** for her Regencies.

Karen Witmer-Gow created the name **Elizabeth Kary** for her famous Civil War historicals, while Sylvia Baumgartner opted for **Louisa Rawlings.**

Many romance editors have had a say about names. Recently, Dee Hendrickson's editor told her that **Emily Hendrickson** was more becoming a Regency novel, so Dee now also answers to Emmy on occasion!

As you may know, men's names are sometimes disguised behind pseudonyms. **Jennifer Wilde** certainly inspires more visions of historical frolic and romance than Tom Huff. Ditto for **Vanessa Royale**, a.k.a. Mike Hinkemeyer, and **Leigh Nichols,** a.k.a. Dean Koontz. Certainly **Marie de Jourlet**, author of the Windhaven series, is more exotic a *nom-de-plume* than Paul Little!

Paul Little, a.k.a. Paula Minton, Marie de Jourlet, and a string of other names, was one of the most prolific writers in America. He died a few years ago, but his many, many names and over 600 titles live on.

Often pseudonyms are used for writing teams. Some of the memorable ones are **Sergeanne Golon, Judith Michael, Fern Michaels, Laura London,** and **Lynda Trent.**

Occasionally a prolific author can write more books than her publisher wishes to print. (The result is that some wholesalers object to seeing more than two books a year from the same author.) Therefore, many prolific writers, such as **Carol Finch, Rosanne Bittner,** and **Karen Harper,** may take another name because they love to write more books than their publisher is willing to publish.

Now that the romance publishers have thinned their ranks and a variety of authors have reached different plateaus financially, there's a reevaluation of the pseudonym situation and a concentrated effort to use an author's legal name.

After all, the amount of effort and nurturing it takes to make an author's name recognizable in the highly competitive field of paperbacks is difficult enough without having to do it two or three times!

But in the meantime, there are thousands of authors, and some do and some don't use pseudonyms.

Since 1981, when *Romantic Times* was first published, we have always brought our readers the latest information on who's who in romantic fiction.

Thanks to Melinda Helfer, we have printed hundreds of her excellent cross-references of pseudonyms, in alphabetical order, for over six years in her column. But by 1989 we were only up to P! And what about all the new names that had come along in the meantime? Thus this Handbook was born!

In many cases, as you will see, **it is not possible to know the legal name** of an author. Some have passed on, and many more could not be reached by mail for verification. Although this part of the listing is incomplete, at least in some instances you will know *not* to look for a book under an author's real name.

If you come upon two italicized names, it refers to the author's maiden name and later, to her married name. At one time or another, both names were legal for her!

We have also included a special page called *NOTES* at the end of each section for when you find new additions.

Like new books and new authors, there will always be many new pseudonyms for one reason or another.

The ROMANCE READER'S HANDBOOK will be updated every three years, if we all live so long! ❤

# The Pseudonym Sleuth

by Melinda Helfer

*It was a dark and stormy night. As the wind whipped through the leaves of the nearby trees, a momentary light gleamed furtively through the curtain-draped windows. A shadowy figure could be seen hunched over the big desk, rapidly turning the pages of a small, dusty book.*

*"Ah!" The cry rang out triumphantly as the mysterious intruder closed the volume with a snap. "It's true! Stephanie James IS Jayne Castle!"*

*Then, after a fiendish chuckle echoed eerily against the walls, the light was snuffed out and a door closed softly. As the storm continued to batter at the windows, all was silent within.*

*The Pseudonym Sleuth had struck again!*

You may laugh, but in my years of collecting pseudonyms, I have often felt like a cross between Sherlock Holmes and Harry Black. In my quest to discover the true identity behind the name on a book, I have roamed the dusty stacks of numerous libraries, poured over what seems like a million copyrights, wheedled names out of sympathetic editors and attacked every author within reach. Sherlock Holmes could not pay more attention to the smallest detail, and Harry Black could know no greater thrill than when I finally "bag" an author's pseudonym.

How did this all get started, you ask? Through frustration primarily. Taking a sabatical from my career as a computer programmer to be at home with my then two small sons, I often found myself with nothing to read. This was truly a fate worse than death for a voracious reader.

Like most such fanatics, I chose most of my reading material by author, although I was always on the lookout for new and interesting things. In my naiveté, it never occurred to me that someone might write with more than one name, and I often bemoaned the lack of a new book from one of my favorite authors.

Imagine my outrage, if you will, when I accidentally discovered that **Barbara Michaels** and **Elizabeth Peters** were one and the same person! How could the publishers have dared to hide such a critically important fact! How many books might I have missed because of this iniquitous practice?

It was at that moment that my pseudonym list was born.

In time I came to moderate my views on the theory and practice of pseudonyms. After all, it is very handy for an author to use a different name when writing a different type of book. While **Jean Plaidy**, **Philippa Carr** and **Victoria Holt** are all the same person, each pseudonym represents quite a different type book. By using different names, this author makes it easy for me to know exactly what kind of a read I am actually getting.

Then, of course, there's something to be said for the image an author's name can evoke. For years publishers encouraged writers with somewhat more unusual names, names that were either difficult to spell or pronounce, to assume a name that could be easily promoted.

Consider the case of Marie Rydzynski, who went through the names of Marie Charles, Marie Michael and Marie Nicole before she finally settled on **Marie Ferrarella**.

And pity poor **Jo Ann Algermissen** who was told that her name was too long to fit on a book cover. Eventually Silhouette found a way, but not before Jo Ann had used the name of Anna Hudson.

And, of course, using a pseudonym makes it easier for an author to keep his or her personal life separate from a professional career. The fictitious Joan Wilder was always getting approached by fans, often in the strangest of places. Sometimes that was very good, as in *Romancing the Stone,* and sometimes it was very, very bad, as in *Jewel of the Nile.*

Last and definitely least in many a reader's opinion is the publishers' wish to safeguard their investment in an author's career by requiring the use of an exclusive pseudonym. But even this oft maligned practice has its bright side.

Modern technology often makes an author a prisoner of numbers, locking in future orders against the performance of past books. While this is certainly legitimate to a certain degree, overkill often freezes an author into one and only one type of book, with little opportunity provided for the author to grow and mature, much less increase sales. A pseudonym can give new life and new opportunity to even the most popular of authors.

It seems clear that, despite efforts to the contrary, the use of pseudonyms will continue to flourish. Every attempt has been made to make this list as accurate as possible. If there are errors, and there are bound to be, I apologize in advance and hope that you will give me the chance to correct them. Meanwhile, in the ongoing struggle to bring order out of chaos, you may be sure that I will continue to wield both magnifying glass and butterfly net with equal abandon.

**Until we next meet, I remain,**
*The Pseudonym Sleuth, a.k.a. Melinda P. Helfer.* ❤

# What's In A Name?

### by Heather Graham
### Shannon Drake,
### Heather Graham Pozzessere

*I* never really meant to use a pseudonym. I encountered the name Pozzessere very young in life—well, I wasn't as young as I was when I encountered Graham, since I was born with it—but I was still only fifteen and I remember that when I first came home, madly in love with a boy I'd met at a Halloween party, my mother wasn't in the least impressed.

"What's his name?" she had asked me, and I had pronounced Pozzessere to the best of my ability. "There will be others," she sighed, like any teen-ager's mom, "less difficult to remember."

He and I stuck together through high school, and by the time I graduated, she had learned to spell the name—it was necessary for the wedding invitations.

I've grown accustomed to spelling it out slowly for Southern Bell and Florida Power and Light.

"No, no, two Zs, an E, and two Ss."

But when I sold my first book—after the days of being shocked and elated and wondering if it was really true—I decided that I wanted to write under the name Graham. It had been my father's name, and I had loved him very much. I learned about the world and believing in myself and in dreams from him and though he was gone, writing under the name that he had given me seemed to be the thing to do.

That was fine with Dell Publishing Company—they didn't have anything against the name Pozzessere, they just thought that it had a few too many Zs or Ss or something. "People will not buy a book by an author if they can't pronounce the name."

In my contracts, Heather Graham went down as a pseudonym for Dell Publishing. I meant to explain that it wasn't a pseudonym, it was really my name but I never did.

When I later sold the novel *Tomorrow the Glory* to Pinnacle, I was told I needed a pseudonym, and publishing being publishing, they needed the name in less than five minutes.

While I was standing there with a totally blank mind, still on the phone, my sons Shayne and Derek walked into the room. I put them together for Shayne Derek. I tried Derek Shayne, but that didn't sound much better, not unless I went into men's action/adventure. But then Shayne Derek turned into Shannon Drake, and my alter-ego was born.

We discovered not long ago that my six-year-old daughter thought that Shannon Drake was her middle name. "Bryee-Annon Shannon Drake Pozzessere." Now that would be one for a book cover.

I was recently at an autographing and had a name plaque for Heather and one for Shannon. There was a wonderful lady who came up and bought a Heather Graham book and chatted delightfully for a while, then cleared her throat, and asked if I would mind moving and find Shannon Drake for her. It really was a lot of fun. I felt like a twin and she couldn't wait to run home and tell her daughter that I was one and the same person.

When I sold to Silhouette, I wanted to use my own name, and so I broached the subject of the Pozzessere. No one seemed to mind the Ss and the Zs. In fact, the idea of them seemed rather cheerful.

"If someone can't say Pozzessere, they'll just go in and ask for the author with all the Ss and Zs in the names!"

So far, it's worked out rather well. I feel that the best use of pseudonyms is when you really change your style of writing. For historical works an author might use one name, for mystery or contemporary writing she might use another.

I never became involved with pseudonyms on purpose, I was naive and new to the business and rather fell into it.

There are books that I hope to write in the future that I'm not sure if I would use a new pseudonym with or not—it can be very important.

One of the things that an author always hopes to avoid is irritating or alienating the readers.

Readers come to expect certain things from the authors they read. To have them pick up a book with a heroine who has several affairs when they are looking for a one-on-one love story is often disappointing. And vice-versa. And our readers are the most important people in the whole scheme of things.

Someday I'd love to write a horror novel. If I do, I'll definitely change my name, and I will use initials! At the moment, Shannon Drake remains with Berkley, and she writes long books, hopefully with a wealth of mood and tapestry within them. Heather Graham remains at Dell where the length is a bit shorter and the friction is perhaps a bit more fierce; and Heather Graham Pozzessere remains at Harlequin and Silhouette.

To all of our readers, we (Heather Graham, Shannon, and Heather G. Pozzessere) would like to say thank you so very much—none of us would exist without you.♥

# Jennifer Wilde Reveals Himself!

## by Tom Huff

*Why did you choose a female pseudonym?*
In 1976 when *Love's Tender Fury* was about to appear, publishers felt that there would be opposition to a male writing an historical romance, so they felt it was necessary that I have a female pseudonym.

*Why did you choose Jennifer Wilde?*
The publishers wanted something that was both sexy and aristocratic. Something that would remind them of those old swashbuckling movies starring Maureen O'Hara and Cornell Wilde. They thought that Jennifer was an aristocratic first name.
But a name to go with it. Jennifer O'Hara? No.
Jennifer Wilde? That's It! Thus Jennifer Wilde was born.

*What names did you reject?*
Prunella Dobson wouldn't cut it. Lavinia Languish seemed a bit much. Penelope Trueheart was stretching it a bit. And Barbara Cartland had already been used. No pun intended!

*How does it feel to be famous under a pseudonym?*
I love it. I can enjoy the success, do my work without interruption, and enjoy my anonymity. The only problem is when fans request photographs. Kathryn Falk has the only decent photograph of me, and magazines and publishers have been borrowing it for years.

*Do women resent the fact that you're a man writing romances?*
On the contrary, they think it's terrific and wonder how I know so much about women.

*How do you know so much about women?*
A great many of my friends are women and they talk incessantly. Every woman likes a good listener and I listen very well.
Women love to talk about their emotional lives. I feel that I've learned a great deal about the female psyche from the charming la-

dies, and when I write about women I try to employ this knowledge.

I really think that men probably know more about women and women know more about men.

Some of the greatest books about women have been written by men. For example, *Anna Karenina* and *Madame Bovary*.

On the other hand some of the greatest male characters have been created by women, witness Rhett Butler and Heathcliff.

When you are writing about the opposite sex, gender does not get in the way. The only problem I have ever really had is when I was writing *Marabelle* in which the narrator was a male writer. I found that there was far too much of myself creeping into the character.

### How many books have you written?

God, I don't know, pushing 30 I think.

### Have you ever written under your own name?

*Marabelle*, a novel based loosely on the life of Talulah Bankhead was published in hardcover under the name Tom E. Huff.

I did use the name T.E. Huff for *Nine Bucks Row*, a novel about Jack the Ripper, and *Meet a Dark Stranger*, a contemporary mystery.

### What about your other pseudonyms?

I wrote a number of Gothic mysteries as Edwina Marlow and Beatrice Parker. When I wrote my first novel, *The Master of Phoenix Hall,* I was teaching high school English and we were reading *She Stoops to Conquer* by Oliver Goldsmith in which there was a character named Marlow. I liked the name.

One of my favorite movies was the "Rains of Ranchipur", in which Lana Turner played a gloriously wicked and sophisticated lady named Edwina. When informed I would need a female pseudonym I decided on Edwina Marlow. Beatrice Parker is my mother's maiden name. I also wrote one novel as Katherine St. Clair, utilizing the names of two friends, Katherine and Clair.

### Do men need female pseudonyms to write romances today?

Publishers have discovered that readers are much more sophisticated and knowledgeable than they first believed, and accept the fact that men know quite a bit about women and vice versa.

Many women are writing about war and military affairs and many men are putting more romance into their books and writing from a woman's viewpoint.

### If you had to choose a new pseudonym, what would be your choice for the 1990s?

Judging from today's market, "Candace Came" might be appropriate. But seriously, in the 1990s, a female pseudonym would not be necessary. ❤

# A.K.A. Jayne Ann Krentz

## by Herself!

*I*'d like you to meet a few of my very closest friends—
Jayne Castle, Stephanie James, Amanda Glass, Jayne
Bentley, and Jayne Taylor. It is quite possible that in the
future I shall acquire a few more very close friends.

Fortunately my friends and I get along very well and that is probably because we all share something in common, namely me. At various points in my career I have written books under each of these
names.

Why pseudonyms? There are a great many reasons why authors re-
sort to using names other than their own on the covers of their
books. I can think of several, right off hand. The use of pseudonyms
is an extremely common practice, especially in the romance genre.
Most of my sister authors in the field have used pseudonyms at one
time or another.

A lot of people wonder if the chief reason an author resorts to using a pseudonym is because she is secretly ashamed of what she has
created. That's nonsense. It is the one reason for using a pseudonym
that almost never applies.

No one I know, including myself, has ever used a pseudonym because she is embarrassed by what she has written.

The explanation for why this reason is seldom applicable is very
simple. Romance novels are primarily novels of strong emotion.
Take it from me, you don't get strong emotion out of a book unless
you put strong emotion into it. A romance novel is an extraordinarily
personal thing to the author—very much an extension of herself—
very much her baby. A great deal of creative energy, time, effort,
sweat, blood and tears are invested in it.

You don't send it out into the world if you are ashamed of it. You
could not bear to hand it over to anyone to look at, let alone an editor, if you weren't satisfied with it.

But there are other explanations for using pseudonyms and believe
me, most of the time the writer is no more in favor of the practice
than the poor reader who is trying to track down all the books written by her favorite author.

Unfortunately, pseudonyms are a fact of life in the business of publishing. Here are a handful of reasons why one might end up going on the cover of a book.

*a)* The publisher insists.

It is not at all rare in the romance genre for a publisher to insist that new authors choose pseudonyms. Editors sometimes threaten not to buy the manuscript unless the author agrees to use another name on the finished book.

Romance publishers, especially those publishing the series books, want pseudonyms because they can tie an author to a specific line by legally tying up the pseudonym. They see the practice as a way of controlling the quality of the lines. It also controls the author's future.

An author's biggest asset is her name. If she is not free to take it to another publisher, she loses her primary negotiating point when she signs a contract with a new publishing house. Having her name tied up can severely handicap her career. But she may have no choice if she wishes to get a career of any kind started.

*b)* To avoid confusing the audience.

An author's audience soon comes to expect a certain type of story from that author. Readers generally don't like it when their favorite novelist experiments with another kind of story. This is true in all genres and mainstream publishing, not just the romance genre.

A writer of successful glitz novels who chooses to try a mystery risks losing a vast number of faithful glitz readers and vice versa. A writer of horror fiction who decides to do a western novel cannot expect the horror audience to follow him into another field. Nor does he want to mislead that audience.

A romance novelist who does a book with a science fiction setting risks confusing her regular romance readers who don't care for highly unusual twists on their favorite kind of story.

When the audience gets confused, it stops reading and no one wants to create that situation.

Therefore, many authors who want to tell a different kind of story will use a different name for those books to avoid confusing and annoying either of the two groups of readers involved.

*c)* To get a fresh start in the business.

In this day and age when everything, including an author's sales, are tracked by computers, some editors are asking authors to choose a different name in order to get a fresh start.

If an author has been publishing in midlist, the sales figures will generally not be very impressive. This is not the author's fault, it simply reflects the way midlist books are distributed and sold in this country. They have a certain niche and rarely do they break out of that niche on their own. The breakout into bestsellerdom is made with the help of a big push from the publisher who has decided an author's time has come.

When this time comes, the publisher may try to ensure that book-sellers and wholesalers aren't biased against taking a large number of copies of the new title by computer records that show only midlist level sales on previous books by that writer. To avoid the bias created by records of midlist sales, the author goes out under a pseudonym.

There are other reasons why an author may choose to use a pseudonym. For instance, it is not unknown for a very successful writer to see if he can recreate his own success under a new name. The author sees it as a challenge and has enough success under his belt to risk playing games of this sort. But such reasons tend to be extremely uncommon.

The raw truth is that, like everything else in the publishing industry, choosing a pseudonym is almost always done for remarkable, straightforward, business reasons. It is certainly never done to confuse or annoy readers.❤

# Pseudonyms

Names in *italics* indicate an author's legal name which does not appear on books. She or he uses pseudonym (s) only.

Names <u>underlined</u> indicate that the author uses legal name for works and may or may not use pseudonym (s).

Aallyn, Alysse
  Melissa Clark
Abbey, Anne Merton
  *Jean Brooks-Janowiak,*
  Janet Brooks, Valerie Vayle
Abbey, Christina
  Nancy John, Nancy Buckingham,
  Hilary London, Erica Quest,
  *Nancy & John Sawyer*
Abbey, Margaret
  Joanna Makepeace, Elizabeth York,
  Margaret York
Abbey, Ruth
  *Ruth Pattison*
Abbott, Alice
  *Kathryn Borland & Helen Ross Speicher*
Abbott, Francesca
Abbott, Jane Worth
  <u>Virginia Myers</u> & <u>Stella Cameron</u>,
  Alicia Brandon
Abbott, Jeanne
*Abbott, Mary Jeanne*
  Elizabeth Hewitt
Abbott, Rose Marie
Abbott, Sandra
Abercrombie, Patricia
  Patricia Barnes
*Abrahamsen, Christine*
  Cristabel, Kathleen Westcott
Absalom, Stacy
Acaster, Linda
Adams, Alicia
Adams, Audra
  Marie Tracy

Adams, Candice
  Rebecca Ashley, Sabrina Myles,
  <u>Lois A. Walker</u>
Adams, Daniel
  Leslie Arlen, Mark Logan,
  Simon McKay, Alison York,
  Christopher Nicole, Robin Cade,
  Peter Grange, Christina Nicholson
  Andrew York
Adams, Jolene
  JoAnna Brandon, <u>Olivia Harper</u>
Adams, Kasey
  <u>Valerie Whisenand</u>
Adams, Kat
Adams, Kelly
Adams, Melodie
Adams, Pepper
  *Debrah Morris* & *Pat Shaver,*
  Dianne Thomas, Jo Ann Stacey,
  Joanna Jordan
Adams, Tracy
  Arlene Hale, Gail Everett,
  Mary Hale, Lynn Williams,
  Mary Tate
Adams, Tricia
*Adams-Manson, Pat*
  Julia Howard
*Adelson, Jean*
  Amanda Mack
Adelson, Sandra
Adrian, Francis
<u>Aeby, Jacquelyn</u>
  Jocelyn Carew, Vanessa Gray
<u>Aghadjian, Mollie</u>
  Moeth Allison, Mollie Ashton

27

Ahearn, Pamela Gray
*Ahearn, Pat*
 Kate Fairchild, Caitlin Murray,
 Kate Meriwether
Aid, Frances
Aiken, Joan
Aimes, Angelica
 *Lita Scotti*
Ainsley, Alix
*Ainsworth, Harriet*
 Elizabeth Cadell
Ainsworth, Patricia
 *Patricia N. Bigg*
Airlie, Catherine
 Jean S. MacLeod
Aitken, Kate
*Alan, Jane*
 Lilian Chisholm, Anne Lorraine
*Albano, Peter*
 Andrea Robbins
Albrand, Martha
 *Heidi Loewengard*,
 Katrin Holland
Albright, Elizabeth
 *Karen Lahey*
*Albritton, Carol*
 Elizabeth Trehearne
Alcott, Cynthia
Alcott, Julia
 Maureen Norris, Edythe Lachlan,
 Nicole Norman, Edythe Cudlipp,
 Rinalda Roberts, Bettina
 Montgomery
Alden, Elizabeth
 Charlene Talbot, Lucy Lee
Alderton, Therese
 Theresa Grazia, Alberta Sinclair
Alerding, Kathy
 *Kathy Puyear-Alerding*
Alers, Rochelle
 Rena McLeary
Alexander, Brandi
 Janelle Taylor, DiAnne Taylor
Alexander, Donna
 Donna Kimel Vitek
Alexander, Jan
 V. J. Banis, Lynn Benedict,
 Elizabeth Monterey

Alexander, Joan
 Joan Pepper
Alexander, Karen
Alexander, Kate
 Tania Langley, Tilly Armstrong
Alexander, Margaret
 Margaret Walker
Alexander, Marsha
Alexander, Megan
 *Mildred T. Fish*
Alexander, Serena
 Candice Arkham, *Alice Ramirez*
Alexander, Susan
Alexie, Angela
 *Angela Talias*
Algermissen, Jo Ann
 Anna Hudson
Allan, Jeanne
 Jeanne Allen
Allardyce, Paula
 Charlotte Keppel, Charity Blackstock,
 *Ursula Torday*
Allen, Barbara
 *Violet Vivian Mann*, Vivian Stuart,
 Robyn Stuart, Alex Stuart,
 William Stuart Long
*Allen, Catherine*
 Catherine Moorhouse
Allen, Elizabeth Evelyn
Allen, Emily Ann
 Diana Reep
Allen, Jeanne
 Jeanne Allan
Allen, Laine
 *Elaine Lakso*
*Allen, Mary Elizabeth*
 Kitty Grey
*Allen, Sheila Rosalynd*
 Sheila O'Hallion
Allis, Sarah
Allison, Elizabeth
 Alice Harron Orr, Morgan Starr
Allison, Moeth
 *Mollie Aghadjian*, Mollie Ashton
Allison, Penny
 Rosalynn Carroll, *Carol Katz*
Allister, Barbara
 *Barbara Teer*

28

Allyn, Ashley
Evelyn Grey, Susan Leslie
Allyn, Jennifer
Allyne, Kerry
Allyson, Kym
Ann Ashton, Katheryn Kimbrough,
Jean Kimbro, John Kimbro,
Charlotte Bramwell
Alpers, Mary Rose
Sarah Campion
*Alred, Margaret*
Anne Saunders
<u>*Alsobrook, Rosalyn*</u>
Jalynn Friends, Gina Delaney
*Amerski, Beth*
Beth Stanley, Elizabeth Anderson
Ames, Jennifer
Maysie Greig, Ann Barclay,
*Mary D. Warre*
Ames, Leslie
Ellen Randolph, Rose Dana,
Ruth Dorset, Ann Gilmor,
Miriam Leslie, Jane Rossiter,
<u>Dan Ross</u>, W. E. D. Ross,
Clarissa Ross, Marilyn Ross,
Diana Randall, Dana Ross,
Rose Williams, Marilyn Carter
Ames, Winter
<u>Phyllis Taylor Pianka</u>
Amis, Breton
Rayleigh Best, *Ray Bentinck*,
Leigh Haddow, Terrence Hughes,
Desmond Roberts, Leslie Wilde
*Amman, Marilyn M.*
Amanda Stevens, Marilyn Medlock
Anders, Donna
Andersen, Jan
Andersen, Linda
*Anderson, Adeline*
Catherine Anderson
Anderson, Ann
Anderson, Blaine
*Anderson, Adeline Catherine*
Catherine Anderson
*Anderson, Dana*
Laura Pender
Anderson, Elizabeth
Beth Stanley, *Beth Amerski*

Anderson, Gail
Anderson, Marlene J.
Joan Lancaster
Anderson, Rachel
Rachel Bradby
*Anderson, Roberta*
Fern Michaels
*Anderson, Susan M.*
Lindsay Randall
*Anderson, Virginia*
Megan Ashe
*Andersson, Nina*
Jane Archer, Asa Drake,
*Nina Romberg*
Andre, Alix
*Andresen, Julia*
Julia Joyce, Julie Tetel
Andrews, Alex
Mary Mackie, Mary Christopher,
Cathy Christopher, Susan Stevens
Caroline Charles
Andrews, Barbara
Andrews, Elizabeth
Andrews, Felicia
Deborah Lewis, <u>Charles L. Grant</u>
Andrews, Jo
Andrews, Lucilla
Diana Gordon, Joanna Marcus,
Lucilla Crichton
Andrews, Nicola
Ann Paris, <u>Orania Papazoglou</u>
Andrews, Susan
Annabella
*Charlotte Lowe*
Annandale, Barbara
Belinda Dell, *Jean Bowden,*
Avon Curry, Jocelyn Barry
*Ansle, Dorothy P.*
Hebe Elsna, Laura Conway,
Vicky Lancaster, Lyndon Snow,
Margaret Campbell Barnes
Anthony, Barbara
Antonia Barber
Anthony, Diana
Diana Lyndon, *Diane Antonio*
Anthony, Page
*Page & Anthony Traynor*

Lois A. Walker
**Ashley, Sarah**
**Ashley, Suzanne**
 *Susan Brown*
**Ashton, Andrea**
**Ashton, Ann**
 Jean Kimbro, John M. Kimbro,
 Kym Allyson, Charlotte Bramwell,
 Katheryn Kimbrough
**Ashton, Elizabeth**
**Ashton, Fiona**
**Ashton, Kate**
 Catherine Lyndell, *Margaret Ball*
 Kathleen Fraser
**Ashton, Katherine**
 Katherine Talbot
**Ashton, Laura**
**Ashton, Lorayne**
**Ashton, Mollie**
 Moeth Allison, *Mollie Aghadjian*
**Ashton, Sharon**
 Helen Van Slyke
**Ashton, Violet**
**Asquith, Nan**
 Susannah Broome, *Nancy Pattison*
**Astin, Cynthia**
**Astley, Juliet**
 Norah Lofts, Peter Curtis
*Astrahan, Syrie Ann*
 Syrie James
**Atkin, Jane**
*Atkins, Jane*
 Sarah Keene
**Atwood, Kathryn**
 <u>*Kathy Ptacek,*</u> Anne Mayfield
*Aubert, Rosemary*
 Lucy Snow
**August, Elizabeth**
 Betsy Page, *Bettie Wilhite,*
 Elizabeth Douglas
*Aumente, Joy*
 Joy Darlington, Joy Gardner
**Austin, Brett**
 Lee Floren, Lisa Franchon,
 Claudia Hall, Grace Lang,
 Matt Harding, Marguerite Nelson,
 Lee Thomas, Len Turner,
 Maria S. Sterling, Will Watson

**Austen, Charlotte**
 *Adele Leone*
**Austin, Deborah**
 Jacqueline Marshall
**Austin, Sarah**
**Austin, Stephanie**
**Avallone, Michael Angelo**
 Priscilla Dalton, Nick Carton,
 Troy Conway, Mark Dane,
 Steve Michaels, Dorothea Nile,
 Edwina Noone, Jean-Anne DePre,
 Vance Stanton, Sidney Stuart
**Avery, Lynn**
 Caroline Arnett, *Lois Cole Taylor*,
 Nancy Dudley, Allan Dwight,
 Anne Lattin
**Avery, Ruby D.**
 Vicki Page
**Awbrey, Elizabeth**
 *Elizabeth Beach*, Elizabeth Stuart
**Ayers, Rose**
**Aylesford, Susan**
**Ayre, Jessica**
**Ayres, Janet**
**Ayres, Ruby M.**

------

*Notes*

**A**

*Notes*

Names in *italics* indicate an author's legal name which does not appear on books. She or he uses pseudonym (s) only.

Names <u>underlined</u> indicate that the author uses legal name for works and may or may not use pseudonym (s).

Bacon, Nancy
*Baczewski, Janice*
    Kay Kirby, Janice Stevens,
    Kay Bartlett, Janice Kay Johnson
Bade, Tom
    Robin St. Thomas
Badger, Rosemary
Badgley, Anne V.
*Baggett, Nancy*
    Amanda Lee
Baer, Tracy
*Bagnara, Elsie Poe*
    Norah Hess
Bagwell, Stella
Bainbridge, Norma
Baird, Jaqui
Baker, Allison
    *Alice Crumbaker*
Baker, Anne
    Nancy Cross
*Baker, Betty*
    Elizabeth Renier
*Baker, Christine*
    Christine West
*Baker, Darlene*
    Heather Lang
<u>Baker, Fran</u>
    Judith Baker, Cathlyn McCoy
Baker, Judith
    <u>Fran Baker</u> & *Judith Noble*,
    Cathlyn McCoy
Baker, Lucinda
Baker, Madeline
*Baker, Marceil*
    Marcia Miller

Baker, Marjorie
    Alison McMaster
Baker, Mary Gladys
    Sheila Stuart
Baker, Sarah
Bakker, Kit
Baldwin, Cathryn
    Cathryn Ladd, *Cathryn LaDame*
Baldwin, Cynthia
Baldwin, Faith
    *Faith Cuthrell*
Baldwin, Rebecca
    Helen Chappell
Bale, Karen A.
Balkey, Rita
    *Rita Balkey Oleyar*
<u>Ball, Donna</u>
    Rebecca Flanders, Donna Carlisle,
    Leigh Bristol
*Ball, Margaret*
    Kathleen Fraser, Kate Ashton,
    Catherine Lyndell
<u>Balogh, Mary</u>
Balser, Joan
*Bamberger, Helen*
    Helen Berger
Bancroft, Iris May
    Andrea Layton, Ingrid Nielson,
    Iris Brent
<u>Banis, V. J.</u>
    Jan Alexander, Lynn Benedict,
    Elizabeth Monterey
Banks, Barbara
*Bannister, Patricia*
    Patricia Veryan, Gwyneth Moore

**33**

**Barber, Antonia**
Barbara Anthony
**Barber, Lenora**
Janet Wing
**Barbieri, Elaine**
**Barclay, Alisha**
**Barclay, Ann**
Jennifer Ames, Maysie Greig,
*Mary D. Warre*
**Barclay, Vera C.**
Margaret Beech
**Barker, Becky**
**Barker, Margaret**
**Barker, Megan**
Rosalind Erskine, Ivor Drummond,
Roger Longrigg
**Barkley, Jessica**
*Cori Deyoe*
**Barlow, Linda**
*Barnard, Judith*
Judith Michael
**Barnes, Elizabeth**
**Barnes, Margaret Campbell**
Hcbe Elsna, Laura Conway,
Vicky Lancaster, Lyndon Snow,
*Dorothy P. Ansle*
**Barnes, Patricia**
*Patricia B. Abercrombie*
**Barr, Elisabeth**
Irene Edwards
**Barraclough, June**
**Barret, Helen**
Justin Channing
**Barrett, Elizabeth**
Cara McLean, Christine Collins
**Barrett, Jean**
*Lee Rogers*
**Barrett, Max**
Maye Barrett
**Barrett, Maye**
Max Barrett
*Barricklow, Patti*
Patricia Burroughs
**Barrie, Monica**
Jenifer Dalton, Marilyn Davids,
David Wind
**Barrie, Susan**
Jane Beaufort, Rose Burghley,

Anita Charles, Pamela Kent,
Ida Pollock, Barbara Rowan,
Mary Whistler
**Barron, Ann Forman**
Annabel Erwin
**Barron, Elizabeth**
*Susan B. Twaddle,* Susan Bowden
**Barry, Andrea**
*Annette Bartle*
**Barry, Eileen**
Kathleen Ash, Pauline Ash,
Emily Walker, Christine Lawson,
Sara Devon, Jane Lester,
Delia Foster, Cora Mayne,
Jill Murray, Quenna Tilbury,
Kathleen Treves, Heather Vincent,
Honor Vincent, Kay Winchester
**Barry, Jocelyn**
Barbara Annandale, Belinda Dell,
Avon Curry, *Jean Bowden*
**Bartell, Linda Lang**
**Bartholomew, Barbara**
**Bartholomew, Dale**
**Bartholomew, Jean**
Patricia Beatty
**Bartle, Annette**
Andrea Barry
**Bartlett, Kay**
*Janice Baczewski*, Janice Stevens,
Janice Kay Johnson
**Bartlett, Lynn M.**
**Bartlett, Marie**
Rowena Lee, Valerie Rift
**Bartlett, Stephanie**
**Basile, Gloria**
Michaela Morgan
**Basset, Aubriel**
**Bassett, Marjorie**
**Bassett, Sara Ware**
**Bates, Jenny**
Maura Seger, Laurel Winslow,
Sara Jennings, Anne MacNeill,
Maeve Fitzgerald
*Battye, Gladys*
Margaret Lynn
**Bauer, Marsha**
**Bauer, Pamela**
*Pamela Muelbauer*

Bauling, Jayne
Bauman, Lauren
Baumann, Margaret
  Marguerite Lees
*Baumgardner, Cathie*
  Cathie Linz
*Baumgarten, Sylvia*
  Ena Halliday, Louisa Rawlings
Baxter, Elizabeth
  Elizabeth Holland
Baxter, Judy
  *Judith Simpson* & *June Haydon,*
  Sara Logan, Rosalind Foxx,
  Taria Hayford
Baxter, Mary Lynn
Baxter, Olive
  Fay Ramsay, Helen Eastwood
*Beach, Elizabeth*
  Elizabeth Awbrey,
  Elizabeth Stuart
*Bear, Joan E.*
  Elizabeth Mayhew
Beatty, Patricia
  Jean Bartholomew
Beauchamp, Kathleen
  Katherine Mansfield
Beauchamp, Margary
Beaudry, Antoinette
Beaufort, Jane
  Susan Barrie, Rose Burghley,
  Anita Charles, Pamela Kent,
  Ida Pollock, Barbara Rowan,
  Mary Whistler
<u>Beauman, Sally</u>
  Vanessa James
Beaumont, Helen
  Jill Eckersley, Anna Stanton,
  Jill Sanderson, Denise Emery
Beaumont, Lisa
Bechko, Peggy
Beckford, Grania
Beckman, Patti
  *Patti & Charles Boeckman*
Beckwith, Lillian
  *Lillian Comber*
Bedford, Debbi
  *Deborah Lynn Bedford*
*Bedford, Deborah Lynn*

  Debbi Bedford
*Beebe, Elswyth*
  Elswyth Thane
Beech, Jane
Beech, Margaret
  Vera C. Barclay
Bell, Anthea
Bell, Donna
Bell, Georgiana
Belle, Pamela
Belmont, Kate
  Kathryn Belmont, Gwen
  Fairfax, <u>Mary Jo Territo</u>
Belmont, Kathryn
  Kate Belmont, Gwen Fairfax,
  <u>Mary Jo Territo</u>
Benedict, Barbara
Benedict, Rachel
  Kay Stephens, Jane Beverley,
  Doreen Stephens
Benet, Deborah
  <u>Elaine Camp</u>, Delaine Tucker,
  Deborah Camp, Elaine Tucker,
  Delayne Camp
Benjamin, Linda
  Jessica Douglass, *Linda H. Wallerich*
Benjamin, Nikki
  *Barbara Vosbein*
Bennett, Barbara
Bennett, Christine
  Joan Garrison, Norma Newcomb,
  Rebecca Marsh, Jan Hathaway,
  William Arthur, *William Neubauer*
Bennett, Clarissa
Bennett, Connie
  *Constance Bennett*
*Bennett, Constance*
  Connie Bennett
Bennett, Corintha
  *Carolyn Wheat*
Bennett, Dorothy
  Laura Kingsley
Bennett, Emma
  Micah Leigh, <u>Emma Merritt</u>
<u>Bennett, Janice</u>
  Eileen Witton
Bennett, Rebecca
  Constance Conrad, Lillian Marsh,

*Ruby Frankel*
**Bennetts, Pamela**
Helen Ashfield, Margaret James
*Bensen, Ronald*
Julia Thatcher
Benson, Anne
Anne Hillary, Kathryn Jessup,
Andrea Edwards, Erika Bryant
Adrienne Edwards, Anne Kolaczyk
Benson, Nella Jane
*Bentinck, Ray*
Breton Amis, Rayleigh Best,
Leigh Haddow, Terrence Hughes,
Desmond Roberts, Leslie Wilde
Bentley, Barbara
*Barbara B. Diamond*
Bentley, Jayne
Jayne Castle, Stephanie James,
Jayne Taylor, Jayne Ann Krentz,
Amanda Glass
Bentley, Pauline
Bentley, Patricia
Julie Ellis, Susan Marino,
Marilyn Ellis, Susan Marvin,
Richard Marvin, Susan Richard,
Alison Lord, Jeffrey Lord,
Linda Michaels, Joan Ellis,
Jill Monte
Benton, Darla
Jessica Dare, Joanna Leslie
Benton, Elsie
**Berencsi, Susan**
**Berenson, Laurien**
Laurien Blair
Bergen, Fran
*Frances de Talavera Berger*
Frances Flores,
*Berger, Daranna*
Caitlin Cross
*Berger, Frances de Talavera*
Frances Flores, Fran Bergen
Berger, Helen
*Helen Bamberger*
**Berger, Nomi**
Alyssa Welles
**Bergstrom, Kay**
Cassie Miles

Berk, Ariel
Thea Frederick, Judith Arnold,
*Barbara Keiler*
*Berland, Nancy*
Nancy Landon
Bernadette, Ann
*Karen Ray & D.H. Gadzak*
Bernard, Dorothy Ann
Dorothea Hale, *Dorothy Weller*
Berne, Karin
*Michaela Karni & Sue Burrell,*
Diana Burke
Berrisford, Mary
Christianna Brand, Mary Lewis,
China Thompson
Best, Carol Ann
Susan Ashe, Con Darlington,
Ann Martin, Marcia Wayne
Best, Rayleigh
Breton Amis, Ray Bentinck,
Leigh Haddow, Terrence Hughes,
Desmond Roberts, Leslie Wilde
Betteridge, Anne
Margaret Potter, Margaret Evans,
*Margaret Neuman*, Anne Melville
*Betz, Ingrid*
Monica Martin
Bevan, Gloria
Beverley, Jane
Kay Stephens, Rachel Benedict,
Doreen Stephens
Beverley, Jo
*Bianchi, Jacqui*
Teresa Denys
Bianchin, Helen
*Bidwell, Marjory*
Mary Ann Gibbs
**Bieber, Janet**
Janet Joyce, Jenna Lee Joyce
**Bierce, Jane**
*Bigg, Patricia N.*
Patricia Ainsworth
*Bils, Sharon & Robert*
Sarah Edwards
Bingham, Charlotte
Bingham, Lisa
*Biondi, Diana*
Diana Guest

Bird, Beverly
  *Beverly Helland*
*Bird, Sara*
  Tory Cates
Bishop, Cassandra
  Robin Lynn, *Robin Latham*
Bishop, Claudia
  Jane Feather
Bishop, Leslie
  Robin Tolivar
Bishop, Mary
Bishop, Natalie
  *Nancy Bush*
Bishop, Sheila
Bissell, Elaine
  Whitney Faulkner
Bittner, F. Rosanne
  Jessie Belle Sage
Black, Amanda
Black, Cheryl
Black, Dorothy
  Kitty Black
Black, Hermina
Black, Jackie
  Jacqueline Ashley, *Jacqueline Casto*
Black, Kitty
  Dorothy Black
Black, Laura
Black, Maureen
  Veronica Black, Sharon Whitby,
  Maureen Peters, Elizabeth Law,
  Judith Rothmann, Catherine Darby,
  Levanah Lloyd
Black, Veronica
  Maureen Black, Sharon Whitby,
  Maureen Peters, Elizabeth Law,
  Judith Rothmann, Catherine Darby,
  Levanah Lloyd
Blackburn, Claire
  Linda C. Jacobs
Blackman, Lynne
Blackmon, Laura
Blackmore, Jane
Blackstock, Charity
  Paula Allardyce, Charlotte Keppel,
  *Ursula Torday*
Blacktree, Barbara
  Barbara Coultry

Blackwell, Judith
  Judy Myers, *Judith Blackwell Myers*
Blair, Cynthia
Blair, Jennifer
  Adeline McElfresh, Jane Scott,
  Elizabeth Wesley
Blair, Joan
Blair, Kathryn
  Rosalind Brett, Celine Conway
Blair, Laurien
  Laurien Berenson
Blaisdell, Anne
  Elizabeth Linington,
  Lesley Egan, Egan O'Neill,
  Dell Shannon
Blake, Andrea
  Anne Weale, Anne Wilson
Blake, Antonia
  Sarah James, *Mildred Juskevice*
Blake, Jennifer
  Patricia Maxwell, Maxine Patrick,
  Elizabeth Trehearne, Patricia Ponder
Blake, Jillian
Blake, Karen
Blake, Laurel
  Elaine Fowler Palencia
Blake, Margaret Glaiser
Blake, Sally
  Rowena Summers, Jean Innes,
  Jean Saunders
Blake, Stephanie
  *Jack Pearl*
Blake, Vanessa
  *May Brown*, Mandy Brown
Blake, Veronica
Blakelee, Alexandra
  *Alexandra Hine*, Lilla Brennan
*Blanchard, Angela Ortiz*
  Rebecca Blanchard
Blanchard, Rebecca
  *Angela Ortiz Blanchard*
Blanford, Virginia
  Sarah Crewe
Blanshard, Audrey
Blayne, Diana
  Diana Palmer, Katy Currie,
  Susan Kyle
Blayne, Sara

Blayney, Mary
Blickle, Katinka
*Blocklinger, Betty*
  Peggy O'More, Jeanne Bowman
Blood, Marje
  Paige McKenzie
Bloom, Jill
Bloom, Ursula
  Lozania Prole, Sheila Burns,
  Mary Essex, Ursula Harvey,
  Deborah Mann, Rachel Harvey
*Blundell, Judith*
  Jude O'Neill
Blundell, V. R.
  Kathleen Nixon
Blyth, Juliet
  *Stella Riley*
Blythe, Leonora
  *Leonora Burton*
Blythe, Megan
  Michalann Perry
Boatner, Patricia
Bockoven, Georgia
Bode, Margo
*Boeckman, Patti & Charles*
  Patti Beckman
*Bodine, Sherrill*
  Leslie Lynn, Lynn Leslie
*Boese, Dawn C.*
  Dawn Carroll
Bolander, Judith
Bolton, Elizabeth
  Kate Chambers, Norma Johnston,
  Pamela Dryden, Lavinia Harris,
  Adrian Roberts, Nicole St. John,
  Catherine Chambers
Bond, Evelyn
  Janet Templeton, Ian Kavanaugh,
  Sara Rothman, Jessica Wilcox,
  Morris Herschman, Sara Roffman,
  Lionel Webb
Bond, Rebecca
  Rebecca Forster, *Rebecca Czuleger*
Bond-Smith, Sylvia
Bonds, Parris Afton
Bonham, Barbara
  Sara North

*Boon, August*
  Claire Vernon, Hilary Wilde,
  Elinor Caldwell, Clare Breton-Smith
*Booth, Rosemary*
  Frances Murray
Borden, Leigh
Bordill, Judith
*Borland, Kathryn*
  Alice Abbott
*Bosler, Colleen*
  Colleen Quinn
*Bosna, Valerie*
  Valerie King, Sarah Montrose
Bostwick, Angela
  Angela Welles
Boswell, Barbara
  Betsy Osborne
*Boulet, Ada*
  Ada John
Bourne, Caroline
Bourne, Hester
  *Molly Troke*
Bourne, Joanne Watkins
Bowden, Jean
  Belinda Dell, Barbara Annandale,
  Avon Curry, Jocelyn Barry
Bowden, Susan
  Elizabeth Barron, *Susan B. Twaddle*
Bowe, Kate
  Mary Ann Taylor, Cass McAndrew
Bowen, Alice
  Alyce Bowen
Bowen, Alyce
  Alice Bowen
Bowen, Charlene
Bowen, Marjorie
  Hilary Lang
Bowersock, Melissa
Bowes, Florence
Bowman, Jeanne
  Peggy O'More, *Betty Blocklinger*
Bowring, Mary
Boyard, Alexis
*Boyd, Edmond*
  Esther Boyd
Boyd, Elizabeth
  Isabel MacCall

**Boyd, Esther**
*Edmond Boyd*
**Boyd, Prudence**
Claire Ritchie, Nora Gibbs,
Lisette Garland, Noelle Ireland,
Lynne Merrill, Nina Shayne,
Heather Wayne, Sara Whittingham,
Dallas Romaine
**Boyer, Elizabeth**
<u>**Boyle, Ann**</u>
Audrey Brent, Ann Bryan
**Bradby, Rachel**
Rachel Anderson
**Brader, Norma**
*Bradford, Barbara*
Sally Bradford, Barbara Siddon,
<u>**Bradford, Barbara Taylor**</u>
**Bradford, Lily**
**Bradford, Sally**
*Barbara Bradford & Sally Siddon*
Barbara Siddon
**Bradley, Kate**
Kathleen Bryant
**Bradley, Marion Zimmer**
**Bradley, Muriel**
**Bradstreet, Valerie**
Pamela D'Arcy, Georgina Grey,
Mary Wilson, Elisabeth Welles,
Pauline Pryor, <u>Mary Linn Roby</u>
*Braeme, Charlotte N.*
Bertha M. Clay
**Bramsch, Joan**
**Bramwell, Charlotte**
Jean Kimbro, Ann Ashton,
*John M. Kimbro,* Kim Allyson,
Kathryn Kimbrough
**Brand, Christianna**
China Thompson, Mary Lewis,
Mary Berrisford
**Brand, Debra**
Suzanne Rand
**Brand, Susan**
**Brandewyne, Rebecca**
*Mary Rebecca Wadsworth Broc*
**Brandon, Alicia**
*Linda Rice* & <u>Stella Cameron</u>,
Jane Worth Abbott, Linda Walters

**Brandon, Beatrice**
*Robert W. Krepps*
**Brandon, Faith**
**Brandon, JoAnna**
Jolene Adams, <u>Olivia & Ken Harper</u>
**Brandon, Joyce**
**Brandon, Sheila**
Ann Lynton, Ruth Martin,
Claire Rayner
**Brandt, Cate**
<u>**Brauer, Deana**</u>
Dena Rhee, Dana Daniels
*Braunstein, Binnie Syril*
Binnie Syril
<u>**Bremer, Jo**</u>
Joellyn Carroll
**Brendan, Mary**
**Brennan, Jan**
**Brennan, Lilla**
Alexandra Blakelee, *Alexandra Hine*
**Brent, Audrey**
Ann Bryan, <u>Ann Boyle</u>
**Brent, Casey**
**Brent, Iris**
Andrea Layton, Ingrid Nielson,
Iris May Bancroft
**Brent, Madeleine**
**Breton-Smith, Clare**
*August Boon,* Claire Vernon,
Hilary Wilde, Elinor Caldwell
**Brett, Barbara**
**Brett, Katheryn**
*Peg Robarchek*
<u>**Brett, Rosalind**</u>
Kathryn Blair, Celine Conway
**Bretton, Barbara**
**Brew, Cathleen**
**Brewster, Martha**
**Brian, Marilyn**
*Jillian Dagg,* Jillian Fayre,
Faye Wildman
**Bride, Nadja**
Nuria Wood, *Joi Nobisso*
*Bridge, Susan*
Elizabeth Carey
**Brier, Margaret**
**Bright, Elizabeth**
*Robert Liston*

*Bruff, Nancy*
  Nancy Gardner
**Bruyere, Toni Marsh**
**Bryan, Ann**
  Audrey Brent, <u>Ann Boyle</u>
**Bryan, Deborah**
  *Deborah Bryson,* Deborah Joyce
**Bryan, Eileen**
  Alana Smith, <u>Ruth Smith</u>
**Bryant, Erika**
  Anne Benson, Anne Hillary,
  Kathryn Jessop, Andrea Edwards,
  Adrienne Edwards, <u>Anne Kolaczyk</u>
**Bryant, Kathleen**
  Kate Bradley
**<u>Bryant, La Ree</u>**
**Bryant, Lynn Marie**
*Bryer, Judy*
  Brenna Drummond, Eve O'Brien,
  Allison Lawrence
*Bryson, Deborah*
  Deborah Joyce, Deborah Bryan
**Buchan, Kate**
**<u>Buchan, Stuart</u>**
  Pamela Foxe, Becky Stuart
**Buchanan, Laura**
  Florence King
**<u>Bucheister, Patt</u>**
  Patt Parrish
**Buck, Carole**
  *Carol Buckman*
**<u>Buck, Gayle</u>**
*Buckholder, Marta*
  Marta Lloyd
*Buckholtz, Eileen*
  Alyssa Howard, Amanda Lee,
  Rebecca York, Samantha Chase
**Buckingham, Nancy**
  Nancy John, Hilary London,
  Erica Quest, Christina Abbey,
  *Nancy & John Sawyer*
*Buckman, Carol*
  Carole Buck
**Budd, Carol**
*Bullard, Ann Elizabeth*
  Casey Stuart
*Bullinger, Maureen*
  Samantha Quinn

*Burak, Linda*
  Alicia Meadowes
**Burchell, Mary**
  *Ida Cook*
**Burford, Eleanor**
  Victoria Holt, Kathleen Kellow,
  Ellalice Tate, Jean Plaidy,
  Eleanor Hibbert, Elbur Ford,
  Philippa Carr
**Burford, Lolah**
**Burgess, Joanna**
  <u>Caroline Fireside</u>
*Burgess, Justine*
  Joanna Harris
**Burgess, Mallory**
  *Mary Sandra Hingston,*
  Catherine Fitzgerald
**Burghley, Rose**
  Susan Barrie, Jane Beaufort,
  Anita Charles, Pamela Kent,
  Ida Pollock, Barbara Rowan,
  Mary Whistler
**Burke, Diana**
  *Sue Burrell & Michaela Karni,*
  Karin Berne
**Burkhardt, Mary**
**Burn, Helen Jean**
**Burnes, Caroline**
  *Carolyn Haines*
*Burns, Carol*
  Samantha Holder
**Burns, Patricia**
**Burns, Sheila**
  Lozania Prole, Ursula Bloom,
  Mary Essex, Rachel Harvey,
  Deborah Mann, Ursula Harvey
*Burrell, Sue*
  Diana Burke, Karin Berne
**Burroughs, Patricia**
  *Patti Barricklow*
**Burrows, Marjorie**
**Burton, Katherine**
*Burton, Kristin*
  Susanna Christie
**Burton, Leonora**
  Leonora Blythe
*Burton, Rebecca*
  Rebecca Winters

**Busbee, Shirlee**
*Bush, Kim*
  Kimberleigh Caitlin, Kimberly Cates
**Bush, Nancy**
  Natalie Bishop
*Bushyhead, Anne*
  Nicole Jordan
**Butler, Gwendoline**
  Jennie Melville
**Butler, Mary**
**Butler, Rae**
  Raymond Ragan Butler
**Butler, Rose**
*Butterworth, William E.*
  Eden Hughes
*Buxton, Anne*
  Anne Maybury, Katherine Troy
**Byers, Cordia**
**Byfield, Sue**
*Byington, Kaa*
  Sybil LeGrand, Octavia Street
**Byrne, Beverly**

---

*Notes*

Names in *italics* indicate an author's legal name which does not appear on books. She or he uses pseudonym (s) only.

Names <u>underlined</u> indicate that the author uses legal name for works and may or may not use pseudonym (s).

**Cade, Robin**
    Daniel Adams, Leslie Arlen,
    Mark Logan, Christopher Nicole,
    Simon McKay, Alison York,
    Christina Nicholson, Peter Grange,
    Andrew York
**Cadell, Elizabeth**
    *Harriet Ainsworth*
<u>**Caimi, Gina**</u>
<u>**Caine, Rebecca**</u>
    Margery Hilton, *Margery Woods*
**Caird, Janet**
**Caitlin, Kimberleigh**
    Kimberly Cates, *Kim Bush*
<u>**Cajio, Linda**</u>
**Caldwell, Elinor**
    *August Boon,* Hilary Wilde,
    Claire Vernon, Clare Breton-Smith
**Caldwell, Taylor**
    Max Renier
**Caldwell-Wilson, Marolyn**
**Callahan, Elizabeth**
**Callender, Joan**
**Calloway, Jo**
**Cameron, Ann**
**Cameron, Barbara**
    *Barbara C. Smith*
**Cameron, Blair**
    *Mary K. Scamehorn* &
    *Karen B. Parker*
**Cameron, Claire**
**Cameron, Caryn**
    Karen Harper,
**Cameron, Elizabeth Jane**
    Jane Duncan

**Cameron, Kate**
    *Beverly McGlamry*
**Cameron, Kate**
    Elizabeth DuBreuil, Lorinda Hagen,
    Margaret Maitland
**Cameron, Kay**
    <u>Virginia Coffman</u>, Jeanne Duval,
    Ann Stanfield, Victor Cross,
    Diana Saunders
**Cameron, Lacey**
**Cameron, Lorna**
**Cameron, Lou**
    Mary Louise Manning
**Cameron, Miranda**
    Amanda Troy, *Mary Kahn*
<u>**Cameron, Stella**</u>
    Alicia Brandon, Jane Worth Abbott
<u>**Camp, Candace**</u>
    Lisa Gregory, Kristin James,
    Sharon Stephens
**Camp, Deborah**
    <u>Elaine Camp</u>, Deborah Benet,
    Delaine Tucker, Elaine Tucker,
    Delayne Camp
**Camp, Delayne**
    See <u>Elaine Camp</u>
<u>**Camp, Elaine**</u>
    Deborah Camp, Deborah Benet,
    Delaine Tucker, Elaine Tucker,
    Delayne Camp
**Campbell, Bethany**
    *Sally McClusky*
**Campbell, Caroline**
    *Leslie A. Safford*
**Campbell, Diane**

*Campbell, Hope*
  True Summers
**Campbell, Jane**
  Jane Edwards
**Campbell, Joanna**
  Jo Ann Simon
**Campbell, Wanza J.**
**Campion, Sarah**
  Mary Rose Alpers
**Canaday, Lee**
  Juliet Ashby, Louise Lee Outlaw
*Canadeo, Anne*
  Anne Cavaliere, Alyssa Douglas
**Canavan, Jean**
**Canfield, Dorothy**
  Dorothea Fisher, Dorothy Fletcher,
  Miriam Canfield
**Canfield, Miriam**
  Dorothy Fletcher, Dorothea Fisher,
  Dorothy Canfield
**Canfield, Sandra**
  Sandi Shane, Karen Keast
**Canham, Marsha**
**Canon, Mary**
*Carboni, Susan G.*
  Susan Gordon
**Cardiff, Sara**
**Carew, Jocelyn**
  Jacquelyn Aeby, Vanessa Gray
**Carey, Diane**
  *Diane & Greg Brodeur,* Lydia Gregory
**Carey, Elizabeth**
  *Susan Bridge*
**Carey, Suzanne**
  *Verna Carey*
*Carey, Verna*
  Suzanne Carey
**Carfax, Catherine**
**Carl, Lillian**
**Carles, Riva**
  Alicia Grace, Gail St. John,
  Anita Grace, Irving Greenfield
**Carlisle, Amanda**
**Carlisle, Carris**
**Carlisle, Donna**
  Donna Ball, Rebecca Flanders,
  Leigh Bristol
**Carlisle, Sarah**

**Carlson, Janice**
  Laura Ashcroft, Laura Price,
  Ashland Price
**Carlson, Nancy**
*Carlton, Cathleen*
  Kaye Wilson Klem
**Carlton, Lori**
  Lori Leigh
**Carmichael, Emily**
  *Emily Krokosz*
**Carnell, Lois**
**Carpenter, Amanda**
**Carpenter, Cyndy**
**Carpenter, Brooke**
**Carr, Eleni**
  Helen Carter, Helen Carras,
  *Helen Maragakis*
**Carr, Kerry**
  Jane Joyce, Ena Young
**Carr, Madeleine**
**Carr, Philippa**
  Victoria Holt, Jean Plaidy,
  Eleanor Hibbert, Kathleen Kellow,
  Ellalice Tate, Elbur Ford,
  Eleanor Burford
**Carr, Roberta**
  Irene Roberts, Iris Rowland,
  Elizabeth Harle, Ivor Roberts,
  Irene Shaw
**Carr, Robyn**
**Carr, Sherry**
  Sara Chance, Sydney Ann Clary
**Carr, Victoria**
**Carras, Helen**
  Eleni Carr, Helen Carter,
  *Helen Maragakis*
**Carrington, Glenda**
  Karen Glenn
**Carro, Patricia**
  *Patricia Markham*
**Carroll, Dawn**
  *Dawn C. Boese*
**Carrol, Kathleen**
  Kathleen Creighton, *Kathleen Modrovich*
**Carrol, Shana**
  Christina Savage, Peter Gentry,
  *Frank Schaefer & Kerry Newcomb*
**Carroll, Enid**

Carroll, Joellyn
Jo Bremer & *Carol Wagner,*
Malissa Carroll, Marisa Carroll
Carroll, Joy
Heather Hill
Carroll, Malissa
*Carol Wagner & Marian Scharf,*
Joellyn Carroll, Marisa Carroll
Carroll, Marisa
*Carol Wagner & Marian Scharf,*
Joellyn Carroll, Malissa Carroll
Carroll, Mary
Anne Shore, Lisa St. John,
Meg Dominique, Anne Starr,
*Annette Sanford*
Carroll, Rosalynn
Penny Allison, *Carol Katz*
Carroll, Samantha
Carroll, Susan
Susan Coppula
Carsley, Anne
Carson, Angela
Sue Peters
Carson, Christine
Carson, Rosalind
Margaret Chittenden
Carstens, Netta
Christina Laffeaty, *Martha Fortina*
Carter, Ann
Anne Tedlock Brooks
Carter, Ashley
Blaine Stevens, Harry Whittington
Carter, Helen
Eleni Carr, Helen Carras,
*Helen Maragakis*
Carter, Janice
Janice Hess
Carter, Marilyn
W.E.D. Ross, Dan Ross, Dana Ross,
Rose Dana, Ruth Dorsett,
Diana Randall, Marilyn Ross,
Clarissa Ross, Ann Gilmor,
Miriam Leslie, Leslie Ames,
Jane Rossiter, Rose Williams,
Ellen Randolph
Carter, Noel Vreeland
Carter, Rosemary
Carteret, Cindy

Cartier, Lynn
Cartland, Barbara
*Barbara McCorquodale*
Carton, Nick
Michael Avallone, Troy Conway,
Priscilla Dalton, Mark Dane,
Jean-Anne DePre, Edwina Noone,
Steve Michaels, Dorothea Nile,
Vance Stanton, Sidney Stuart
Cartwright, Vanessa
Case, Barbra
*Casey, June E.*
Casey Douglas, Melissa Ash,
Constance Ravenlock, June Trevor
Cass, Zoe
Lois Low, Lois Paxton,
Dorothy Mackie Low
Cassidy, Becca
Jamie West, *Beverly Vines-Haines*
Cassity, Joan
Casstevens, Jeanne S.
Castell, Megan
Jeanne Crecy, Kristin Michaels,
Deirdre Rowan, Megan Stuart,
Jeanne Williams, Jeanne Foster
Castle, Brenda
Georgina Ferrand
Castle, Jayne
Stephanie James, Jayne Bentley,
Jayne Taylor, Jayne Ann
Krentz, Amanda Glass
Castle, Jill
*Linda Neukrug*
Castle, Philippa
Marilyn M. Lowery
*Casto, Jacqueline*
Jackie Black, Jacqueline Ashley
*Castoro, Laura*
Laura Parker
Caswell, Anne
Mary Orr
Caswell, Helen
Catalani, Victoria
*Carola Haas*
Cates, Kimberly
Kimberleigh Caitlin, Kim Bush
Cates, Tory
*Sara Bird*

Catley, Melanie
Catlin, Barbara
  *Barbara C. Craven*
Catlin, Maranda
  *Martha R. Hix & Barbara C. Craven,*
  Martha Hicks
Cato, Nancy
Causeway, Jane
  Barry Cook
Cavaliere, Anne
  *Anne Canadeo,* Alyssa Douglas
Cavanagh, Helen
  Honey Christopher
Cavanna, Betty
  Elizabeth Harrison, Elizabeth Headley
Chace, Isobel
  Elizabeth Hunter, Elisie B. Rider,
  *Elizabeth de Guise*
Chadwick, Cleo
  *Lois Smith*
Chadwick, Elizabeth
Chamberlain, Diane
Chambers, Catherine
  Elizabeth Bolton, Kate Chambers,
  Pamela Dryden, Lavinia Harris,
  Norma Johnston, Adrian Roberts,
  Nicole St. John
Chambers, Ginger
Chambers, Kate
  Elizabeth Bolton, Adrian Roberts,
  Catherine Chambers, Lavinia Harris,
  Pamela Dryden, Norma Johnston,
  Nicole St. John
Chance, Lisbeth
  Leigh Daniels
Chance, Sara
  Sherry Carr, Sydney Ann Clary
Chandler, Laurel
  Nancy Holder, Wendi Davis,
  Nancy Jones
Chandos, Fay
  Jan Tempest, Theresa Charles,
  *Irene Mossop*, Virginia Storm,
  Leslie Lance, *Charles &*
  *Irene Swatridge*
Channing, Justin
  *Helen Barret & Karen Kitzig*

Chapel, Ashley
  Harper McBride, *Judith Weaver*
Chapman, Margaret
*Chappelyear, Laurie*
  Laurie Grant
Chappell, Helen
  Rebecca Baldwin
Charles, Anita
  Susan Barrie, Jane Beaufort,
  Rose Burghley, Pamela Kent,
  Ida Pollock, Barbara Rowan,
  Mary Whistler
Charles, Caroline
  Mary Mackie, Mary Christopher,
  Cathy Christopher, Susan Stevens,
  Alex Andrews
Charles, Iona
  *Carolyn Nichols & Stanlee*
  *Miller Coy,* Cissie Miller
Charles, Maggi
  Meg Hudson, Carole Standish,
  Russell Mead, *Margaret Koehler*
Charles, Marie
  Marie Michael, Marie Rydzynski,
  Marie Nicole, Marie Ferrarella
Charles, Theresa
  Jan Tempest, Fay Chandos,
  *Irene Mossop*, Virginia Storm,
  Leslie Lance, *Charles &*
  *Irene Swatridge*
Charleton, Madeline
Charlton, Ann
Charlton, Josephine
  *Josephine C. Hauber*
Chase, Carolyn
Chase, Elaine Raco
Chase, Loretta
  *Loretta Chekani*
Chase, Marian
Chase, Samantha
  Ruth Glick & Eileen Buckholtz,
  Alexis Hill, Alexis Hill Jordan,
  Alyssa Howard, Rebecca York,
  Tess Marlowe, Amanda Lee
Chastain, Sandra
  Jenna Darcy
Chater, Elizabeth
  Lisa Moore

**Chatfield, Susan**
 *Susan C. Fasshauer*
**Cheatham, Lillian**
*Chekani, Loretta*
 Loretta Chase
**Cheney, Sally**
**Chenier, Blanche**
**Chesney, Marion**
 Jennie Tremain, Ann Fairfax,
 Helen Crampton, Sarah Chester
 *Marion Scott-Gibbons*
*Chesnutt, Linda*
 Lindsey Hanks
**Chester, Deborah**
**Chester, Sarah**
 Jennie Tremain, Ann Fairfax,
 Helen Crampton, Marion Chesney,
 *Marion Scott-Gibbons*, Amanda Lee
*Child, Judith*
 Juli Greene
*Childress, Susan*
 Susan Wiggs
**Chimenti, Francesca**
**Chisholm, Lilian**
 Anne Lorraine, *Jane Alan*
**Chittenden, Margaret**
 Rosalind Carson
**Choate, Gwen**
 Kristin Michaels
**Christenberry, Judy**
**Christian, Jill**
 Norrey Ford, *Noreen Dilcock*,
 Christian Walford
**Christie, Colleen**
 *J. S. Bidwell*
**Christie, Michelle**
 Gerri O'Hara, Michelle Michaels
**Christie, Susanna**
 *Susan B. Ossana & Kristin Burton*
**Christopher, Beth**
**Christopher, Cathy**
 Mary Mackie, Mary Christopher,
 Caroline Charles, Susan Stevens,
 Alex Andrews
**Christopher, Jane**
 Nell Kincaid, Joanna Kenyon,
 *Janet Clarke*
**Christopher, Francine**

 *Francine Mandeville*
**Christopher, Honey**
 Helen Cavanagh
**Christopher, Mary**
 Mary Mackie, Cathy Christopher,
 Caroline Charles, Susan Stevens,
 Alex Andrews
**Christopher, Paula**
 Lynn Michaels, *Lynne Smith*
**Church, Emma**
 Elizabeth Graham, *E. Schattner*
**Churchill, Jill**
 (See Janice Young Brooks)
*Cichanth, Elaine*
 Elizabeth Shelley
**Clague, Maryhelen**
 Ashley Snow
**Clair, Daphne**
 Laurey Bright, Claire Lorel,
 *Daphne DeJong*
**Claire, Eva**
 Claire Evans, Claire De Long
**Claire, Evelyn**
**Clamp, Helen**
 Olivia Leigh
**Clare, Cathryn**
 *Cathy Stanton*
**Clare, Ellen**
 Olga Daniels, Olga Sinclair
**Clare, Jane**
 Dinah Shields
**Clare, Samantha**
**Clare, Shannon**
 Linda Harrel
**Clark, Amanda**
**Clark, Blair**
 Blair Foster, Sylvia Clark
**Clark, Cecily**
**Clark, Gail**
 Maggie MacKeever, Grace South,
 Grace Scott
**Clark, Jean**
**Clark, Kathy**
**Clark, Louise**
 Roslyn MacDonald
**Clark, Lydia**
 Lydia Lancaster, Valancy Hunter,
 *Eloise Meaker*

**Clark, Marianne**
Sabina Clark, <u>Marianne Willman</u>
**Clark, Mary Higgens**
**Clark, Melissa**
Alysse Aallyn
**Clark, Norma Lee**
**Clark, Roberta**
**Clark, Sabina**
Marianne Clark, <u>Marianne Willman</u>
**Clark, Sandra**
**Clark, Sylvia**
Blair Clark, Blair Foster
**Clarke, Brenda**
Brenda Honeyman
*Clarke, Janet*
Nell Kincaid, Joanna Kenyon,
Jane Christopher
**Clarke, Marion**
*Marion Schultz*
**Clarke, Pippa**
**Clary, Sydney Ann**
Sara Chance, Sherry Carr
**Clay, Bertha M.**
Charlotte Braeme
**Clay, Rita**
Tira Lacy, <u>Rita Estrada</u>
**Clayford, James**
Peggy Gaddis, Peggy Dern,
*Erolie Dern*, Roberta Courtland,
Joan Sherman, Gail Jordan,
Perry Lindsay, Georgia Craig
**Cleary, Gwen**
**Cleaver, Anastasia**
Natasha Peters
**Cleaves, Margaret Major**
Ann Major
**Clemence, Ruth**
*Clemens-Fox, Carol*
Alicia Fox
*Clement, Ernest*
Candace Connell
**Clements, Abigail**
**Clements, Kaye L.**
Jeanne Kaye Triner, Caylin Jennings
**Clermont, Shana**
McElwain, Dean
**Clifford, Kay**
**Clifton, Suzanne**

**Cloud, Patricia**
Pat Wallace, Vivian Lord,
Pat West, <u>Pat Wallace Strother</u>
**Coate, Evelyn**
**Coates, May**
**Coates, Sheila**
Charlotte Lamb, *Sheila Holland,*
Sheila Lancaster, Laura Hardy,
Victoria Woolf
**Coburn, Jean**
**Cockcroft, Ann**
**Coffaro, Katherine**
*Katherine Kovacs*
**Coffman, Elaine**
**Coffman, Virginia**
Jeanne Duval, Kay Cameron,
Diana Saunders, Ann Stanfield,
Victor Cross
*Coghlan, Peggie*
Jessica Stirling
**Cohen, Anthea**
**Cohen, Jean**
**Cohen, Rhoda**
Eleanora Brownleigh, Diana Loy
**Cohen, Sharron**
*Cohen, Susan*
Elizabeth St. Clair
**Colander, Valerie N.**
**Cole, Hilary**
*Valerie Miller*
**Cole, Jennifer**
*Cheryl Zach*
**Cole, Justine**
*Claire Kiehl* & <u>Susan Phillips</u>
**Cole, Marianne**
Jennifer Dale, <u>Charlotte White</u>
**Cole, Sue Ellen**
Susanna Collins, <u>Susan Gross,</u>
Susana de Lyonne
**Coles, Janis**
**Collier, Leona**
**Collin, Marion Cripes**
**Collins Laurel**
*Linda C. Wiath*
**Collins, Christine**
Cara McLean, <u>Elizabeth Barrett</u>
**Collins, Kathryn**

**Collins, Marion Smith**
  Marion Smith
**Collins, Susanna**
  Susan Gross, Sue Ellen Cole,
  Susana de Lyonne
**Collins, Toni**
**Collinson, Marie**
**Colt, Zandra**
  Zabrina Faire, Ellen Fitzgerald,
  Lucia Curzon, Pamela Frazier,
  Florence Stevenson
**Colter, Cara**
**Colvin, Penny**
*Comber, Lillian*
  Lillian Beckwith
**Combs, Becky**
**Comer, Linda**
  Eileen Jackson, Helen May
**Comfort, Iris**
**Conant, Constance**
*Conarain, Alice*
  Elizabeth Hoy
*Conaway, James*
  Leila Lyons, Vanessa Valcour
**Conlee, Jaelyn**
  Fayrene Preston
**Conn, Phoebe**
  *Phoebe C. Ingwalson*
**Connell, Candace**
  Ernest Clement
*Connell, Ethel*
  Katrina Britt
**Connolly, Vivian**
  Susanna Rosse
**Conrad, Constance**
  Rebecca Bennett, Lillian Marsh,
  *Ruby Frankel*
**Conrad, Helen**
  Jena Hunt, Raye Morgan
**Constant, Jan**
**Conte, Charles**
  Vivian Donald, Iain Torr,
  Charles Stuart, Hilary Rose,
  Graham Montrose, Rory Macalpin,
  Charles R. MacKinnon
**Converse, Jane**
  Adela Gale, Kay Martin,
  *Adela Maritano*

**Conway, Celine**
  Kathryn Blair, Rosalind Brett
**Conway, Jean**
**Conway, Laura**
  Hebe Elsna, Vicky Lancaster,
  Lyndon Snow, *Dorothy P. Ansle*,
  Margaret Campbell Barnes
**Conway, Theresa**
**Conway, Troy**
  Edwina Noone, Michael Avallone,
  Nick Carton, Priscilla Dalton,
  Mark Dane, Jean-Anne DePre,
  Steve Michaels, Dorothea Nile,
  Vance Stanton, Sidney Stuart
*Coogan, Beatrice*
  Claire Lorrimer, Patricia Robins
**Cook, Barry**
  Jane Causeway
**Cook, Bonna Lee**
  Bonna Lee DuBois
*Cook, Deirdre*
  Dorothy Cork
**Cook, Eugenia**
*Cook, Ida*
  Mary Burchell
*Cook, Petronella*
  Margot Arnold
**Cook, Sally**
**Cook, Susan**
**Cooke, Phyl**
**Cookson, Catherine**
  Catherine Marchant,
  Catherine Fawcett
**Coombs, Ann**
  Nina Pykare, Regina Towers,
  Nan Pemberton, Nora Powers,
  Natalie Pryor, Nina Coombs
**Coombs, Nina**
  Nan Pemberton, Nina Pykare,
  Regina Towers, Nora Powers,
  Natalie Pryor, Ann Coombs
**Cooper, Ann**
**Cooper, Barbara A.**
**Cooper, Jilly**
**Cooper, Lynna**
  Gardiner Fox
**Copeland, Lori**
**Copeland, Patricia Ann**

# C

Coppula, Susan
　Susan Carroll
Corbett, Paula
Corbin, Delinda
Corcoran, Barbara
*Corcoran, Dotti*
　DeAnn Patrick
Corey, Gayle
　*Elaine Havptman*
Cork, Dorothy
　*Deirdre Cook*
Corren, Grace
　Susan Jennifer, Robert Hoskins
Corrie, Jane
*Corson, Martha*
　Anne Lacey, Kristin Michaels
Cory, Caroline
　*Mary Fitt*, Kathleen Freeman
Cory, Diane
Cosgrove, Rachel R.
　Rachel Cosgrove Payes
　Joanne Kaye, E. L. Arch
Cott, Christine
Coughlin, Pat
　Liz Grady
Couldrey, Vivienne
Coulson, Juanita
Coulter, Catherine
　*Jean Coulter Pogony*
Coultry, Barbara
　Barbara Blacktree
*Courcelles, Sandra*
　Samantha Day
Court, Katherine
　*Elizabeth K. Schrempp*
Courtland, Roberta
　Peggy Gaddis, Peggy Dern,
　*Erolie Dern,* James Clayford,
　Joan Sherman, Gail Jordan,
　Perry Lindsay, Georgia Craig
Courtney, Caroline
Cousins, Margaret
　Avery Johns, Mary Parrish,
　William Masters
Cowdray, Rosalind
Cox, Eleanor Anne
Cox, Jane
Cox, Joan

Cox, Patricia
　Pat Warren
*Coy, Stanlee Miller*
　Iona Charles, Cissie Miller
Craig, Dolores
　Moira Lord, Claire Vincent,
　Miriam Lynch
Craig, Georgia
Craig, Georgia
　Peggy Gaddis, Peggy Dern,
　*Erolie P. Dern*, Perry Lindsay,
　Roberta Courtland, Gail Jordan,
　James Clayford, Joan Sherman
Craig, Jasmine
　Jasmine Cresswell
Craig, Mary
　Alexis Hill
Craig, Rianna
　*Sharon & Rick Harrington*
Craig, Vera
　Edna Murray, *Donald S. Rowland*
Crampton, Helen
　Ann Fairfax, Marion Chesney,
　Jennie Tremain, Sarah Chester,
　*Marion Scott-Gibbons*
Crane, Leah
　Jean Hager, Amanda McAllister,
　Jeanne Stephens, Sarah North,
　Marlaine Kyle
Cranmer, Kathryn
*Craven, Barbara Catlin*
　Maranda Catlin, Barbara Catlin
Craven, Sara
Crawford, Diane
　Georgette Livingston
Crawford, Lillian
Crawford, Rosemary
Crawley, Aileen
Crecy, Jeanne
　Megan Castell, Kristin Michaels,
　Deirdre Rowan, Megan Stuart,
　Jeanne Williams, Jeanne Foster
Creekmore, Donna
Creel, Catherine
Creese, Bethea
Creighton, Kathleen
　Kathleen Carrol, *Kathleen Modrovich*
Crenshaw, Nadine

**Cresswell, Jasmine**
Jasmine Craig
*Crewe, Sarah*
Virginia Blanford
*Crews, Ethel Maxam*
Mia Maxam
**Crichton, Lucilla**
Diana Gordon, Joanna Marcus,
Lucilla Andrews
**Cristabel**
Kathleen Westcott, *Christine Abrahamsen*
**Cristy, Ann**
Hayton Monteith, Danielle Paul,
Helen Mittermeyer
**Crockett, Christina**
Linda Crockett Gray
**Croissant, Kay**
Catherine Kay
**Cromie, Alice**
*Crompton, Anne*
Anne Eliot
**Cromwell, Elsie**
Elsie Lee, Jane Gordon,
Lee Sheridan, Elsie Sheridan
**Crone, Alla**
**Crose, Susan**
Lisa Jackson, Michelle Mathews
**Cross, Caitlin**
*Daranna Berger*
**Cross, Charlene**
**Cross, Melinda**
**Cross, Nancy**
Anne Baker
**Cross, Peggy**
**Cross, Victor**
Virginia Coffman,
Jeanne Duval, Kay Cameron,
Ann Stanfield, Diana Saunders
**Crowe, Cecily**
**Crowe, Evelyn A.**
*Crumbaker, Alice*
Allison Baker
**Cruz, Joan Carroll**
*Cudlipp, Edythe*
Nicole Norman, Maureen Norris,
Julia Alcott, Bettina Montgomery,
Rinalda Roberts, Edythe Lachlan
**Cuevas, Judith**

*Culver, Colleen*
Colleen Faulkner
**Cumberland, Patricia**
**Cummings, Monette**
**Cummins, Mary**
Susan Taylor
**Cunliffe, Corinna**
*Corinna Wildman*
**Cunningham, Jan**
Chelsey Forrest
**Cunningham, Madelyn**
**Cunningham, Marilyn**
**Currie, Katy**
Diana Blayne, Susan Kyle,
Diana Palmer
**Curry, Avon**
Barbara Annandale, Belinda Dell,
*Jean Bowden*, Jocelyn Barry
**Curry, Elissa**
Nancy Martin
**Curtis, Jean**
**Curtis, Mary**
Mary Haskell
**Curtis, Peter**
Norah Lofts, Juliet Astley
**Curtis, Sharon & Thomas**
Laura London, Robin James
**Curtis, Susannah**
Helen Upshall
**Curzon, Lucia**
Zabrina Faire, Ellen Fitzgerald,
Zandra Colt, Pamela Frazier,
Florence Stevenson
**Cushing, Enid**
**Cust, Barbara**
Caroline Fanshawe, Kate Ward
*Cuthrell, Faith*
Faith Baldwin
*Czuleger, Rebecca*
Rebecca Bond, Rebecca Forster

**C**

*Notes*

Names in *italics* indicate an author's legal name which does not appear on books. She or he uses pseudonym (s) only.

Names underlined indicate that the author uses legal name for works and may or may not use pseudonym (s).

**Dagg, Jillian**
Jillian Fayre, Faye Wildman, Marilyn Brian
**Daheim, Mary**
**Dailey, Janet**
**Dair, Christina**
*Louzana Kaku*
**Daish, Elizabeth**
**Dakers, Elaine**
Jane Lane
**Dale, Jennifer**
Marianne Cole, Charlotte White
**Dale, Ruth Jean**
*Jean Stribling* & *Betty Duran*
**Daley, Kathleen**
Margaret Ripy, Margaret Daley, Patti Moore, Kit Daley
**Daley, Kit**
Margaret Ripy, Margaret Daley, Patti Moore, Kathleen Daley
**Daley, Margaret**
Margaret Ripy, Kathleen Daley, Patti Moore, Kit Daley
**Dallmayr, Ilse**
Heidi Strasser
**Dalton, Elyse**
**Dalton, Gena**
*Genell Dellin Smith*
**Dalton, Jackie**
*Jackie Troutman*
**Dalton, Jenifer**
Monica Barrie, Marilyn Davids, David Wind
**Dalton, Pat**

**Dalton, Priscilla**
Michael Avallone, Edwina Noone, Nick Carton, Troy Conway, Mark Dane, Jean-Anne DePre, Steve Michaels, Dorothea Nile, Vance Stanton, Sidney Stuart
**Daly, Saralyn**
**Dalzell, Helen**
**Damon, Kate**
*Margaret Brownley*
**Damon, Lee**
*Jane H. Look*
**Dana, Erin**
Ellen Langtry, Nancy Elliott
**Dana, Rose**
Dana Ross, Rose Williams, Ellen Randolph, Leslie Ames, Ruth Dorset, Ann Gilmor, Miriam Leslie, W. E. D. Ross, Clarissa Ross, Marilyn Ross, Diana Randall, Dan Ross, Jane Rossiter, Marilyn Carter
**Danbury, Iris**
**Dane, Eva**
Emma Drummond, Edna Dawes, Elizabeth Darrell, Eleanor Drew
**Dane, Mark**
Michael Avallone, Edwina Noone, Priscilla Dalton, Nick Carton, Troy Conway, Jean-Anne DePre, Steve Michaels, Dorothea Nile, Vance Stanton, Sidney Stuart
**Daniel, Elaine**
**Daniel, Megan**
*Donna Meyer*

**Daniels, Carol**
*Carol Viens*
**Daniels, Dana**
Dena Rhee, <u>Deana Brauer</u>
**Daniels, Dorothy**
Angela Gray, Dorothy Daniels,
Danielle Dorsett, Geraldine Thayer,
Suzanne Somers, Helen Gray Weston,
Cynthia Kavanaugh, Helaine Ross
**Daniels, Faye**
**Daniels, Joleen**
*Gayle Malone Schimek*
**Daniels, Jordanna**
**Daniels, Judith**
*Judith Pelfrey*, Rhett Daniels
**Daniels, Kayla**
*Karin Hofland*
**Daniels, Laura**
**Daniels, Leigh**
<u>Lisbeth Chance</u>
**Daniels, Max**
<u>Roberta Gellis</u>, Leah Jacobs,
Priscilla Hamilton
**<u>Daniels, Olga</u>**
Ellen Clare, Olga Sinclair
**Daniels, Rhett**
Judith Daniels, *Judy Pelfrey*
**Dann, Victoria**
Victoria Glenn
**Danton, Rebecca**
Louisa Bronte, Janette Radcliffe,
<u>Janet Louise Roberts</u>
**Daoust, Pamela**
Katharine Kincaid
**Darby, Catherine**
Veronica Black, Maureen Black,
<u>Maureen Peters</u>, Judith Rothmann,
Sharon Whitby, Elizabeth Law,
Levanah Lloyd
**<u>Darcy, Clare</u>**
**Darcy, Emma**
**Darcy, Jenna**
<u>Sandra Chastain</u> & Nancy Knight
**Darcy, Lilian**
**D'Arcy, Pamela**
Georgina Grey, <u>Mary Linn Roby</u>,
Mary Wilson, Elisabeth Welles,
Pauline Pryor, Valerie Bradstreet

**Dare, Jessica**
Darla Benton, Joanna Leslie
**Darke, Hilary**
**Darling, Joan**
Dee Stuart, Doris Stuart,
Ellen Searight
**Darlington, Con**
Susan Ashe, Carol Ann Best,
Ann Martin, Marcia Wayne
**Darlington, Joy**
Joy Gardner, *Joy Aumente*
**Darnell, Berde**
**Darrell, Elizabeth**
Emma Drummond, Eva Dane,
<u>Edna Dawes</u>, Eleanor Drew
**Darrington, Paula**
Paula Williams
**Darwin, Jeanette**
<u>Candace Schuler</u>
**Davenport, Kathryn**
Keller Graves
**Daveson, Mons**
**Davids, Marilyn**
Monica Barrie, Jenifer Dalton,
<u>David Wind</u>
**Davidson, Andrea**
Elise Randolph, *Susan Lowe*
**Davies, Frances**
*Leone Lewensohn*
**Davies, Iris**
Iris Gower
**Davis, Berrie**
**Davis, Deborah**
**<u>Davis, DianeWicker</u>**
Delaney Devers
**Davis, Elizabeth**
Lou Ellen Davis
**Davis, Genevieve**
*Davis, Julie*
Juliana Davison
**Davis, Katherine**
*Mildred Davis*
**Davis, Kathryn**
**Davis, Leslie**
<u>Leslie D. Guccione</u>
**Davis, Lou Ellen**
Elizabeth Davis

Davis, Madeline
  Madeline Garry
**Davis, Maggie**
Davis, Melanie
  Claudette Williams
Davis, Mary
  Rosemary Jordan
Davis, Mildred
  Katherine Davis
**Davis, Suzannah**
Davis, Wendi
  Laurel Chandler, Nancy Holder,
  Nancy Jones
Davison, Juliana
  Julie Davis
**Dawes, Edna**
  Emma Drummond, Eva Dane,
  Elizabeth Darrell, Eleanor Drew
Dawson, Elizabeth
Dawson, Helena
Dawson, Saranne
  Pamela Lind, *Saranne Hoover*
Day, Dianne
Day, Jocelyn
  Lorena McCourtney, Rena McKay,
  Lisa McConnell
Day, Lucinda
  *Marie Flasschoen & Marian Scheirman*
Day, Samantha
  *Sandra Courcelles*
Dayton, Lily
  Linda Hampton
Dean, Dinah
  Marjorie May
Dean, Nell Marr
  *Nell Dean Ratzlaff*, Anne Marr,
  Virginia Roberts
**Dean Rena**
*De Bets, Julie*
  Maura McGiveny
**De Blassis, Celeste**
DeBoer, Marjorie Rockwell
**De Borde, Sherry**
De Coto, Jean
De Coursey, Virginia
*De Covarrubias, Barbara Faith*
  Barbara Faith

Dee, Sherry
  Sheryl Hines Flournoy
*Dees, Catherine*
  Catherine Kay
De Guise, Elizabeth
  Isobel Chace, *Elisie B. Rider*,
  Elizabeth Hunter
Deiterle, Robin
*DeJong, Daphne*
  Laurey Bright, Daphne Clair,
  Claire Lorel
De Jourlet, Marie
  Paula Minton, Paul Little,
  Leigh Franklin James, Paula Little
Delaney, Gina
  Jalynn Friends, *Patricia Wells* &
  Rosalyn Alsobrook
Delatour, Elise
**Delatush, Edith**
  Alyssa Morgan, Edith St. George,
  Edith De Paul
De Lauer, Marjel
**DeLeeuw, Cateau W.**
  Jessica Lyon, Kay Hamilton
*De Leon, Ana Lisa*
  Celina Mullan, Rachel Scott,
  Marisa de Zavala
**Delinsky, Barbara**
  Billie Douglass, Bonnie Drake
Dell, Belinda
  Barbara Annandale, *Jean Bowden*,
  Avon Curry, Jocelyn Barry
Dellamere, Wanda
Delmore, Diana
  *Lois Nollet*
De Long, Claire
  Claire Evans, Eva Claire
De Lyn, Nicole
  Nicole Lindsay, Eva Woodland
De Lyonne, Susana
  Susanna Collins, Susan Gross,
  Sue Ellen Cole
*Demetropoulos, Nicholas*
  Marianne Evans, Jean Evans
Dennis, Roberta
*Dennore, Roberta*
  Rochelle De Nore

**De Nore, Rochelle**
*Roberta Dennore*
<u>Dent, Roxanne</u>
Melissa Masters
**Dentinger, Jane**
**Denton, Kate**
*Carolyn Hake & Jeanie Lambright*
**Denys, Teresa**
*Jacqui Bianchi*
**Deobold, Sue**
**De Paul, Edith**
Alyssa Morgan, Edith St. George,
<u>Edith Delatush</u>
**DePre, Jean-Anne**
Michael Avallone, Edwina Noone,
Priscilla Dalton, Nick Carton,
Troy Conway, Mark Dane,
Steve Michaels, Dorothea Nile,
Vance Stanton, Sidney Stuart
**Dern, Erolie Pearl**
Peggy Gaddis, Peggy Dern,
James Clayford, Gail Jordan,
Perry Lindsay, Joan Sherman
Roberta Courtland, Georgia Craig
**Dern, Peggy**
Peggy Gaddis, *Erolie Dern,*
James Clayford, Gail Jordan,
Perry Lindsay, Joan Sherman
Roberta Courtland, Georgia Craig
*De Sha, Sandra*
Sandra Donovan
**De St. Jeor, Owanna**
**Deveraux, Jude**
*Jude Gilliam White*
**De Vere, Jane**
<u>Julia Fitzgerald</u>, Julia Watson,
Julia Hamilton
**Devers, Delaney**
<u>Diane Davis</u>
**Devin, Flanna**
<u>Karen Juneman</u>
**De Vincent, Eleanora**
**Devine, Thea**
**De Vita, Sharon**
**DeVoe, Lily**
**Devon, Alexandra**
Katherine Kent, <u>Joan Dial,</u>
Amanda York, Katherine Sinclair

**Devon, Anne**
Marian Devon, <u>Marian Pope Rettke</u>
**Devon, Georgina**
*Allison J. Hentges*
**Devon, Lynn**
**Devon, Marian**
Anne Devon, <u>Marian Pope Rettke</u>
**Devon, Sara**
Kathleen Ash, Pauline Ash,
Emily Walker, Eileen Barry,
Delia Foster, Christine Lawson,
Jane Lester, Cora Mayne,
Honor Vincent, Heather Vincent,
Jill Murray, Quenna Tilbury,
Kathleen Treves, Kay Winchester
*De Vore, Mary*
Madelyn Dohrn
**Dewar, Sandra**
**De Winter, Danielle**
<u>Keith Timson</u>
**Deyoe, Cori**
Jessica Barkley
**De Zavala, Marisa**
Celina Mullan, Rachel Scott,
*Ana Lisa de Leon*
<u>Dial, Joan</u>
Katherine Kent, Alexandra Devon,
Amanda York, Katherine Sinclair
*Diamond, Barbara B.*
Barbara Bentley
<u>Diamond, Graham</u>
Rochelle Leslie
**Diamond, Jacqueline**
<u>Jackie Hyman</u>, Jacqueline Jade,
Jacqueline Topaz
**Diamond, Petra**
*Judith Sachs*
**Di Benedetto, Theresa**
**Dickerson, Marilyn**
**Di Donato, Georgia**
*Dilcock, Noreen*
Norrey Ford, Jill Christian,
Christian Walford
*Dillard, Polly Hargis*
Polly Hargis, Pauline Hargis
**Dillon, Catherine**
**Dillon, Patricia**

**Dimick, Cherylle Lindsey**
  Dawn Lindsey
**Dingley, Sally G.**
  Sally Garrett
**Dingwell, Joyce**
  Kate Starr
**Dion, Paula**
**Dix, Dorothy**
  Elizabeth M. Gilmer
**Dix, Isabel**
**Dixon, Diana**
**Dixon, Lesley**
  Kay Vernon, Kathleen R. Vernon
**Dixon, Rhonda**
**Dobkin, Kaye**
**Dobravolsky, Barbara**
**Dobson, Margaret**
**Dohrn, Madelyn**
  *Mary De Vore & Joan Dornsbusch*
**Dominique, Meg**
  Anne Shore, Lisa St. John,
  Anne Starr, Mary Carroll,
  Annette Sanford
**Domning, Joan**
**Donald, Robyn**
**Donald, Vivian**
  Hilary Rose, Iain Torr,
  Charles Conte, Charles Stuart,
  Rory Macalpin, Graham Montrose,
  Charles R. MacKinnon
**Donnelly, Jane**
**Donner, Katherine**
*Donohue, Mary Irene*
  Irene Michaels
**Donovan, Sandra**
  *Sandra De Sha*
**Dore, Christy**
  *Jim Plagakis*
*Dornbusch, Joan*
  Madelyn Dohrn
**Dors, Alexandra**
  Dorothy Mack, *Dorothy McKittrick*
**Dorset, Ruth**
  Dana Ross, Rose Williams
  Ellen Randolph, Leslie Ames,
  Rose Dana, Miriam Leslie,
  Ann Gilmor, W. E. D. Ross,
  Clarissa Ross, Marilyn Ross,

  Diana Randall, Dan Ross,
  Jane Rossiter, Marilyn Carter
**Dorsett, Danielle**
  Angela Gray, Dorothy Daniels,
  Geraldine Thayer, Suzanne Somers,
  Helen Gray Weston, Helaine Ross
*Dorsey, Christine*
  Christine Elliott
**Douglas, Alyssa**
  Anne Cavaliere, *Anne Canadeo*
**Douglas, Barbara**
  Rosalind Laker, Barbara Paul,
  Barbara Ovstedahl
**Douglas, Carole Nelson**
**Douglas, Gail**
**Douglas, Casey**
  June Trevor, *June E. Casey,*
  Constance Ravenlock, Melissa Ash
**Douglas, Elizabeth**
  Betsey Page, Elizabeth Page,
  *Bettie Wilhite*
**Douglas, Gloria**
  *Gloria Upper*
**Douglas, Kate**
**Douglas, Kathryn**
  *Kathryn Ewing*
**Douglas, LaLette**
  Lafayette Hammett
**Douglas, Mary**
  *Mary Tew*
**Douglas, Monica**
**Douglas, Sheila**
**Douglass, Amanda Hart**
**Douglass, Billie**
  Bonnie Drake, Barbara Delinsky
**Douglass, Jessica**
  Linda Benjamin, *Linda H. Wallerich*
**Dowdell, Dorothy**
**Dowling, Shirley**
*Downes, Deirdre*
  Kathleen Downes
**Downes, Kathleen**
  *Deirdre Downes*
**Doyle, Amanda**
**Doyle, Barbara**
**Doyle, Emily**
  Amanda Kent, Betty Henrichs

*Dozier, Zoe*
  Dixie Browning, Bronwyn Williams
**Drake, Asa**
  Jane Archer, *Nina Andersson,*
  *Nina Romberg*
**Drake, Bonnie**
  Billie Douglass, <u>Barbara Delinsky</u>
**Drake, Connie**
  Carol Finch, Gina Robins,
  *Connie Fedderson*
**Drake, Shannon**
  Heather Graham, <u>Heather Pozzessere</u>
**Dressler, Gladys**
  Gladys McGorian
**Drew, Eleanor**
  Emma Drummond, EvaDane,
  Elizabeth Darrell, <u>Edna Dawes</u>
<u>**Dreyer, Eileen**</u>
  Kathleen Korbel
**Drummond, Brenna**
  Allison Lawrence, Eve O'Brien,
  *Judy Bryer*
**Drummond, Emma**
  Eva Dane, Elizabeth Darrell,
  <u>Edna Dawes</u>, Eleanor Drew
**Drummond, Ivor**
  Megan Barker, Rosalind Erskine,
  Roger Longrigg
**Dryden, Pamela**
  Elizabeth Bolton, Kate Chambers,
  Catherine Chambers, Norma Johnston,
  Lavinia Harris, Adrian Roberts,
  Nicole St. John
**Drymon, Kathleen**
**DuBay, Sandra**
**DuBois, Claudia**
**DuBois, Bonna Lee**
  Bonna Lee Cook
**DuBois, Jill**
**DuBois, Sally**
  *Lyn Vincentnathan*
**DuBreuil, Elizabeth Lorinda**
  Kate Cameron, Lorinda Hagen,
  Margaret Maitland
**DuBus, Elizabeth Nell**
*Duckett, Madelaine G.*
  Madelaine Gibson
**Ducoty, Lyn**

**Dudley, Nancy**
  Caroline Arnett, *Lois Cole Taylor,*
  Lynn Avery, Allan Dwight,
  Anne Lattin
**Duffield, Anne**
  *Dorothy Dean Duffield*
*Duffield, Dorothy Dean*
  Anne Duffield
**Duke, Elizabeth**
**Dumbrille, Dorothy**
**Dunaway, Diana**
*Dunaway, Patti*
  Poppy Nottingham
**Dunbar, Inga**
**Dunbar, Jean**
<u>**Duncan, Carol**</u>
**Duncan, Jane**
  Elizabeth Jane Cameron
**Duncan, Judith**
  *Judith Mulholland*
**Dunn, Carola**
**Dunn, Mary**
  *Mary Faid*
**Dunnett, Dorothy**
  *Dorothy Halliday*
**DuPont, Diane**
**DuPont, Ellen**
  Joy St. David
**DuPre, Gabrielle**
  *Dianne M. Kleinschmidt &*
  *Sandra Smith-Ware*
**Dupres, Lenore**
**Duquette, Anne Marie**
*Duran, Betty*
  Ruth Jean Dale
**Durant, Cheryl**
  *Durant Imboden*
**Dureau, Lorena**
**Dureau, Lorna**
**Durham, Anne**
**Dustin, Sarah**
  <u>Hannah Howell</u>
**Duval, Jeanne**
  <u>Virginia Coffman</u>, Kay Cameron,
  Ann Stanfield, Victor Cross,
  Diana Saunders
**Duval, Justine**
**Duval, Nicole**

**DuVal, Nicolette**
**Duvall, Aimee**
   Aimee Martel, <u>Aimee Thurlo</u>
**Dwight, Allan**
   Caroline Arnett, *Lois Cole Taylor*,
   Lynn Avery, Nancy Dudley,
   Anne Lattin
*Dworman, Brenda*
   Brenda Joyce
**Dwyer-Joyce, Alice**
**Dyal, Gloria**
*Dyne, Michael*
   Evelyn Hanna

*Notes*

# D

## Notes

Names in *italics* indicate an author's legal name which does not appear on books. She or he uses pseudonym (s) only.

Names <u>underlined</u> indicate that the author uses legal name for works and may or may not use pseudonym (s).

<u>Eagle, Kathleen</u>
**Earley, Fran**
  *Bob Whearley*
**Eastvale, Margaret**
**Eastwood, Helen**
  Fay Ramsay, Olive Baxter
**Eatock, Marjorie**
**Eaton, Laura**
**Eckersley, Jill**
  Helen Beaumont, Anna Stanton, Jill Sanderson, Denise Emery
**Eckert, Roberta**
**Eden, Dorothy**
  Mary Paradise
**Eden, Laura**
  <u>Claire Harrison</u>
**Edgar, Josephine**
  Mary Howard, *Mary Mussi*
**Edgeworth, Ann**
<u>Edghill, Rosemary</u>
**Edmonds, Janet**
**Edward, Ann**
  Anna West
**Edwards, Adrienne**
  Anne Benson, Anne Hillary, Kathryn Jessup, Erika Bryant, Andrea Edwards, <u>Anne & Ed Kolaczyk</u>
**Edwards, Andrea**
  Anne Hillary, Anne Benson, Kathryn Jessup, Erika Bryant, Adrienne Edwards, <u>Anne & Ed Kolaczyk</u>
**Edwards, Cassie**
**Edwards, Claudia**
**Edwards, Emily Ruth**
**Edwards, Estelle**
  Mollie Gregory
**Edwards, Jane**
  Jane Campbell

**Edwards, Judi**
<u>Edwards, Irene</u>
  Elisabeth Barr
**Edwards, Jaroldeen**
**Edwards, Kathryn**
**Edwards, Paula**
**Edwards, Rachelle**
**Edwards, Samuel**
  <u>Noel B. Gerson</u>, Dana F. Ross, Carter Vaughn, Phillip Vail, Paul Lewis
**Edwards, Sarah**
  *Sharon & Robert Bils*
**Egan, Lesley**
  <u>Elizabeth Linnington</u>, Anne Blaisdell Egan O'Neill, Dell Shannon,
**Eirls, Sandra Lynn**
**Elder, Catherine**
  *Elgin, Betty*
  Kate Kirby
**Elgin, Mary**
**Elgin, Suzette**
**Eliot, Anne**
  *Anne Crompton*
**Eliot, Carolyn**
**Eliot, Jessica**
  *Lois A. Brown & Barbara Levy*
*Eliot, Winslow*
  Ellie Winslow
*Elkins, Charlotte*
  Emily Spenser
**Ellerbeck, Rosemary**
  Anna L'Estrange, Nicola Thorne, Katherine Yorke
**Ellingson, Marnie**
**Elliot, Lucy**
  *Nancy Greenman*
**Elliot, Rachel**

61

*Elliott, Anne*
  Christine Elliott
**Elliott Christine**
  *Christine Dorsey & Anne Elliott*
**Elliott, Emily**
  *Emily Mims*
**Elliott, Nancy**
  Ellen Langtry, Erin Dana
**Elliott, Robin**
  Joan E. Pickart
**Ellis, Alexandra**
  *Carmel B. Reingold*
**Ellis, Audrey**
**Ellis, Delia**
**Ellis, Janine**
**Ellis, Joan**
  Julie Ellis, Marilyn Ellis,
  Susan Marvin, Richard Marvin,
  Susan Marino, Susan Richard,
  Alison Lord, Jeffrey Lord,
  Patricia Bentley, Jill Monte,
  Linda Michaels
**Ellis, Julie**
  Susan Marino, Marilyn Ellis,
  Susan Marvin, Richard Marvin,
  Susan Richard, Joan Ellis,
  Patricia Bentley, Jill Monte,
  Allison Lord, Jeffrey Lord,
  Linda Michaels
**Ellis, Kathy**
**Ellis, Leigh**
  *Anne & Louisa Rudeen*
**Ellis, Marilyn**
  Julie Ellis, Joan Ellis,
  Susan Marvin, Richard Marvin,
  Susan Richard, Susan Marino,
  Alison Lord, Jeffrey Lord,
  Patricia Bentley, Jill Monte,
  Linda Michaels
**Ellis, Patricia**
**Ellison, Marjorie**
  Marjorie Norton, Marjorie Norrell
**Ellison, Suzanne**
**Elsna, Hebe**
  Laura Conway, Vicky Lancaster,
  Lyndon Snow, *Dorothy P. Ansle*,
  Margaret Campbell Barnes
*Elward, James*
  Rebecca James
*Emerson, Kathy Lynn*
  Kaitlyn Gorton
**Emery, Denise**
  Helen Beaumont, Jill Eckersley,

  Anna Stanton, Jill Sanderson
**Emm, Catherine**
  Kay McMahon
**Engels, Mary Tate**
  Tate McKenna, Cory Kenyon,
  Corey Keaton
**English, Genevieve**
  Sarah Patton
**English, Judith**
  Judith Kelly
**Engren, Edith**
  *Edith & Robert McCaig*
**Ensley, Clare**
  Clare Plummer
**Erickson, Lynn**
  *Carla Peltonen & Molly Swanton*
*Eriksen, Barbara*
  Katherine Arthur
**Ernest, Francine**
**Ernest, Jeanette**
  Andra Erskine, *Judy Martin*
**Erskine, Andra**
  Jeanette Ernest, *Judy Martin*
**Erskine, Barbara**
**Erskine, Helen**
  *Helen Santori*
**Erskine, Rosalind**
  Megan Barker, Ivor Drummond,
  Roger Longrigg
**Erwin, Annabel**
  Ann Forman Barron
**Esmond, Harriet**
*Essenmacher, Eugenia Riley*
  Eugenia Riley
**Essex, Marianna**
  *Joan van Nuys*
**Essex, Mary**
  Lozania Prole, Rachel Harvey,
  Ursula Bloom, Sheila Burns,
  Deborah Mann, Ursula Harvey
**Essig, Terry**
**Estrada, Rita**
  Rita Clay, Tira Lacy
**Etheridge, Christina**
**Evanick, Marcia**
**Evanovich, Janet**
  Steffie Hall
**Evans, Claire**
  Eva Claire, Claire De Long
**Evans, Constance M.**
  Mairi O'Nair, Jane Gray
**Evans, Jean**
  Marianne Evans, *Nicholas Demetropoulos*

**Evans, Laurel**
*Ellen Wilson*
**Evans, Margaret**
Margaret E. Potter, Anne Betteridge,
*Margaret Neuman*, Anne Melville
**Evans, Marianne**
Jean Evans, *Nicholas Demetropoulos*
**Evans, Patricia Gardner**
**Evanston, Linell**
**Everest, Francine**
**Everett, Gail**
Arlene Hale, Lynn Williams,
Tracy Adams, Mary Tate,
Mary Hale
*Ewing, Kathryn*
Kathryn Douglas
**Ewing, Tess**
<u>Virginia K. Smiley</u>
**Eyre, Annette**
<u>Anne Worboys</u>, Vicky Maxwell

---

*Notes*

**E**

# Notes

Names in *italics* indicate an author's legal name which does not appear on books. She or he uses pseudonym (s) only.

Names <u>underlined</u> indicate that the author uses legal name for works and may or may not use pseudonym (s).

**Fabian, Erika**
**Fabian, Ruth**
  Erica Lindley, *Aileen Quigley*,
  Aileen Armitage
**Faid, Mary**
  Mary Dunn
**Fain, Michael**
  Judith Maxwell
**Fairchild, Kate**
  Kate Meriwether, Caitlin Murray,
  *Pat Ahearn*
**Fairchilde, Sarah**
**Faire, Zabrina**
  Zandra Colt, Ellen Fitzgerald,
  Lucia Curzon, Pamela Frazier,
  <u>Florence Stevenson</u>
**Fairfax, Ann**
  Jennie Tremain, Marion Chesney,
  Helen Crampton, *Marion Scott-Gibbons*,
  Sarah Chester
**Fairfax, Gwen**
  Kathryn Belmont, Kate Belmont,
  <u>Mary Jo Territo</u>
**Fairfax, Kate**
  Irene Ord
**Fairfax, Lynn**
*Fairman, Paul*
  Paula Fairman, Janet Lovesmith,
  Paulette Warren
**Fairman, Paula**
  *Paul Fairman*, Janet Lovesmith,
  Paulette Warren
**Fairman, Paula**
  Paula Moore, Robert Vaughan
**Faith, Barbara**
  *Barbara Faith de Covarrubias*
**Fanshawe, Caroline**
  Barbara Cust, Kate Ward

**Farland, Kathryn**
  *Kathryn Fladland*
**Farmer, Joan**
**Farnes, Eleanor**
**Farrant, Sarah**
*Fasshauer, Susan C.*
  Susan Chatfield
**Faulkner, Colleen**
  *Colleen Culver*
**Faulkner, Whitney**
  <u>Elaine Bissell</u>
**Faure, Jean**
  Mary Alice Kirk, Mary Kirk
  *Mary Kilchenstein*
**Favor, Erika**
*Favors, Jean*
  Elizabeth Morris
*Fawcett, Catherine*
  Catherine Marchant, Catherine Cookson
**Fayre, Jillian**
  Faye Wildman, *Jillian Dagg*,
  Marilyn Brian
<u>**Feather, Jane**</u>
  Claudia Bishop
<u>**Fecher, Constance**</u>
  Constance Heaven, Christina Merlin
  George Fleming
*Feddersen, Connie*
  Carol Finch, Gina Robins,
  Connie Drake
*Felber, Edith*
  Edith Layton
*Feldman, Gilda*
  Louisa Gillette, Madeline Hale
**Felice, Cynthia**
**Felix, Jenny**
**Felldin, Jeanne**
**Fellows, Catherine**
**Fenwick, Patricia**

**65**

Ferguson, Jo Ann
Fernald, Abby
Ferrand, Georgina
  Brenda Castle
**Ferrarella, Marie R.**
  Marie Charles, Marie Michael,
  Marie Nicole, Marie Rydzynski
Ferrari, Ivy
Ferrars, E. X.
  Morna Brown, Elizabeth Ferrars
Ferrars, Elizabeth
  Morna Brown, E. X. Ferrars
Ferrell, Olivia
Ferris, Gina
  Gina Wilkins
**Ferris, Rose Marie**
  Michelle Roland, Valerie Ferris
  Robin Francis
Ferris, Valerie
  Rose Marie Ferris, Robin Francis,
  Michelle Roland
Field, Karen
Field, Penelope
  *Dorothy Giberson*
Field, Sandra
  Jan MacLean, Jocelyn Haley,
  *Jill MacLean*
Finch, Carol
  Gina Robins, Connie Drake,
  *Connie Feddersen*
*Finkelstein, Roni*
  Janine French
Finley, Glenna
Finlay, Fiona
*Fiorotto, Christine*
  Lucy Gordon
**Fireside, Carolyn**
  Joanna Burgess
Firth, Suzanne
*Fish, Mildred*
  Megan Alexander
Fisher, Dorothea
  Dorothy Canfield, Dorothy Fletcher,
  Miriam Canfield
*Fitt, Mary*
  Caroline Cory, Kathleen Freeman
Fitzgerald, Amber
  Nancy Smith
Fitzgerald, Arlene
Fitzgerald, Barbara
  Jean Stewart, Mona Newman
Fitzgerald, Catherine
  Mallory Burgess, *Mary Sandra Hingston*

Fitzgerald, Ellen
  Pamela Frazier, Zandra Colt,
  Zabrina Faire, Lucia Curzon,
  Florence Stevenson
**Fitzgerald, Julia**
  Jane De Vere, Julia Watson,
  Julia Hamilton
Fitzgerald, Maeve
  Jenny Bates, Anne MacNeill,
  Maura Seger, Sara Jennings,
  Laurel Winslow
Fitzgerald, Catherine
  Mallory Burgess,
  *Mary Sandra Hingston*
Fitzgerald, Nancy
Fitzgerald, Rosemary
Fitzgerald, Sara
Flanders, Rebecca
  Leigh Bristol, Donna Ball,
  Donna Carlisle
**Flannery, Constance O'Day**
*Flasschoen, Marie*
  Lucinda Day
Fladland, Kathryn
  Kathryn Farland
Fleming, Cardine
  Anne Mather, Caroline Fleming,
  *Mildred Grieveson*
Fleming, Caroline
  Anne Mather, Cardine Fleming,
  *Mildred Grieveson*
Fleming, Danielle
  Nancy Morse
Fleming, George
  Constance Heaven, Constance Fecher,
  Christina Merlin
Fleming, Lee
  Ginny Haymond
*Fleming, Kate*
  Jenny McGuire
Fletcher, Aaron
Fletcher, Dorothy
  Miriam Canfield, Dorothea Fisher,
  Dorothy Canfield
Fletcher, Margaret
Fletcher, Violet
Fleury, Jacqueline
  *Jane Fleury*
*Fleury, Jane*
  Jacqueline Fleury
Flindt, Dawn
  Vella Munn
Flixton, Katherine

# F

**Frederick, Thea**
Ariel Berk, Judith Arnold,
*Barbara Keiler*
*Freed, Mary Kay*
Mary Kay Simmons
**Freeman, Jayne**
<u>Freemen, Joy</u>
**Freeman, Kathleen**
Caroline Cory, *Mary Fitt*
**French, Ashley**
<u>Denise Robins</u>, Julia Kane,
Harriet Gray, Francesca Wright
**French, Janine**
<u>Antonia Van-Loon</u> & *Roni Finkelstein*
<u>French, Judith</u>
**Friends, Jalynn**
<u>Rosalyn Alsobrook &
Jean Haught</u>, Gina Delaney
**Fritch, Elizabeth**
Eleanor Frost
**Frost, Eleanor**
*Elsa Frohman*
**Fruchey, Deborah**
**Fulford, Paula**
**Fullbrook, Gladys**
*Patricia Hutchinson*
**Fuller, Kathleen**
*Theodore Mark Gottfried*,
Katherine Tobias, Ted Mark,
Harry Gregory

---

*Notes*

**68**

Names in *italics* indicate an author's legal name which does not appear on books. She or he uses pseudonym (s) only.

Names <u>underlined</u> indicate that the author uses legal name for works and may or may not use pseudonym (s).

Gabhart, Ann
Gabriel, Mary
Gabriel, Tonya
Gaddis, Peggy,
    Peggy Dern, *Erolie Pearl Dern*,
    James Clayford, Perry Lindsay
    Roberta Courtland, Gail Jordan,
    Joan Sherman, Georgia Craig
*Gadzack, D.H.*
    Ann Bernadette
Gaffney, Patricia
Gage, Carol
    Renee Shann
Gage, Elizabeth
Gage, Elsie
Gainer, Kathleen
    Catherine Spencer, Kathy Orr,
    Kathleen Orr
Gair, Diana
Gale, Adela
    Jane Converse, Kay Martin,
    *Adela Maritano*
*Galiardi, Spring*
    *Spring Hermann*
Gallagher, Patricia
Gallagher, Rita
Gallant, Felicia
Gallant, Jennie
    <u>Joan Smith</u>
Galt, Serena
Gamble, M. L.
    *Marsha Nuccio*
Gamel, Nona
<u>Garcia, Nancy</u>
    Kate O'Donnell
Gardner, Joy
    Joy Darlington, *Joy Aumente*
*Gardner, Maria*
    Jillian Hunter

Gardner, Nancy
    Nancy Bruff
Gardner, Toni
Garland, Blanche
    *Ruth Lesko*
Garland, Lisette
    Nora Gibbs, Claire Ritchie,
    Sara Whittingham, Nina Shayne,
    Prudence Boyd, Noelle Ireland,
    Lynne Merrill, Heather Wayne,
    Dallas Romaine
Garland, Sherry
    Lynn Lawrence
<u>Garlock, Dorothy</u>
    Dorothy Phillips, Dorothy Glenn,
    Johanna Phillips
Garnar, Pauline
*Garner, Phyllis A.*
    Phyllis Whitney
Garner, Kathleen
    Catherine Spencer, Kathy Orr,
    Kathleen Orr
Garratt, Maria
Garratt, Mary A.
Garrett, Sally
    *Sally G. Dingley*
<u>Garrett, Sibylle</u>
Garrison, Joan
    Rebecca Marsh, Norma Newcomb,
    William Arthur, Jan Hathaway,
    *William Neubauer*, Christine Bennett
Garrod, Rene J.
Garry, Madeline
    Madeline Davis
*Garvice, Charles*
    Caroline G. Hart, Carolyn Hart
<u>Garwood, Julia</u>
*Gasparotti, Elizabeth*
    Elizabeth Seifert

**69**

Gates, Natalie
Gaud, Priscilla
Gault, Cinda
Gaver, Jessica
Gay, Valerie
Gay, Virginia
Gayle, Emma
Gayle, Margaret
  *Gail Hamilton*
Gayle, Pamela
Gaynor, Anne
*Geach, Christine*
  Christine Wilson, Anne Lowing
*Gee, Evelyn*
  Constance O'Banyon,
  Micah Leigh
Gelles, Sandi
  Nicole Raine
Gellis, Roberta
  Max Daniels, Leah Jacobs,
  Priscilla Hamilton
Gentry, Georgina
  Lynne Murphy
*Gentry, Jane*
  Jane Malcolm
Gentry, Peter
  Shana Carrol, Christina Savage,
  Frank Schaefer & Kerry Newcomb
George, Catherine
*George, Mary*
  Elizabeth Thornton
George, Rebecca
Gerber, Ruth
*Gergich, Millie*
  Millie Grey
Germany, Jo
  Josie King
*Gerritsen, Terry*
  Tess Gerritsen
Gerritsen, Tess
  *Terry Gerritsen*
Gerson, Noel B.
  Samuel Edwards, Carter Vaughan,
  Phillip Vail, Dana Fuller Ross,
  Paul Lewis
Gibbs, Mary Ann
  *Marjory Bidwell*
Gibbs, Nora
  Claire Ritchie, Prudence Boyd,
  Sara Whittingham, Nina Shayne,
  Lisette Garland, Noelle Ireland,
  Lynne Merrill, Heather Wayne,
  Dallas Romaine

*Giberson, Dorothy*
  Penelope Field
*Gibeson, Jacqueline*
  Jacqueline LaTourrette
Gibson, Hanna
*Gibson, Jacqueline*
  Sabina Grant
Gibson, Madelaine
  *Madelaine G. Duckett*
Giddings, Lauren
  *Nancy Gideon*, Dana Ransom
*Gideon, Nancy*
  Lauren Giddings, Dana Ransom
Gideon, Robin
  *K.D. Severson*
Gilbert, Anna
  *Marguerite Lazarus*
Gilbert, Jacqueline
Gilbert, Kate
Gilbert, Nan
  *Mildred Gilbertson*, Jo Mendel
Gilbert, Therese
*Gilbertson, Mildred*
  Nan Gilbert, Jo Mendel
Giles, Katherine
Gill, Judy
Gillen, Cathy
  Cathy Gillen Thacker
Gillen, Lucy
  Rebecca Stratton
Gillenwater, Sharon
Gillespie, Jane
Gillette, Louisa
  *Gilda Feldman & Leslie Rugg*,
  Madeline Hale
Gilliland, Alexis
Gillman, Olga
Gilman, Hilary
Gilmer, Donna
Gilmer, Elizabeth Meriwether
  Dorothy Dix
Gilmor, Ann
  Dana Ross, Rose Williams,
  Ellen Randolph, Leslie Ames,
  Rose Dana, Ruth Dorset,
  Miriam Leslie, W. E. D. Ross,
  Clarissa Ross, Marilyn Ross,
  Dan Ross, Diana Randall,
  Jane Rossiter, Marilyn Carter
Gilmour, Ann
  *Ann Boyce McNaught*
Gilmour, Barbara

Gilpen, Joanna
Christa Merlin, Jan McGowan,
Joanna McGauran
Gilzean, Elizabeth
Elizabeth Houghton, Mary Hunton
Gimbel, Joan
*Ginnes, Judith S.*
Paige Mitchell
Giscard, Valerie
Emily Mesta
*Gladstone, Arthur*
Margaret SeBastian, Cilla Whitmore,
Lisabet Norcross, Maggie Gladstone
Gladstone, Eve
*Herma Werner & Joyce Gleit,*
Roxanne Jarrett
Gladstone, Maggie
Margaret SeBastian,
Cilla Whitmore, Lisabet Norcross,
*Arthur Gladstone*
Glass, Amanda
Jayne Bentley, Jayne Castle,
Jayne Taylor, Stephanie James,
Jayne Ann Krentz
*Gleit, Joyce*
Eve Gladstone
Glenn, Dorothy
Dorothy Phillips, Johanna Phillips,
Dorothy Garlock
Glenn, Elizabeth
Martha Gregory
Glenn, Karen
*Glenda Carrington*
Glenn, Victoria
*Victoria Dann*
Glick, Ruth
Alyssa Howard, Amanda Lee,
Tess Marlowe, Rebecca York,
Alexis Hill Jordan
Gluyas, Constance
*Goff, Jacqueline*
Jenna Ryan
*Goforth, Ellen*
Pat Louis, Dorothy Francis
Goldenbaum, Sally
Natalie Stone
*Golding, Morton J.*
Patricia Morton
Goldrick, Emma
Good, Susanna
Gooding, Katherine
*Goodman, Irene*
Diana Morgan

Goodman, Jo
Goodman, Liza
*Goodman, Ruth*
Meagan McKinney
Goodwin, Hope
Linda Lee
*Goold, Christine R.*
Christine Robb
*Gordon, Deborah*
Brooke Hastings
Gordon, Diana
Lucilla Andrews, Joanna Marcus,
Lucilla Crichton
Gordon, Ethel E.
Gordon, Jane
Elsie Lee, Jane Gordon,
Elsie Cromwell, Elsie Sheridan
Gordon, Katharine
Gordon, Lucy
*Christine Fioretto*
Gordon, Martha
Martha Starr
Gordon, Susan
*Susan G. Carboni*
Gordon, Victoria
Goring, Anne
Gorton, Kaitlyn
*Kathy Lynn Emerson*
Gosling, Paula
*Gottfried, Theodore Mark*
Kathleen Fuller, Katherine Tobias,
Ted Mark, Harry Gregory
Goulart, Ron
Jillian Kearny
Gower, Iris
Iris Davies
Grace, Alicia
Riva Carles, Irving Greenfield,
Anita Grace, Gail St. John
Grace, Anita
(see above)
Grady, Liz
Pat Coughlin
Graham, Elizabeth
Emma Church, *E. Schattner*
Graham, Heather
Shannon Drake,
Heather Graham Pozzessere
Graham, Lynne
Graham, Marteen D.
Grames, Selwyn Anne
Gramm, Nancy
Granbeck, Marilyn

*Grand, Natalie*
  Susannah Hart
**Grandower, Elissa**
  <u>Hillary Waugh</u>
**Grandville, Louise**
  *Daniel Streib*
**Grange, Peter**
  Daniel Adams, Leslie Arlen,
  Mark Logan, Christina Nicholson,
  Simon McKay, Alison York,
  Christopher Nicole, Robin Cade,
  Andrew York
**Granger, George**
  *Georgia Granger*
**Granger, Georgia**
  George Granger
**Granger, Katherine**
  Katherine Ransom,
  *Mary Sederquest*
<u>**Grant, Charles L.**</u>
  Felicia Andrews, Deborah Lewis
**Grant, Hilda**
  Kay Grant, Jan Hilliard
**Grant, Jeanne**
  Jessica Massey, Jennifer Greene,
  *Alison Hart*
*Grant, Joan & Tracy*
  Anthea Malcolm
**Grant, Kathryn**
  Kathleen Maxwell
**Grant, Kay**
  Hilda Grant, Jan Hilliard
**Grant, Laurie**
  *Laurie Chappelyear*
**Grant, Sabina**
  *Jacqueline Gibson*
**Grant, Sara**
  <u>Marianne Irwin</u>
**Grant, Vanessa**
  *Vanessa Oltman*
**Graves, Keller**
  *Kathryn Davenport & Evelyn Rogers*
**Graves, Tricia**
**Gray, Alison**
  *Alma Moser*
**Gray, Angela**
  Dorothy Daniels, Suzanne Somers,
  Danielle Dorsett, Geraldine Thayer,
  Cynthia Kavanaugh, Helen Gray Weston,
  Helaine Ross
**Gray, Ginna**
  *Virginia Gray*

**Gray, Harriet**
  Ashley French, Julia Kane,
  Francesca Wright, Denise Robins
**Gray, Jane**
  Constance M. Evans, Mairi O'Nair
**Gray, Janet**
  Sybil Russell
**Gray, Janice**
**Gray, Juliet**
**Gray, Kerrie**
**Gray, Linda Crockett**
  Christina Crockett
*Gray, Lori*
  Marcy Gray
**Gray, Marcy**
  *Lori Gray*
**Gray, Valerie**
**Gray, Vanessa**
  <u>Jacquelyn Aeby</u>, Jocelyn Carew
*Gray, Virginia*
  Ginna Gray
<u>**Grazia, Theresa**</u>
  Therese Alderton, Alberta Sinclair
<u>**Green, Billie June**</u>
**Green, Elaine**
*Green, Grace*
  Grace Reid
**Greenaway, Gladys**
  Julia Manners
*Greenberg, Jan*
  Jill Gregory
**Greene, Jennifer**
  Jeanne Grant, Jessica Massey,
  *Alison Hart*
**Greene, Juli**
  *Judith Child & Lisa Neher*
**Greene, Maria**
<u>**Greenfield, Irving**</u>
  Alicia Grace, Riva Carles,
  Anita Grace, Gail St. John
**Greenlea, Denice**
**Greenleaf, Jeanne M.**
*Greenman, Nancy*
  Lucy Elliot
**Greenwood, Leigh**
  *Harold Lowery*
**Greer, Francesca**
  Saliee O'Brien, *Frankie-Lee Janas*
**Gregg, Meredith**
**Gregor, Carol**
**Gregory, Harry**
  Kathleen Fuller, Katherine Tobias,
  Ted Mark, *Theodore Mark Gottfried*

G

**Gregory, Jill**
*Jan Greenberg*
**Gregory, Kay**
**Gregory, Lisa**
Kristin James, <u>Candace Camp</u>,
Sharon Stephens
**Gregory, Lydia**
*Diane & Greg Brodeur*, Diane Carey
*Gregory, Martha*
Elizabeth Glenn, Marty Gregory
**Gregory, Mollie**
Estelle Edwards
**Gregory, Veronica**
*Victoria Shakarjian*
**Greig, Maysie**
Jennifer Ames, Ann Barclay,
*Mary D. Warre*
**Grey, Belinda**
**Grey, Charlotte**
**Grey, Evelyn**
*Susan Leslie*, Ashley Allyn
**Grey, Georgina**
Pamela D'Arcy, <u>Mary Linn Roby</u>,
Mary Wilson, Elisabeth Welles,
Pauline Pryor, Valerie Bradstreet
**Grey, Kitty**
*Mary Elizabeth Allen*
**Grey, Millie**
*Millie Gergich*
**Grey, Naidra**
**Grey, Shirley**
**Greyland, Valerie**
*Valerie Siebond*
**Grice, Julia**
*Julia Haughey*
**Grieg, Sylvia**
**Grierson, Linden**
*Grieveson, Mildred*
Caroline Fleming, Anne Mather,
Cardine Fleming
**Griffin, Anne**
*Arthur Griffin*
*Griffin, Arthur*
Anne Griffin
**Griffin, Jocelyn**
Laura Sparrow, *Laura Halford*
**Grimstead, Hettie**
Marsha Manning
*Grisanti, Mary Lee*
Perdita Shepherd
**Gronau, Mary Ellen**
<u>Gross, Susan</u>
Susanna Collins, Sue Ellen Cole,

Susana De Lyonne
**Grove, Joan**
**Grundman, Donna**
<u>Guccione, Leslie D.</u>
Leslie Davis
**Guest, Diane**
*Diana Biondi*
**Gunn, Virginia**
<u>Guntrum, Suzanne</u>
Suzanne Simmons, Suzanne Simms

_Notes_

73

**G**

*Notes*

Names in *italics* indicate an author's legal name which does not appear on books. She or he uses pseudonym (s) only.

Names <u>underlined</u> indicate that the author uses legal name for works and may or may not use pseudonym (s).

*Haaf, Beverly*
  Beverly Terry
*Haas, Carola*
  Victoria Catalani
**Habersham, Elizabeth**
  *Madeline Porter & Shannon Harper*,
  Madeline Harper, Anna James,
  Leigh Bristol
*Hacsi, Jacqueline*
  Jacqueline Hope, Jacqueline Louis
**Hadary, Simone**
**Haddow, Leigh**
  Breton Amis, Rayleigh Best,
  *Ray Bentinck*, Terence Hughes,
  Desmond Roberts, Leslie Wilde
**Hadley, Liza**
**Hagan, Patricia**
**Hagar, Judith**
  Helen Kent, Judith Stewart,
  <u>Judith Anna Polley</u>, Valentina Luellan
**Hagen, Lorinda**
  Kate Cameron, Elizabeth DuBreuil,
  Margaret Maitland
<u>Hager, Jean</u>
  Marlaine Kyle, Jeanne Stephens,
  Sarah North, Leah Crane,
  Amanda McAllister
*Hahn, Lynn L.*
  Lynn Lowery
**Hailey, Johanna**
  *Marcia Y. Howl & Sharon Jarvis*,
  Pauline York
*Haines, Carolyn*
  Caroline Burnes
*Hake, Carolyn*
  Kate Denton
**Haldeman, Linda**
**Hale, Antoinette**
  <u>Antoinette Stockenberg</u>, Antoinette Hardy

**Hale, Arlene**
  Gail Everett, Lynn Williams,
  Tracy Adams, Mary Tate,
  Mary Hale
**Hale, Dorothea**
  Dorothy Bernard, <u>Dorothy Weller</u>
**Hale, Katherine**
**Hale, Madeline**
  *Gilda Feldman & Leslie Rugg*,
  Louisa Gillette
**Hale, Mary**
  Gail Everett, Arlene Hale,
  Lynn Williams, Mary Tate,
  Tracy Adams
**Haley, Andrea**
  Irene M. Pascoe
**Haley, Jocelyn**
  Sandra Field, Jan MacLean,
  *Jill MacLean*
*Halford, Laura*
  Jocelyn Griffin, Laura Sparrow
*Hall, Carolyn*
  Carole Halston
**Hall, Claudia**
  Lisa Franchon, Lee Floren,
  Austin Brett, Lee Thomas,
  Matt Harding, Len Turner,
  Marguerite Nelson, Grace Lang,
  Will Watson, Maria S. Sterling
**Hall, Gillian**
<u>Hall, Gimone</u>
**Hall, Libby**
  Laurie Paige, *Olivia M. Hall*
*Hall, Olivia M.*
  Laurie Paige, Libby Hall
**Hall, Steffie**
  <u>Janet Evanovich</u>
**Halldorson, Phyllis Taylor**

**Halliday, Dorothy**
Dorothy Dunnett
**Halliday, Ena**
Louisa Rawlings, *Sylvia Baumgarten*
*Hallin, Emily*
Elaine Harper
*Halsall, Penny*
Penny Jordan
**Halston, Carole**
*Carolyn Hall*
**Halter, Caroline**
**Hamilton, Audrey**
Neely Powell,
*Jan Hamilton Powell*
**Hamilton, Daphne**
**Hamilton, Diana**
*Hamilton, Gail*
Margaret Gayle
**Hamilton, Julia**
Jane De Vere, Julia Watson,
Julia Fitzgerald
**Hamilton, Kay**
*Cateau W. DeLeeuw*, Jessica Lyon
**Hamilton, Lucy**
*Julia A. Rhyne*
**Hamilton, Paula**
**Hamilton, Priscilla**
Roberta Gellis, Max Daniels,
Leah Jacobs
*Hamilton, Steve & Melinda*
Linda Vail, Linda Stevens
**Hamilton, Violet**
**Hamlin, Dallas**
Dallas Schulze
**Hammett, Lafayette**
LaLette Douglas
**Hammond, Mary Ann**
*Mary Ann Slojkowski*, DeAnn Patrick
**Hammond, Rosemary**
Hampson, Anne
Jane Wilby
**Hampton, Georgia**
Hampton, Linda
Lily Dayton
**Hampton, Nora**
**Hanchar, Peggy**
**Hancock, Lucy Agnes**
**Handy, Toni**
**Hanks, Lindsey**
*Linda Chesnutt & Georgia Pierce*
**Hanna, Evelyn**
*Michael Dyne & Ethel Frank*

*Hansen, Anne*
Anne Peters
**Hansen, Kim**
**Hansen, Peggy**
Margaret Westhaven
**Hanson, Jeanne F.**
**Hanson, Mary Catherine**
**Hara, Monique**
*Madge Harrah*
**Harbringer, April**
**Hardcastle, Catherine**
Phyllis Thatcher
**Harding, Christina**
**Harding, Matt**
Lisa Franchon, Lee Floren,
Austin Brett, Maria S. Sterling,
Len Turner, Claudia Hall,
Lee Thomas, Will Watson,
Marguerite Nelson, Grace Lang
**Harding, Nancy**
*Hardter, Frances*
Frances Williams
**Hardy, Antoinette**
Antoinette Hale, Antoinette Stockenberg
**Hardy, Laura**
Sheila Holland, Charlotte Lamb,
Sheila Lancaster, Victoria Woolf,
Sheila Coates
**Hargis, Pauline**
Polly Hargis, Polly H. Dillard
**Hargis, Polly**
Pauline Hargis, Polly H. Dillard
**Harkness, Judith**
**Harle, Elizabeth**
Irene Roberts, Roberta Carr,
Iris Rowland, Ivor Roberts,
Irene Shaw
**Harper, Elaine**
*Emily W. Hallin*
Harper, Karen
Caryn Cameron
**Harper, Madeline**
*Shannon Harper & Madeline Porter*,
Anna James, Leigh Bristol,
Elizabeth Habersham
Harper, Olivia & Ken
JoAnna Brandon, Jolene Adams
*Harper, Shannon*
Anna James, Madeline Harper,
Elizabeth Habersham, Leigh Bristol
*Harrah, Madge*
Monique Hara

**Harrell, Anne**
Carla Neggers, Amalia James
**Harrel, Linda**
Shannon Clare
**Harrington, Emma**
Virginia Brown & *Jane Harrison*
*Harrington, Sharon & Rick*
Rianna Craig
**Harris, Andrea**
Irma Walker
**Harris, Joanna**
*Justine Burgess*
**Harris, Lane**
Monica Harris
**Harris, Lavinia**
Elizabeth Bolton, Kate Chambers,
Catherine Chambers, Pamela Dryden,
Norma Johnston, Adrian Roberts,
Nicole St. John
**Harris, Louise**
**Harris, Marilyn**
**Harris, Melinda**
Melinda McKenzie, Melinda Snodgrass
**Harris, Monica**
Lane Harris
**Harris, Rosemary**
**Harris, Sandra**
Brittany Young, *Sandra Young*,
Abigail Wilson
**Harris, Vivian**
*Vivian H. Tichenor*
**Harrison, Claire**
Laura Eden
**Harrison, Elizabeth**
Betty Cavanna, Elizabeth Headley
*Harrison, Jane*
Emma Harrington
**Harrison, Janis**
**Harrison, Sarah**
**Harrowe, Fiona**
Florence Hurd, Flora Hiller
*Hart, Alison*
Jessica Massey, Jeanne Grant,
Jennifer Greene
**Hart, Caroline G.**
*Charles Garvice*, Carolyn Hart
**Hart, Carolyn**
*Charles Garvice*, Caroline G. Hart
**Hart, Carrie**
Jackie Merritt, *Carolyn Joyner*
**Hart, Catherine**
*Diane Tidd*

**Hart, Elizabeth**
**Hart, Joan Mary**
**Hart, Mallory Dorn**
**Hart, Samantha**
**Hart, Shirley**
Shirley Larson
**Hart, Susannah**
*Natalie Grand*
**Hart, Virginia L.**
**Harte, Marjorie**
Marjorie McEvoy
**Harte, Samantha**
*Hartman, Jan & Lorie*
Susannah Lawrence
**Harvey, Judy**
**Harvey, Marianne**
Mary Williams
**Harvey, Rachel**
Lozania Prole, Mary Essex,
Ursula Bloom, Ursula Harvey,
Sheila Burns, Deborah Mann
**Harvey, Samantha**
**Harvey, Ursula**
Ursula Bloom, Lozania Prole,
Mary Essex, Rachel Harvey,
Sheila Burns, Deborah Mann
**Haskell, Leigh**
**Haskell, Mary**
Mary Curtis
**Hastings, Brooke**
Deborah Gordon
**Hastings, Charlotte**
Charlotte Wisely
**Hastings, Julia**
**Hatcher, Robin Lee**
**Hathaway, Jan**
Joan Garrison, Rebecca Marsh,
Norma Newcomb, William Arthur,
*William Neubauer*, Christine Bennett
**Hauber, Josephine C.**
Josephine Charlton
*Haughey, Julia*
Julia Grice
**Haught, Jean**
Patricia Pellicane, Jalynn Friends
**Haviland, Diana**
*Florence Hershman*, Diana Browning
**Haviland, Meg**
Helen Ketcham
*Havptman, Elaine*
Gayle Corey

# H

Hawkes, Sarah
Hawthorne, Alaine
 *Alaine Richardson*
Hawthorne, Violet
 Christopher Rainone
Hay, Suzanne
Haycraft, Molly Costain
*Haydon, June*
 Judy Baxter, Rosalind Foxx,
 Sara Logan, Taria Hayford
Haye, Jan
 Juliet Shore, Anne Vinton
Hayford, Taria
 *June Haydon & Pat Rutherford,*
 Rosalind Foxx, Judy Baxter,
 Sara Logan
Hayle, Felicity
Haymond, Ginny
 Lee Fleming
Haynesworth, Susan
 *Susan E. Robertson*
Hays, Lee
 Sarah Nichols
Hazard, Barbara
 Lillian Lincoln
Headley, Elizabeth
 Betty Cavanna, Elizabeth Harrison
Healy, Catherine
*Healy, Christine*
 Erin Yorke
Healy, Letitia
Heath, Sandra
 Sandra Wilson
Heathcott, Mary
 Mary Raymond, Mary Constance Keegan
Heaton, Dorothy
Heaven, Constance
 Constance Fecher, George Fleming,
 Christina Merlin
Hedley, Catherine
Heland, Victoria
 Josephine Janes
Heley, Veronica
*Helland, Beverly*
 Beverly Bird
*Heller, Arnie*
 Eve O'Brian
Hely, Sara
Hemmings, Lauren
Henaghan, Rosalie
*Hendrickson, Doris E.*
 Emily Hendrickson

Hendrickson, Emily
 *Doris E. Hendrickson*
Henke, Shirl
 Shirl Henke & *Carol Reynard*
Henley, Virginia
Henrichs, Betty L.
 Emily Doyle, Amanda Kent
Henry, Anne
 *Judith Wall*
Henry, Elizabeth
*Hentges, Alison J.*
 Georgina Devon
Hepburne, Melissa
 Lisa Lenore, *Howard Brouder*
Hermann, Nancy
 Jessica Jeffries, Renee Russell,
 Samantha Scott
Hermann, Spring
 *Spring Galiardi*
Herrmann, Phyllis
Herrick, Susannah
Herries, Anne
Herring, Christina
Herrington, Terri
 Tracy Hughes
*Hershman, Florence*
 Diana Haviland, Diana Browning
Hershman, Morris
 Janet Templeton, Evelyn Bond,
 Sara Rothman, Jessica Wilcox,
 Ian Kavanaugh, Sara Roffman,
 Lionel Webb
*Herter, Loretta M.*
 Lori Herter
Herter, Lori
 *Loretta M. Herter*
Hervey, Evelyn
Hess, Janice
 Janice Carter
Hess, Norah
 *Elsie Poe Bagnara*
Hewitt, Elizabeth
 *Mary Jeanne Abbott*
Heydron, Vicki Ann
Heywood, Philippa
Heywood, Sally
Hibbert, Eleanor
 Victoria Holt, Jean Plaidy,
 Philippa Carr, Kathleen Kellow,
 Elbur Ford, Eleanor Burford,
 Ellalice Tate

**Hicks, Daisy**
  Daisy Thomson, *M. S. Roe*,
  Jonathon H. Thompson
**Hicks, Helen B.**
*Hicks, Joan Wilson*
  Kit Windham
**Hicks, Martha**
  *Martha Hix*, Maranda Catlin
*Highet, Helen*
  Helen MacInnes
**Higgins, Joyce**
**Hill, Alexis**
  Mary Craig
**Hill, Alexis**
  Ruth Glick & Louise Titchener,
  Alexis Hill Jordan, Alyssa Howard,
  Clare Richards, Jane Silverwood,
  Anne Silverlock, Rebecca York,
  Clare Richmond, Tess Marlowe,
  Samantha Chase
**Hill, Anne**
  Netta Muskett
**Hill, Fiona**
  *Ellen Pall*
**Hill, Heather**
  Joy Carroll
**Hill, Johanna**
**Hill, Rosa**
**Hillary, Anne**
  Anne Benson, Kathryn Jessup,
  Andrea Edwards, Erika Bryant,
  Adrienne Edwards, Anne &
  Ed Kolaczyk
**Hiller, Flora**
  Florence Hurd, Fiona Harrowe
**Hilliard, Jan**
  Hilda Grant, Kay Grant
**Hilliard, Nerina**
**Hills, Ida**
**Hilton, Linda**
**Hilton, Margery**
  Rebecca Caine, Margery Woods
*Himrod, Brenda*
  Megan Lane, Brenda Trent
**Hinchman, Jane**
*Hine, Alexandra*
  Alexandra Blakelee, Lilla Brennan
**Hines, Charlotte**
  Judith McWilliams
**Hines, Jeanne**
  Rosamond Royal, Valerie Sherwood
**Hingston, Mary Sandra**
  Mallory Burgess, Catherine Fitzgerald

**Hinkemeyer, Michael T.**
  Vanessa Royall
**Hintze, Naomi**
*Hinz, Diana*
  Diana Whitney
**Hitzig, Karen**
  Justin Channing
*Hix, Martha Rand*
  Maranda Catlin, Martha Hicks
**Hoag, Tami**
**Hobbs, Margaret**
**Hocker, Karla**
**Hockett, Kathryn**
**Hodge, Jane Aiken**
*Hodges, Doris Marjorie*
  Charlotte Hunt
*Hodgson, Eleanor*
  Eleanor Howard, Norah Parker
*Hofland, Karin*
  Kayla Daniels
**Hohl, Joan M.**
  Amii Lorin, Paula Roberts
**Holbrook, Cindy**
*Holden, Lisa*
  Monique Holden
**Holden, Monique**
  *Lisa Holden*
**Holder, Nancy**
  Laurel Chandler, Wendi Davis,
  Nancy Jones
**Holder, Samantha**
  *Deborah Jones & Carol Burns*
**Holdsworth, Diana**
**Holland, Elizabeth**
  Elizabeth Baxter
**Holland, Isabelle**
**Holland, Katrin**
  *Heidi Loewengard*, Martha Albrand
**Holland, Margot**
**Holland, Sarah**
**Holland, Sheila**
  Charlotte Lamb, Laura Hardy,
  Sheila Lancaster, Sheila Coates,
  Victoria Woolf
**Holliday, Dolores**
**Holliday, Judith**
**Hollis, Erica**
**Holloway, Tess**
  Tess Oliver, *Teri Kovack*,
  Teri Shapiro
**Hollyock, Dulcie**
**Holmes, Clare Frances**
**Holmes, Mary Mayer**

**H**

**Hughes, Cally**
  Lass Small
**Hughes, Charlotte**
**Hughes, Eden**
  *William E. Butterworth*
**Hughes, Rose**
**Hughes, Samantha**
  Susan Hufford
**Hughes, Terence**
  Breton Amis, Rayleigh Best,
  *Ray Bentinck*, Leigh Haddow,
  Leslie Wilde, Desmond Roberts
**Hughes, Tracy**
  Terri Herrington
**Hull, Beverly Wilcox**
**Hunt, Beverly**
  *Beverly Allen*
**Hunt, Charlotte**
  *Doris Marjorie Hodges*
**Hunt, Jena**
  Helen Conrad, Raye Morgan
**Hunter, Diane**
**Hunter, Elizabeth**
  Isobel Chace, Elisie B. Rider,
  Elizabeth de Guise
**Hunter, Jillian**
  *Maria Gardner*
**Hunter, Joan**
  Jeanne Montague, *Jeanne Yarde*
**Hunter, Julia**
**Hunter, Margaret**
  Delphine Marlowe, *Ron Singer*
**Hunter, Valancy**
  Lydia Lancaster, Lydia Clark,
  *Eloise Meaker*
**Hunton, Mary**
  Elizabeth Gilzean, Elizabeth Houghton
**Hurd, Florence**
  Fiona Harrowe, Flora Hiller
**Hurley, Ann**
  *Ann Salerno*
**Husted, Darrell**
**Hutchinson, Bobby**
**Hutchinson, Patricia**
  Gladys Fullbrook
**Hyatt, Betty Hale**
**Hylton, Sara**
**Hyman, Ann**
**Hyman, Jackie**
  Jacqueline Jade, Jacqueline Topaz,
  Jacqueline Diamond
*Hynnes, Lucetta*
  Caroline Light

*Notes*

**H**

*Notes*

Names in *italics* indicate an author's legal name which does not appear on books. She or he uses pseudonym (s) only.

Names <u>underlined</u> indicate that the author uses legal name for works and may or may not use pseudonym (s).

Ibbotson, Eva
*Imboden, Durant*
  Cheryl Durant
Ingram, Grace
*Ingwalson, Phoebe C.*
  Phoebe Conn
Innes, Jean
  Sally Blake, Rowena Summers,
  <u>Jean Saunders</u>
Ireland, Jane
  Jackie Potter
Ireland, Noelle
  Nora Gibbs, Nina Shayne,
  Heather Wayne, Lynne Merrill,
  Claire Ritchie, Prudence Boyd,
  Lisette Garland, Sara Whittingham,
  Dallas Romaine
<u>Irwin, Marianne</u>
  Sara Grant
Ison, Dorothy
Ives, Averil

*Notes*

83

# *Notes*

Names in *italics* indicate an author's legal name which does not appear on books. She or he uses pseudonym (s) only.

Names <u>underlined</u> indicate that the author uses legal name for works and may or may not use pseudonym (s).

**Jackson, Angela & Sandra**
Lia Sanders
**Jackson, Betty**
<u>Jackson, Eileen</u>
Helen May, Linda Comer
**Jackson, Lisa**
Michelle Mathews, Susan Crose
**Jacobs, Leah**
<u>Roberta Gellis</u>, Max Daniels,
Priscilla Hamilton
**Jacobs, Linda C.**
Claire Blackburn
**Jade, Jacqueline**
Jacqueline Diamond, <u>Jackie Hyman</u>
Jacqueline Topaz
**James, Amalia**
<u>Carla Neggers</u>, Anne Harrell
**James, Anna**
*Madeline Porter & Shannon Harper*,
Madeline Harper, Leigh Bristol,
Elizabeth Habersham
**James, Arlene**
*Deborah Rather*
<u>James, BJ</u>
**James, Dana**
**James, Deana**
*Mona Sizer*
**James, Janice**
**James, Kristin**
Candace Camp, Lisa Gregory,
Sharon Stephens
**James, Leigh Franklin**
Paula Minton, Marie de Jourlet,
Paul Little, Paula Little
**James, Livia**
**James, Margaret**
Helen Ashfield, <u>Pamela Bennetts</u>
**James, Melanie**

**James, Rebecca**
*James Elward*
**James, Robin**
<u>Sharon & Thomas Curtis</u>, Laura London
**James, Sally**
Joyce Wilson
**James, Sandra**
<u>Sandra Kleinschmit</u>
**James, Sarah**
*Mildred Juskevice*
**James, Stephanie**
Jayne Castle, Jayne Bentley,
<u>Jayne Ann Krentz</u>, Jayne Taylor,
Amanda Glass
**James, Susannah**
**James, Syrie**
*Syrie Ann Astrahan*
**James, Vanessa**
<u>Sally Beauman</u>
**Jameson, Claudia**
**Jamison, Amelia**
Sally M. Singer
**Janas, Frankie-Lee**
Francesca Greer, Saliee O'Brien
**Janes, Josephine**
Victoria Heland
**Janney, Kate**
**Jantz, Carolyn**
**Jarrett, Bella**
Bella Thorne
**Jarrett, Roxanne**
Eve Gladstone, *Herma Werner*
**Jarvis, Sharon**
Johanna Hailey
**Jason, Veronica**
Velda Johnston
*Jay, Amanda Moor*
Laura Kinsale
**Jeffrey, Elizabeth**

**Jeffries, Jessica**
  Samantha Scott, <u>Nancy Hermann</u>,
  Renee Russell
**Jeffries, Julia**
  <u>Lynda Ward</u>
**Jenkins, Kate**
  *Linda Jenkins-Nutting*
**Jenkins, Sara Lucille**
  Joan Sargent
**Jenner, Suzanne**
  *Sally Netzel & Gretchen Johnson*
**Jennifer, Susan**
  Grace Corren, <u>Robert Hoskins</u>
**Jennings, Sara**
  <u>Maura Seger</u>, Jenny Bates,
  Laurel Winslow, Anne MacNeill,
  Maeve Fitzgerald
**Jennings, Caylin**
  <u>Jeanne Triner</u> & *Kaye L. Clements*,
  Jeanne Kaye Triner
<u>**Jerina, Carol**</u>
*Jensen, Dorothea*
  Catherine Moorhouse
**Jensen, Muriel**
*Jeske, Colleen*
  Colleen Shannon
**Jessop, Kathryn**
  Anne Benson, Anne Hillary,
  Andrea Edwards, Erika Bryant,
  Adrienne Edwards, <u>Anne &</u>
  <u>Ed Kolaczyk</u>
**Jett, Judtih**
**Jewel, Carolyn**
<u>**Johansen, Iris**</u>
**John, Ada**
  *Ada Boulet*
**John, Nancy**
  Hilary London, Nancy Buckingham,
  Erica Quest, Christina Abbey,
  Nancy & *John Sawyer*
**Johns, Avery**
  Margaret Cousins, Mary Parrish,
  William Masters
**Johns, Karen**
  *Karen Kimpel-Johns*
*Johnson, Ellen Argo*
  Ellen Argo
*Johnson, Gretchen*
  Suzanne Jenner
**Johnson, Janice Kay**
  Kay Barlett, Janice Stevens,
  Kay Kirby, *Janice Baczewski*

*Johnson, Mary*
  M. J. Rodgers
**Johnson, Maud**
<u>**Johnson, Norma Tadlock**</u>
  Kay Kirby
*Johnson, Renate*
  Ellen Tanner Marsh
<u>**Johnson, Susan**</u>
**Johnston, Corinne**
<u>**Johnston, Joan**</u>
**Johnston, Norma**
  Elizabeth Bolton, Kate Chambers,
  Catherine Chambers, Pamela Dryden,
  Lavinia Harris, Adrian Roberts,
  Nicole St. John
**Johnston, Velda**
  Veronica Jason
**Jones, Annabel**
**Jones, Beth Carsley**
*Jones, Deborah*
  Samantha Holder
**Jones, Diane McClure**
  Phoebe Matthews
**Jones, Elinor**
**Jones, Jan**
  Caron Welles
**Jones, Kathy**
**Jones, Kit O'Brien**
**Jones, Marian**
**Jones, Minka**
**Jones, Nancy**
  Laurel Chandler, Wendi Davis,
  <u>Nancy Holder</u>
**Jones-Wolf, Gloria**
**Jordan, Alexis Hill**
  <u>Ruth Glick & Louise Titchener</u>,
  Amanda Lee, Anne Silverlock,
  Alyssa Howard, Clare Richards,
  Jane Silverwood, Rebecca York,
  Clare Richmond, Samantha Chase
**Jordan, Carrie**
*Jordan, Debbie*
  Rosemary Jordan
**Jordan, Gail**
  Peggy Gaddis, Peggy Dern,
  Erolie P. Dern, Perry Lindsay,
  James Clayford, Joan Sherman,
  Roberta Courtland, Georgia Craig
**Jordan, Joanna**
  *Debrah Morris & Pat Shaver*,
  Pepper Adams, JoAnn Stacey,
  Dianne Thomas

**Jordan, Laura**
 <u>Sandra Brown</u>, Rachel Ryan,
 Erin St. Claire
**Jordan, Maggie**
 Myra Rowe
**Jordan, Nicole**
 *Anne Bushyhead*
**Jordan, Penny**
 *Penny Halsall*
**Jordan, Rosemary**
 *Mary Davis & Debbie Jordan*
**Joseph, Joan**
**Joseph, Robin**
 Robert Joseph
**Joyce, Brenda**
 *Brenda Dworman*
**Joyce, Deborah**
 *Deborah Bryson* & <u>Joyce Porter</u>,
 Deborah Bryan
**Joyce, Jane**
 Kerry Carr, Ena Young
**Joyce, Janet**
 <u>Janet Bieber & Joyce Thies</u>,
 Jenna Lee Joyce, Melissa Scott
**Joyce, Jenna Lee**
 Janet Joyce, Melissa Scott,
 <u>Janet Bieber & Joyce Thies</u>
**Joyce, Julia**
 Julie Tetel, *Julie Andresen*
**Joyce, Marianne**
*Joyner, Carolyn*
 Jackie Merritt, Carrie Hart
*Julien, Isobel*
 Carola Salisbury
**Juneman, Karen**
 Flanna Devin
*Jurin-Reid, Barbara*
 Leslie Reid
*Juskevice, Mildred*
 Sarah James, Antonio Blake
**Justin, Jennifer**
 Jennifer West

*Notes*

# Notes

Names in *italics* indicate an author's legal name which does not appear on books. She or he uses pseudonym (s) only.

Names <u>underlined</u> indicate that the author uses legal name for works and may or may not use pseudonym (s).

*Kachelmeier, Glenda S.*
 Glenda Sands, Glenda Sanders
*Kahn, Mary*
 Amanda Troy, Miranda Cameron
**Kaiser, Janice**
**Kaye, Joanne**
 Rachel Cosgrove Payes, E. L. Arch,
 Rachel R. Cosgrove
*Kaku, Louzana*
 Christina Dair
**Kalman, Yvonne**
**Kalmes, Susan**
**Kamada, Annalise**
*Kamaroff, Alex*
 Diana Morgan
*Kamien, Marcia*
 Marcia Rose
**Kane, Julia**
 Ashley French, Harriet Gray,
 Denise Robins, Francesca Wright
*Karni, Michaela*
 Diana Burke, Karin Berne
**Karr, Lee**
 Leona Karr
**Karr, Leona**
 Lee Karr
**Karr, Phyllis Ann**
**Karron, Kris**
 <u>Carol Norris</u>
**Kary, Elizabeth N.**
 *Karyn Witmer Gow*
**Kasey, Michelle**
 Kasey Michaels, <u>Kathie Seidick</u>
*Katz, Carol*
 Penny Allison, Rosalynn Carroll
**Katz, Molly**
*Kaukas, Bevlyn M.*
 Bevlyn Marshall
**Kavaler, Rebecca**

**Kavanaugh, Cynthia**
 Dorothy Daniels, Suzanne Somers,
 Danielle Dorsett, Angela Gray,
 Geraldine Thayer, Helen Gray Weston,
 Helaine Ross
**Kavanaugh, Ian**
 Janet Templeton, Evelyn Bond,
 Sara Rothman, Jessica Wilcox,
 <u>Morris Hershman</u>, Sara Roffman,
 Lionel Webb
**Kay, Catherine**
 *Catherine Dees* & *Kay Croissant*,
 Kate McKenzie
**Kaye, Barbara**
 *Barbara Walker*
**Kaye, M. M.**
**Kayle, Hilary**
**Keane, Lucy**
**Kearny, Jillian**
 <u>Ron Goulart</u>
**Keast, Karen**
 Sandi Shane, <u>Sandra Canfield</u>
**Keaton, Corey**
 *Vicki L. Thompson* &*Mary Tate Engels*,
 Cory Kenyon, Tate McKenna
**Keegan, Mary Constance**
 Mary Raymond, Mary Heathcott
**Keene, Sarah**
 *Jane Atkins*
*Keiler, Barbara*
 Ariel Berk, Judith Arnold,
 Thea Frederick
**Keinzley, Francis**
**Keller, Barbara**
**Keller, Kathy**
*Kelman, Ellen*
 Leonora Woodbury

**Kellow, Katherine**
Victoria Holt, Jean Plaidy,
Eleanor Hibbert, Elbur Ford,
Eleanor Burford, Ellalice Tate,
Phillipa Carr
**Kells, Susannah**
**Kelly, Carla**
**Kelly, Judith**
Judith English
**Kelly, Susan**
**Kelrich, Victoria**
**Kemp, Shirley**
**Kendall, Julia Jay**
Katherine Kingsley
**Kendall, Katherine**
*Katherine Applegate*
**Kennedy, Marilyn**
**Kent, Amanda**
Emily Doyle, Betty Henrichs
**Kent, Andrea**
**Kent, Fortune**
Jocelyn Wilde, John Toombs
**Kent, Helen**
Judith Hagar, Judith Anne Polley,
Valentina Luellan, Judith Stewart
**Kent, Jean Salter**
Kathryn Kent
**Kent, Katherine**
Joan Dial, Alexandra Devon,
Amanda York, Katherine Sinclair
**Kent, Kathryn**
Jean Salter Kent
**Kent, Pamela**
Susan Barrie, Jane Beaufort,
Rose Burghley, Anita Charles,
Ida Pollock, Barbara Rowan,
Mary Whistler
**Kenyon, Bruce**
Meredith Leigh, Daisy Vivian
**Kenyon, Cory**
Mary Tate Engels & Vicki L. Thompson,
Tate McKenna, Corey Keaton
**Kenyon, Joanna**
Nell Kincaid, Jane Christopher,
*Janet Clarke*
**Keppel, Charlotte**
Paula Allardyce, *Ursula Torday*,
Charity Blackstock
**Ker, Madeleine**
**Kerr, Katharine**
*Ketcham, Helen*
Meg Haviland

*Ketter, Pam*
Pamela Browning, Melanie Rowe
**Keyworth, Anne**
*Kichline, Linda*
Allyson Ryan, Carin Rafferty
**Kidd, Elisabeth**
*Linda Triegel*
**Kidd, Flora**
*Kiehl, Claire*
Justine Cole
**Kihlstrom, April**
*Kilchenstein, Mary*
Jean Faure, Mary Alice Kirk,
Mary Kirk
**Kilmer, Wendela**
Karen Van der Zee, Moran van Wieren
**Kimbro, Jean**
Ann Ashton, Charlotte Bramwell,
Katheryn Kimbrough, *John Kimbro*,
Kym Allyson
*Kimbro, John M.*
Ann Ashton, Katheryn Kimbrough,
Jean Kimbro, Kym Allyson,
Charlotte Bramwell
**Kimbrough, Colleen**
Kay Porterfield
**Kimbrough, Katheryn**
Ann Ashton, *John M. Kimbro*,
Jean Kimbro, Kym Allyson,
Charlotte Bramwell
*Kimpel-Johns, Karen*
Karen Johns
**Kincaid, Katharine**
*Pamela Daoust*
**Kincaid, Nell**
Joanna Kenyon, Jane Christopher,
*Janet Clarke*
**King, Alison**
Theresa Martini, *Teri Martini*,
Wendy Martin
**King, Carol**
**King, Christine**
Thea Lovan
**King, Dianne**
Pamela Wallace & *Elnora King*
*King, Elnora*
Dianne King
**King, Florence**
Laura Buchanan
**King, Josie**
Jo Germany
**King, Valerie**
Sarah Montrose, *Valerie Bosna*

Kingsley, Katherine
  Julia Kendall
Kingsley, Laura
  Dorothy Bennett
Kingston, Kate
Kingston, Meredith
  Meredith Lindley,
  Meredith Brucker
Kingston, Roberta
Kinsale, Laura
  *Amanda Moor Jay*
Kirby, Kate
  *Betty Elgin*
Kirby, Kay
  *Norma T. Johnson & Janice
  Baczewski,* Janice Kay Johnson,
  Kay Bartlett, Janice Stevens
Kirby, Rowan
Kirk, Alexandra
  Suzanne Sherrill, Sherryl Ann Woods
Kirk, Mariel
Kirk, Mary Alice
  Jean Faure, *Mary I. Kilchenstein &
  Nancy Richards-Akers,* Mary Kirk
Kirk, Risa
  *Janis Flores*
Kistler, Julie
Kistler, Mary
  Jean Reece
Kitt, Sandra
Klass, Harriet
  *Harriet Kossoff*
Kleeb, Pamela
*Kleinsasser-Testerman, Lois*
  Cait Logan, Cait London
*Kleinschmidt, Dianne*
  Gabrielle DuPre
Kleinschmit, Sandra
  Sandra James
Klem, Kaye Wilson
  Cathleen Carleton
Kleypas, Lisa
Knight, Alanna
  Margaret Hope
Knight, Alicia
  Lucretia Wright
Knight, Allison
  Martha Kreiger
Knight, Barbara
*Knight, Joan Giezey*
  Iris Summers
Knight, Nancy
  Jenna Darcy

Knoll, Patricia
  Charlotte Nichols, Patricia Forsythe
*Knowles, Mabel Winnifred*
  Wynne May
*Koehler, Margaret Hudson*
  Maggi Charles, Meg Hudson,
  Carole Standish, Russell Mead
Kohake, Rosanne
Kolaczyk, Anne & Ed
  Anne Benson, Anne Hillary,
  Andrea Edwards, Kathryn Jessop,
  Erika Bryant, Adrienne Edwards
Koontz, Dean
  Leigh Nichols
*Koppel, Lillian & Shelley*
  Lillian Shelley
Korbel, Kathleen
  Eileen Dreyer
*Kossoff, Harriet*
  Harriet Klass
*Koumalats, Jodi*
  Jodi Thomas
*Kovack, Teri*
  Tess Holloway, Tess Oliver,
  Teri Shapiro
Kovacs, Katherine
  Katherine Coffaro
Kovats, Nancy
Krahn, Betina
Kramer, Katherine
  Katherine Vickery
*Kreiger, Martha*
  Allison Knight
Krentz, Jayne Ann
  Jayne Bentley, Jayne Castle,
  Stephanie James, Jayne Taylor,
  Amanda Glass
*Krepps, Robert*
  Beatrice Brandon
*Krokosz, Emily*
  Emily Carmichael
*Kuczir, Mary*
  Fern Michaels, Iris Summers
*Kuether, Edith Lyman*
  Margaret Malcolm
*Kuhlin, Suzanne J.*
  Jennifer Mikels
Kuhn, Phyllis
Kurr, Maureen
Kwock, Laureen
  Clarice Peters

**Kyle, Marlaine**
  <u>Jean Hager</u>, Jeanne Stephens,
  Sarah North, Leah Crane,
  Amanda McAllister
**<u>Kyle, Susan</u>**
  Diana Blayne, Diana Palmer,
  Katy Currie

*Notes*

Names in *italics* indicate an author's legal name which does not appear on books. She or he uses pseudonym (s) only.

Names <u>underlined</u> indicate that the author uses legal name for works and may or may not use pseudonym (s).

**Lacey, Anne**
  Kristin Michaels, *Martha Corson*
**Lachlan, Edythe**
  Julia Alcott, Maureen Norris, Nicole Norman, Bettina Montgomery, Rinalda Roberts, *Edythe Cudlipp*
**Lacy, Tira**
  Rita Clay, <u>Rita Estrada</u>
*LaDame, Cathryn*
  Cathryn Ladd, Cathryn Baldwin
**Ladd, Cathryn**
  *Cathryn LaDame,* Cathryn Baldwin
<u>**Ladd, Linda**</u>
  Jillian Roth
**Laden, Janis**
  *Janis Laden Shiffman*
**Laffeaty, Christina**
  Netta Carstens, Martha Fortina
*Lahey, Karen*
  Elizabeth Albright
**Laine, Annabel**
**Lake, Patricia**
**Lake, Rozella**
  Roberta Leigh, Rachel Lindsay, Roumelia Lane, Janey Scott
**Laker, Rosalind**
  Barbara Douglas, Barbara Paul, <u>Barbara Ovstedahl</u>
*Lakso, Elaine*
  Laine Allen
**Lamb, Charlotte**
  Laura Hardy, Sheila Lancaster, <u>Sheila Holland,</u> Victoria Woolf, Sheila Coates
*Lambert, Bill*
  Willa Lambert
**Lambert, Elizabeth**
**Lambert, Willa**
  *Bill Lambert*

*Lambright, Jeanie*
  Kate Denton
<u>**Lamont, Marianne**</u>
  Joanne Marshall, Alexandra Manners
**Lancaster, Joan**
  Marlene J. Anderson
**Lancaster, Lisa**
  Elizabeth Lane
**Lancaster, Lydia**
  Valancy Hunter, Lydia Clark, *Eloise Meaker*
**Lancaster, Sheila**
  Charlotte Lamb, Laura Hardy, <u>Sheila Holland</u>, Victoria Woolf, Sheila Coates
**Lancaster, Vicky**
  Hebe Elsna, Laura Conway, Lyndon Snow, *Dorothy P. Ansle,* Margaret Campbell Barnes
**Lance, Leslie**
  Jan Tempest, Theresa Charles, Fay Chandos, *Irene Mossop,* Virginia Storm, *Charles & Irene Swatridge*
**Lancour, Gene**
  Jeanne Lancour, Gene Louis Fisher
**Lancour, Jeanne**
  Gene Louis Fisher, Gene Lancour
**Land, Jane**
**Landis, Jill Marie**
**Landon, Nancy**
  *Nancy Berland*
**Lane, Elizabeth**
  Lisa Lancaster
**Lane, Jane**
  *Elaine Dakers*
**Lane, Kami**
  *Elaine Smith*

**93**

**Lane, Megan**
Brenda Trent, *Brenda Himrod*
**Lane, Roumelia**
Roberta Leigh, Rachel Lindsay,
Rozella Lake, Janey Scott
**Lang, Eve**
Ruth Langan
**Lang, Grace**
Lee Floren, Lisa Franchon,
Austin Brett, Maria S. Sterling,
Marguerite Nelson, Len Turner,
Claudia Hall, Lee Thomas,
Matt Harding, Will Watson
**Lang, Heather**
*Darlene Baker*
**Lang, Hilary**
Marjorie Bowen
**Lang, Maud**
**Lang, Miriam**
Margot Leslie
**Langan, Ruth**
Eve Lang
**Lange, Emma**
**Langford, Sandra**
Olivia Sinclair
**Langley, Tania**
Tilly Armstrong, Kate Alexander
**Langtry, Ellen**
*Nancy Elliott*, Erin Dana
**Lanigan, Catherine**
Joan Wilder
**Lansdale, Nina**
*Marilyn Meeske Sorel*
**Lansing, Jessica**
David Ritz, Ester E. Pearl
**Larkin, Elinor**
*Diane Lefer*
**Larkin, Rochelle**
**Larson, Shirley**
Shirley Hart
*Larson, Susan*
Suzanne Michelle
**LaRosa, Linda**
**LaRue, Brandy**
*Latham, Robin*
Cassandra Bishop, Robin Lynn
**LaTourrette, Jacqueline**
*Jacqueline Gibeson*
**Lattin, Anne**
Caroline Arnett, *Lois Cole Taylor*,
Lynn Avery, Nancy Dudley,
Allan Dwight

**Laven, Marti**
*Marti Laven O'Laimhin*
**Lavender, Gwyn**
**Law, Elizabeth**
Maureen Black, Veronica Black,
Catherine Darby, Sharon Whitby,
Maureen Peters, Judith Rothman,
Levanah Lloyd
**Lawrence, Allison**
Brenna Drummond, *Judy Bryer*
Eve O'Brian
**Lawrence, Jacqueline**
**Lawrence, Juliet**
**Lawrence, Katy**
Kat & Larry Martin,
*Kathleen Kelly Martin*
**Lawrence, Lynn**
Sherry Garland
**Lawrence, Mary Margaret**
*Lawrence, Mary Terese*
Terry Lawrence
**Lawrence, Susannah**
*Jan & Lorie Hartman*
**Lawrence, Terry**
*Mary Terese Lawrence*
**Lawson, Christine**
Kathleen Ash, Pauline Ash,
Emily Walker, Eileen Barry,
Sara Devon, Quenna Tilbury,
Jane Lester, Delia Foster,
Cora Mayne, Jill Murray,
Kathleen Treves, Honor Vincent,
Heather Vincent, Kay Winchester
**Lawton, Lynna**
**Laye, Patricia**
**Laymon, Carla**
**Layton, Andrea**
Iris May Bancroft, *Ingrid Nielson*
**Layton, Edith**
Edith Felber
*Lazarus, Marguerite*
Anna Gilbert
**Leabo, Karen**
**Lear, Caty**
*Le Compte, Jane*
Jane Ashford
**Lee, Amanda**
Ruth Glick & *Eileen Buckholtz*,
*Nancy Baggett*, Rebecca York,
Alyssa Howard, Samantha Chase
Alexis Hill Jordan, Tess Marlowe
**Lee, Devon**
*Robert Warren Pohle*

Lee, Doris
Lee, Elsie
   Elsie Cromwell, Jane Gordon,
   Lee Sheridan, Elsie Sheridan
Lee, Joyce
Lee, Katherine
Lee, Linda
   Hope Goodwin
Lee, Lucy
   Elizabeth Alden, *Charlene Talbot*
Lee, Lydia
   Rose Marie Lima
Lee, Maureen
Lee, Rowena
   Marie Bartlett, Valerie Rift
Lee, Sandra
   Sandra Lee Smith
Lee, Sherry
Lees, Marguerite
   Margaret Baumann
Lefer, Diane
   Elinor Larkin
LeGrand, Sybil
   *Kaa Byington,* Octavia Street
Lehr, Helene
   Helene Sinclair
Leigh, Ana
Leigh, Jackie
   Jacqueline Lennox, Deborah Smith
Leigh, Lori
   *Lori Carlton*
Leigh, Meredith
   Daisy Vivian, Bruce Kenyon
Leigh, Micah
   *Emma Merritt & Evelyn Gee,*
   Constance O'Banyon, Emma Bennett
Leigh, Olivia
   Helen Clamp
Leigh, Petra
   *Peter Ling*
Leigh, Roberta
   Rachel Lindsay, Rozella Lake,
   Roumelia Lane, Janey Scott
Leigh, Susannah
*Lemberger, Le Ann*
   Leigh Michaels
*Lemery, Alysse*
   Alysse S. Rasmussen
LeMon, Lynn
   Lynette Wert
Lennox, Jacqueline
   Jackie Leigh, Deborah Smith

Lenore, Lisa
   Melissa Hepburne, *Howard Brouder*
Leonard, Lila
Leonard, Phyllis G.
   Isabel Ortega
*Leone, Adela*
   Charlotte Austen
Le Roy, Irene
   *Sally Svee*
*Lesko, Ruth*
   Blanche Garland
Leslie, Alice
Leslie, Joanna
   Jessica Dare, Darla Benton
Leslie, Lynne
   *Elaine Sima & Sherrill Bodine,*
   Lynn Leslie
Leslie, Margot
   Miriam Lang
Leslie, Miriam
   Dana Ross, Rose Williams,
   Ellen Randolph, Leslie Ames,
   Rose Dana, Ruth Dorset,
   Ann Gilmor, W. E. D. Ross,
   Clarissa Ross, Marilyn Ross,
   Diana Randall, Dan Ross,
   Jane Rossiter, Marilyn Carter
Leslie, Rochelle
   Graham Diamond
Leslie, Susan
   Evelyn Grey, Ashley Allyn
Lesoing, Jan
Lester, Jane
   Kathleen Ash, Pauline Ash,
   Christine Lawson, Eileen Barry,
   Emily Walker, Kathleen Treves,
   Sara Devon, Kay Winchester,
   Delia Foster, Cora Mayne,
   Jill Murray, Quenna Tilbury,
   Heather Vincent, Honor Vincent
Lester, Samantha
   *Lester Roper*
L'Estrange, Anna
   Rosemary Ellerbeck, Nicola Thorne,
   Katherine Yorke
LeVarre, Deborah
   *Deborah Varlinsky*
Levitt, Diana
Levy, Barbara
   Jessica Elliot
*Lewensohn, Leone*
   Frances Davies

Lewis, Deborah
  Felicia Andrews, <u>Charles L. Grant</u>
Lewis, Mary
  Christianna Brand, Mary Berrisford,
  China Thompson
Lewis, Maynah
Lewty, Marjorie
Ley, Alice Chetwynd
*Leyton, Sophie*
  Sheila Walsh
*Lichte, Prudence Bingham*
  Prudence Martin, Henrietta Houston
Lide, Mary
Light, Caroline
  *Lucetta Hynnes*
*Lima, Rose Marie*
  Lydia Lee
Lincoln, Lillian
  <u>Barbara Hazard</u>
Lind, Pamela
  Saranne Dawson, *Saranne Hoover*
Linden, Catherine
Linden, Deanna
  *Dana Rae Pugh*
Lindley, Erica
  Aileen Armitage, Ruth Fabian,
  *Aileen Quigley*
Lindley, Meredith
  Meredith Kingston, Meredith Brucker
Lindsay, Devon
  <u>Cynthia Wright</u>
Lindsay, Nicole
  Nicole De Lyn, Eva Woodland
Lindsay, Perry
  Peggy Gaddis, Peggy Dern,
  *Erolie P. Dern,* James Clayford,
  Gail Jordan, Joan Sherman,
  Roberta Courtland, Georgia Craig
Lindsay, Rachel
  Roberta Leigh, Rozella Lake,
  Roumelia Lane, Janey Scott
Lindsey, Betina
Lindsey, Dawn
  *Cherylle Lindsey Dimick*
Lindsey, Johanna
*Ling, Peter*
  Petra Leigh
Lingard, Joan
<u>Linington, Elizabeth</u>
  Dell Shannon, Lesley Egan,
  Egan O'Neill, Anne Blaisdell
Link, Gail
Linley, Elinor

Linz, Cathie
  *Cathie Baumgardner*
Lippencott, Dorothy
*Liston, Robert*
  Elizabeth Bright
<u>Little, Paul</u>
  Marie de Jourlet, Paula Minton,
  Leigh Franklin James, Paula Little
Little, Paul
  Marie DeJourlet, Paul Little,
  Leigh Franklin James, Paula Minton
Livingston, Alice
Livingston, Georgette
  Diane Crawford
Livingston, Margaret
  Mary Flynn
Lloyd, Adrien
Lloyd, Frances
Lloyd, Levanah
  Catherine Darby, <u>Maureen Peters</u>,
  Maureen Black, Veronica Black,
  Sharon Whitby, Elizabeth Law,
  Judith Rothman
Lloyd, Marta
  *Marta Buckholder*
*Loewengard, Heidi*
  Martha Albrand, Katrin Holland
Lofts, Norah
  Juliet Astley, Peter Curtis
Logan, Cait
  *Lois Kleinsasser-Testerman,*
  Cait London
Logan, Daisy
  <u>Sara Orwig</u>
Logan, Jessica
  *Lawrence & Pauline Foster*
Logan, Leandra
Logan, Mark
  Daniel Adams, Andrew York,
  Christopher Nicole, Leslie Arlen,
  Simon McKay, Alison York,
  Peter Grange, Christina Nicholson,
  Robin Cade
Logan, Sara
  *June Haydon & Judith Simpson,*
  Judy Baxter, Rosalind Foxx,
  Taria Hayford
Loghry, Lizabeth
London, Anne
  Leslie Morgan, Ann Miller
London, Cait
  *Lois Kleinsasser-Testerman,*
  Cait London

**London, Hilary**
  Nancy John, Nancy Buckingham,
  Erica Quest, Christina Abbey,
  *Nancy & John Sawyer*
**London, Laura**
  Sharon & Thomas Curtis, Robin James
**London, Victoria**
**Long, Jean M.**
**Long, William Stuart**
  Alex Stuart, Vivian Stuart,
  Barbara Allen, Robyn Stuart,
  *Violet V. Mann*
**Longrigg, Roger**
  Megan Barker, Rosalind Erskine,
  Ivor Drummond
*Look, Jane H.*
  Lee Damon
**Lopez, Dee**
  Dee Norman
**Lord, Alexandra**
  *Patricia A. Williams & Catherine Seibert*
**Lord, Alison**
  Julie Ellis, Patricia Bentley,
  Joan Ellis, Linda Michaels,
  Marilyn Ellis, Susan Marino,
  Susan Marvin, Susan Richard,
  Jill Monte, Richard Marvin,
  Jeffrey Lord
**Lord, Bette Bao**
**Lord, Jeffrey**
  Alison Lord, Julie Ellis,
  Susan Marvin, Richard Marvin,
  Joan Ellis, Patricia Bentley,
  Jill Monte, Linda Michaels,
  Susan Marino, Susan Richard,
  Marilyn Ellis
**Lord, Moira**
  Miriam Lynch, Dolores Craig,
  Claire Vincent
**Lord, Vivian**
  Patricia Cloud, Pat Wallace,
  Pat West, Pat Wallace Strother
**Lorel, Claire**
  Daphne Clair, Laurey Bright,
  *Daphne DeJong*
**Lorin, Amii**
  Joan M. Hohl, Paula Roberts
**Loring, Jenny**
  Lee Sawyer, Martha Sans
**Lorraine, Anne**
  Lilian Chisholm, *Jane Alan*
**Lorraine, Marian**
  Marian L. Horton

**Lorrimer, Claire**
  Beatrice Coogan, Patricia Robins
**Louis, Jacqueline**
  Jacqueline Hope, *Jacqueline Hacsi*
**Louis, Pat**
  Ellen Goforth, Dorothy Francis
**Lovan, Thea**
  Christine King
**Lovelace, Jane**
  Dixie McKeone, Lee McKeone
**Lovesmith, Janet**
  *Paul Fairman*, Paula Fairman,
  Paulette Warren
**Low, Dorothy Mackie**
  Lois Paxton, Lois Low, Zoe Cass
**Low, Lois**
  Lois Paxton, Dorothy Mackie Low,
  Zoe Cass
*Lowe, Charlotte*
  Annabella
*Lowe, Susan*
  Elise Randolph, Andrea Davidson
**Lowell, Elizabeth**
  Ann Maxwell
**Lowell, Lydia**
**Lowery, Lynn**
  *Lynn L. Hahn*
**Lowery, Marilyn**
  Philippa Castle
**Lowing, Anne**
  *Christine Geach*, Christine Wilson
*Lowery, Harold*
  Leigh Greenwood
**Loy, Diana**
  Eleanor Brownleigh, Rhoda Cohen
**Lozano, Wendy**
**Lucas, Mary Mayo**
**Luellan, Valentina**
  Judith Anne Polley, Judith Hagar,
  Helen Kent, Judith Stewart
**Luke, Mary**
*Lutyens, Mary*
  Esther Wyndham
**Lyle, Elizabeth**
**Lynch, Miriam**
  Moira Lord, Dolores Craig,
  Claire Vincent
**Lynch, W. Ware**
**Lyndell, Catherine**
  Kathleen Fraser, Kate Ashton,
  *Margaret Ball*
**Lyndon, Amy**
  *Richard F. Radford*

**Lyndon, Diana**
  Diana Antony, *Diane Antonio*
**Lynley, Elinor**
**Lynn, Karen**
  *Karen Maxfield & Lynn Taylor*
**Lynn, Margaret**
  *Gladys Battye*
**Lynn, Mary**
  Angel Milan, Elizabeth Nelson,
  *Elizabeth Neibor*
**Lynn, Robin**
  Cassandra Bishop, Robin Latham
**Lynne, Deborah**
**Lynne, Leslie**
  Sherrill Bodine & Elaine Sima
**Lynne, Suzanne**
**Lynton, Ann**
  Sheila Brandon, Ruth Martin,
  Claire Rayner
**Lyon, Jessica**
  Cateau W. DeLeeuw, Kay Hamilton
**Lyons, Jacqueline**
  Veronica Flynn
**Lyons, Leila**
  Vanessa Valcour, *James Conaway*
**Lyons, Maggie**
**Lyons, Mary**

*Notes*

Names in *italics* indicate an author's legal name which does not appear on books. She or he uses pseudonym (s) only.

Names <u>underlined</u> indicate that the author uses legal name for works and may or may not use pseudonym (s).

*Maas, Donald*
  Stephanie St. Clair
**McAllister, Amanda**
  <u>Jean Hager</u>, Jeanne Stephens, Leah Crane, Sarah North, Marlaine Kyle
**McAllister, Anne**
  *Barbara Schenck*
**Macalpin, Rory**
  Vivian Donald, Iain Torr, Stuart, Hilary Rose, Graham Montrose, Charles Conte, Charles Roy MacKinnon
**McAndrew, Cass**
  <u>Mary Ann Taylor</u>, Kate Bowe
**McAneny, Marjorie**
**McBain, Laurie**
**McBride, Harper**
  Ashley Chapel, *Judith Weaver*
**McBride, Kate**
**McCaffree, Sharon**
  *Sharon Shallenberger*
**McCaffrey, Anne**
*McCaig, Edith & Robert*
  Edith Engren
**MacCall, Isabel**
  Elizabeth Boyd
**McCall, Kathleen**
**McCall, Virginia**
  <u>Virginia Nielsen</u>
**McCallum, Kristy**
**McCarrick, Marsha**
**McCarry, Charles**
**McCarthy, Candace**
**MacCarthy, Dorothy**
**McCarthy, Susanne**

**McCartney, Brenna**
**McCarty, Betsy**
**McClure, Anna**
  *Roy Sorrels*
*McCluskey, Sally*
  Bethany Campbell
**McComas, Mary Kay**
**McConnell, Lisa**
  Jocelyn Day, Rena McKay, Lorena McCourtney
**McCormick, Marsha**
*McCorquodale, Barbara*
  Barbara Cartland
**McCourtney, Lorena**
  Jocelyn Day, Rena McKay, Lisa McConnell
*McCoy, Cathlyn*
  Judith Baker, <u>Fran Baker</u>
**McCoy, Susan Hatton**
<u>**McCue, Noelle Berry**</u>
  Nicole Monet
**McCulloch, Sara**
  <u>Jean Ure</u>
**McCullough, Helen**
**McDaniel, Jan**
**McDonald, Colleen**
**MacDonald, Elisabeth**
  Sabrina Ryan
**McDonald, Kay L.**
**MacDonald, Roslyn**
  Louise Clark
**MacDonald, Sue**
**MacDonnell, Megan**
  <u>Serita Stevens</u>, Shira Stevens

McDonnell, Margie
  Margie Michaels
McDowell, Donna
McElfresh, Adeline
  Jennifer Blair, Jane Scott,
  Elizabeth Wesley
McElhaney, Carole
*McElwain, Dean*
  Shana Clermont
McEvoy, Marjorie
  *Marjorie Harte*
McFather, Nelle
McGauran, Joanna
  Christa Merlin, Jan McGowan,
  Joanna Gilpen
*McGee, Emilie*
  Emilie Richards
McGiveny, Maura
  *Julie de Bets*
*McGlamry, Beverly*
  Kate Cameron
McGorian, Gladys
  *Gladys M. Dressler*
McGowan, Jan
  Christa Merlin, Joanna Gilpen,
  Joanna McGauran
McGrath, Kay
McGrath, Laura
McGraw, Terry
MacGregor, Miriam
McGuire, Jenny
  *Nancy Morgan & Kate Fleming*
McGuire, Sarah
Machin, Meredith Land
MacInnes, Helen
  *Helen Highet*
McIntyre, Hope
  Ruth B. Tucker
Mack, Amanda
  *Jean Adelson*
Mack, Dorothy
  Alexandra Dors, *Dorothy McKittrick*
McKay, Rena
  Lorena McCourtney, Jocelyn Day,
  Lisa McConnell
McKay, Simon
  Leslie Arlen, Mark Logan,
  Peter Grange, Alison York,

  Christopher Nicole, Daniel
  Adams, Robin Cade, Christina
  Nicholson, Andrew York
McKean, Margarett
*McKee, Janice*
  Jan McKee
MacKeever, Maggie
  Grace South, Gail Clark,
  Grace Scott
McKenna, RoseAnne
  Lynn Patrick, Patricia Rosemoor,
  *Patricia Pinianski*
McKenna, Tate
  Cory Kenyon, Corey Keaton,
  Mary Tate Engels
McKenna, Lindsay
  Beth Brookes, Eileen Nauman
McKenzie, Kate
  *Catherine Dees & Kay Croissant*,
  Catherine Kay
MacKenzie, Maura
McKenzie, Melinda
  Melinda Harris, Melinda Snodgrass
McKenzie, Paige
  Marje Blood
McKeone, Dixie
  Jane Lovelace, Lee McKeone
McKeone, Lee
  Jane Lovelace, Dixie McKeone
*Mackesy, Leonora*
  Leonora Starr, Dorothy Rivers
Mackey, Mary
Mackie, Mary
  Mary Christopher, Alex Andrews
  Cathy Christopher, Caroline Charles,
  Susan Stevens
McKinney, Georgia
  *Ardia Poteet*
McKinney, Meagan
  *Ruth Goodman*
MacKinnon, Charles R.
  Iain Torr, Vivian Donald,
  Hilary Rose, Charles Stuart,
  Graham Montrose, Charles Conte,
  Rory Macalpin
Mackintosh, May
*McKittrick, Dorothy*
  Alexandra Dors, Dorothy Mack

**Manners, Alexandra**
  Joanne Marshall, Anne Rundle,
  Marianne Lamont, Jean Sanders
**Manners, Julia**
  Gladys Greenaway
**Manning, Jo**
  Irene Robinson
**Manning, Liza**
**Manning, Marilyn**
**Manning, Marsha**
  Hettie Grimstead
**Manning, Mary Louise**
  Lou Cameron
**Mansell, Joanna**
**Mansfield, Elizabeth**
  *Paula Reibel*, Paula Schwartz
**Mansfield, Katherine**
  Kathleen Beauchamp
*Maragakis, Helen*
  Helen Carter, Eleni Carr,
  Helen Carras
*Marath, Laurie*
  Suzanne Roberts
**March, Jessica**
**March, Lindsay**
*March, Stella*
  Marguerite Mooers Marshall
**Marchant, Catherine**
  Catherine Cookson, *Catherine Fawcett*
**Marchant, Jessica**
**Marcus, Joanna**
  Lucilla Andrews, Diana Gordon,
  Lucilla Crichton
**Mardon, Deirdre**
**Marie, Susan**
**Marino, Carolyn**
**Marino, Susan**
  Julie Ellis, Marilyn Ellis,
  Alison Lord, Jeffrey Lord,
  Susan Marvin, Richard Marvin,
  Susan Richard, Jill Monte,
  Joan Ellis, Patricia Bentley,
  Linda Michaels
*Maritano, Adela*
  Adela Gale, Jane Converse,
  Kay Martin
**Mark, Ted**
  Kathleen Fuller, Katherine Tobias,

Harry Gregory, *Theodore Mark Gottfried*
*Markham, Patricia*
  Patricia Carro
**Marks, Joanna**
*Marliss, Deanna*
  Diana Mars, Diana Moore
**Marlow, Edwina**
  Tom E. Huff, Katherine St. Clair,
  Beatrice Parker, Jennifer Wilde
**Marlowe, Ann**
**Marlowe, Delphine**
  Margaret Hunter, *Ron Singer*
**Marlowe, Tess**
  *Ruth Glick* & *Louise Titchenor*,
  Alyssa Howard, Amanda Lee,
  Rebecca York, Alexis Hill,
  Alexis Hill Jordan, Samantha Chase
**Marnay, Jane**
**Marr, Anne**
  Nell Marr Dean, Virginia Roberts,
  *Nell Dean Ratzlaff*
**Marrs, Pauline Draper**
**Mars, Diana**
  Diana Moore, *Deanna Marliss*
**Marsh, Ellen Tanner**
  *Renate Johnson*
**Marsh, Lillian**
  Rebecca Bennett, Constance Conrad,
  *Ruby Frankel*
**Marsh, Rebecca**
  Joan Garrison, Norma Newcomb,
  William Arthur, Jan Hathaway,
  *William Neubauer*, Christine Bennett
**Marsh, Valerie**
**Marshall, Bevlyn**
  *Bevlyn M. Kaukas*
**Marshall, Jacqueline**
  Deborah Austin
**Marshall, Joanne**
  Alexandra Manners, Anne Rundle,
  Marianne Lamont, Jean Sanders
**Marshall, Margaret Mooers**
  *Stella March*
**Marshall, Marilyn**
**Martel, Aimee**
  Aimee Duvall, Aimee Thurlo
**Marten, Jacqueline**

Max, Barbara
  Justina Valenti, Vanessa Victor
Maxam, Mia
  *Ethel Maxam Crews*
*Maxfield, Karen*
  Karen Lynn
Maxwell, Ann
  Elizabeth Lowell
Maxwell, Kathleen
  Kathryn Grant
Maxwell, Patricia
  Jennifer Blake, Patricia Ponder,
  Elizabeth Trehearne, Maxine Patrick
Maxwell, Vicky
  Anne Worboys, Annette Eyre
May, Helen
  Eileen Jackson, Linda Comer
May, Janis
May, Marjorie
  Dinah Dean
May, Wynne
  *Mabel W. Knowles*
Maybury, Anne
  Katherine Troy, *Anne Buxton*
Mayfield, Anne
  Kathryn Atwood, Kathy Ptacek
Mayhew, Elizabeth
  *Joan E. Bear*
Mayhew, Margaret
Mayne, Cora
  Kathleen Ash, Pauline Ash,
  Emily Walker, Christine Lawson,
  Eileen Barry, Quenna Tilbury,
  Kathleen Treves, Sara Devon,
  Jane Lester, Delia Foster,
  Heather Vincent, Honor Vincent,
  Jill Murray, Kay Winchester
Mayo, Margaret
*Mayson, Marina*
  Rosemary Rogers
Meacham, Leila
Mead, Russell
  Maggi Charles, Meg Hudson,
  Carole Standish, *Margaret Keohler*
Meadowes, Alicia
  *Linda Burak & Joan Zeig*
*Meaker, Eloise*
  Valancy Hunter, Lydia Clark,

  Lydia Lancaster
Meaney, Dee Morrison
Medlock, Marilyn
  Amanda Stevens, *Marilyn M. Amman*
Meeks, Dianna
Melahn, Martha
Melbourne, Alix
Mellings, Rose
Melville, Anne
  Anne Betteridge, Margaret Evans,
  Margaret E. Potter, *Margaret Neuman*
Melville, Jennie
  Gwendoline Butler
Mendel, Jo
  *Mildred Gilbertson*, Nan Gilbert
Menitt, Jackie
Menzel, Lois
Mercer, June
Mercer, Peggy
Meredith, Jane
Meriwether, Kate
  Kate Fairchild, *Pat Ahearn*
*Merkt, Frankie*
  Ann Richards
Merlin, Christa
  Joanna Gilpen, Jan McGowan,
  Joanna McGauran
Merlin, Christina
  Constance Heaven, George Fleming,
  Constance Fecher
Merrill, Jean
Merrill, Lynne
  Claire Ritchie, Prudence Boyd,
  Lisette Garland, Noelle Ireland,
  Nina Shayne, Sara Whittingham,
  Heather Wayne, Nora Gibbs,
  Dallas Romaine
*Merrit, William*
  Lee Williams, Leigh Anne Williams
Merritt, Elizabeth
Merritt, Emma
  Emma Bennett, Micah Leigh
Merritt, Jackie
  *Carolyn Joyner*, Carrie Hart
*Mertz, Barbara*
  Barbara Michaels, Elizabeth Peters
Merwin, Lucy

**Messman, Jon**
Pamela Windsor, Colleen Moore,
Claudette Nicole, Claudia Nicole
**Mesta, Emily**
*Valerie Giscard*
**Metzger, Barbara**
*Meyer, Donna*
Megan Daniel
*Meyers, Barrie*
Jeanne Sommers
**Meyers, Julie**
Judith Blackwell, *Judith Blackwell Myers*
**Meyrick, Polly**
**Michael, Judith**
*Judith Barnard & Michael Fain*
**Michael, Marie**
Marie Charles, Marie Rydzynsky,
Marie Nicole, Marie Ferrarella
**Michaels, Barbara**
Elizabeth Peters, *Barbara Mertz*
**Michaels, Elizabeth**
**Michaels, Fern**
*Roberta Anderson & Mary Kuczir*,
Iris Summers
**Michaels, Irene**
*Mary Irene Donohue*
**Michaels, Jan**
Jan Mathews, Jan Milella
**Michaels, Kasey**
Michelle Kasey, Kathie Seidick
**Michaels, Kristin**
Gwen Choate, Martha Corson,
Jeanne Williams, Sue Long Turner
**Michaels, Leigh**
*Le Ann Lemberger*
**Michaels, Linda**
Julie Ellis, Patricia Bentley,
Alison Lord, Jeffrey Lord,
Susan Marvin, Richard Marvin,
Joan Ellis, Susan Richard,
Jill Monte, Susan Marino,
Marilyn Ellis
**Michaels, Lynn**
Paula Christopher, *Lynne Smith*
**Michaels, Margie**
Margie McDonnell
**Michaels, Michelle**
Gerri O'Hara, Michelle Christie

**Michaels, Steve**
Priscilla Dalton, Nick Carton,
Michael Avallone, Mark Dane,
Troy Conway, Dorothea Nile,
Edwina Noone, Vance Stanton,
Jean-Anne DePre, Sidney Stuart
**Michel, Freda**
**Michelle, Suzanne**
*Barbara Michels & Susan Larson*
*Michels, Barabara*
Suzanne Michelle
**Mickles, Linda**
**Miesel, Sandra**
**Mikels, Jennifer**
*Suzanne J. Kuhlin*
**Milan, Angel**
Elizabeth Nelson, Mary Lynn
*Elizabeth Neibor*
**Milella, Jan**
Jan Mathews, Jan Michaels
**Miles, Cynthia**
**Miles, Cassie**
Kay Bergstrom
**Miles, Deborah**
**Miller, Ann**
Leslie Morgan, Anne London
**Miller, Cissie**
Iona Charles, *Stanlee Coy Miller*
**Miller, Linda Lael**
**Miller, Marcia**
*Marceil Baker*
*Miller, Valerie*
Hilary Cole
**Millhiser, Marlys**
**Mills, Anita**
**Mills, Catherine**
**Mills, Frances**
**Milne, Rosaleen**
*Mims, Emily*
Emily Elliott
**Minger, Elda**
**Minger, Miriam**
**Minton, Paula**
Marie De Jourlet, Paul Little,
Leigh Franklin James, Paula Little
**Mireles, Sandra**
**Mitchell, Allison**
**Mitchell, Ann**

**Mitchell, Erica**
**Mitchell, Jay**
 Jennifer O'Green, Jennifer Roberson
**Mitchell, Paige**
 *Judith S. Ginnes*
**Mittermeyer, Helen**
 Ann Cristy, Hayton Monteith,
 Danielle Paul
**Mixon, Veronica**
 Nigella Weston
**Modean, Mary**
 Modean Moon
*Modrovich, Kathleen*
 Kathleen Creighton, Kathleen Carrol
*Moffett, Paula*
 Vanessa Richards
**Monet, Nicole**
 Noelle Berry McCue
*Monroe, Schere*
 Jessica Howard, Abigail Winter,
 Jean K. Schere
**Monson, Christine**
**Montague, Jeanne**
 Joan Hunter, *Jeanne Yarde*
**Montague, Lisa**
 *Sandra Dawn Shulman*
**Monte, Jill**
 *Julie Ellis*, Patricia Bentley,
 Allison Lord, Jeffrey Lord,
 Susan Marvin, Richard Marvin,
 Joan Ellis, Linda Michaels,
 Susan Marino, Susan Richard,
 Mariln Ellis
**Monteith, Hayton**
 Ann Cristy, Helen Mittermeyer,
 Danielle Paul
**Monterey, Elizabeth**
 Jan Alexander, V. J. Banis,
 Lynn Benedict
**Montgomery, Bettina**
 Nicole Norman, *Edythe Cudlipp*,
 Julia Alcott, Maureen Norris,
 Rinalda Roberts, *Edythe Lachlan*
**Montgomery, Marianne**
 D.H. Allen
**Montrose, Graham**
 Vivian Donald, Rory Macalpin,
 Charles Stuart, Charles Conte,

 Hilary Rose, Iain Torr,
 Charles Roy MacKinnon
**Montrose, Sarah**
 Valerie King, *Valerie Bosna*
**Moon, Modean**
 Mary Modean
**Mooney, Mary Alice**
**Moore, Anne**
**Moore, Aurora**
 *Arthur Moore*
*Moore, Arthur*
 Aurora Moore
**Moore, Colleen**
 Jon Messman, Pamela Windsor,
 Claudette Nicole, Claudia Nicole
**Moore, Diana**
 Diana Mars, *Deanna Marliss*
**Moore, Emily**
**Moore, Gwyneth**
 Patricia Veryan, *Patricia Bannister*
**Moore, Jill**
**Moore, Lisa**
 Elizabeth Chater
**Moore, Marjorie**
**Moore, Mary**
**Moore, Mary Ellen**
**Moore, Miriam**
 Miriam Morton
**Moore, Patti**
 Margaret Ripy, Kathleen Daley,
 Margaret Daley, Kit Daley
**Moore, Paula**
 *Robert Vaughan*, Paula Fairman
**Moore, Rayanne**
**Moorhouse, Catherine**
 *Catherine Allen & Dorothea Jensen*
**Morel, Angela**
**Morel, Jimmie**
**Moreland, Peggy**
 *Peggy B. Morse*
*Moren, Sally*
 Jane Morgan
**Morgan, Alice**
**Morgan, Alyssa**
 Edith Delatush, Edith De Paul,
 Edith St. George
**Morgan, Diana**
 *Alex Kamaroff & Irene Goodman*

Morgan, Faye
  Doreen Owens Malek
Morgan, Jane
  *Sally Moren*
Morgan, Leslie
  Anne London, Ann Miller
Morgan, Marley
Morgan, Meredith
Morgan, Michaela
  Gloria Basile
*Morgan, Nancy*
  Jenny McGuire
Morgan, Raye
  Jena Hunt, Helen Conrad
Morgan, Virginia
Morland, Lynnette
  Karen O'Connell
*Morris, Debrah*
  Pepper Adams, JoAnn Stacey,
  Dianne Thomas, Joanna Jordan
Morris, Elizabeth
  *Jean Favors*
Morris, Ira J.
Morris, Janet
Morris, Kathleen
*Morrison, Patricia*
  Patricia Kennealy
Morrison, Roberta
  Jean Francis Webb
Morse, Nancy
  Danielle Fleming
*Morse, Peggy B.*
  Peggy Morehead
Mortimer, Carole
Morton, Miriam
  Miriam Moore
Morton, Patricia
  *Morton J. Golding*
*Moser, Alma*
  Alison Gray
Moss, Jan
Motheral, Nancy
  Laura Shaw
Motley, Annette
Moulton, Nancy
Mountjoy, Roberta
  Jerry Sohl
Moyer, Florence

*Muelbauer, Pamela*
  Pamela Bauer
Muir, Jean
Muir, Lucy
*Mulholland, Judith*
  Judith Duncan
Mullan, Celina
  Marisa De Zavala, Rachel Scott,
  *Ana Lisa de Leon*
*Mullen, Dore*
  Dorothy Mullen
Mullen, Dorothy
  *Dore Mullen*
*Mulvihill, Rochelle A.*
  Rochelle Wayne
Munn, Vella
  Dawn Flindt
*Munro, Mary*
  Doris Howe, Newlyn Nash
*Murphy, Lynne*
  Georgina Gentry
Murray, Annabel
  *Marie Murray*
Murray, Beatrice
  *Richard Posner*
Murray, Caitlin
  Kate Fairchild, Kate Meriwether,
  *Pat Ahearn*
Murray, E. P.
Murray, Edna
  Vera Craig, *Donald S. Rowland*
Murray, Frances
  *Rosemary Booth*
Murray, Jill
  Pauline Ash, Kathleen Ash,
  Emily Walker, Christine Lawson,
  Sara Devon, Quenna Tilbury,
  Delia Foster, Jane Lester,
  Eileen Barry, Cora Mayne,
  Kathleen Treves, Honor Vincent,
  Heather Vincent, Kay Winchester
Murray, Julia
*Murray, Marie*
  Annabel Murray
Murray, Rachel
Murrey, Jeneth
*Musgrave, David & Margaret*
  Jacqueline Musgrave

**Musgrave, Jacqueline**
*David & Margaret Musgrave*
**Muskett, Netta**
Anne Hill
*Mussi, Mary*
Josephine Edgar, Mary Howard
**Mutch, Karen**
**Myers, Eve**
Myers, Helen R.
*Myers, Judith Blackwell*
Judith Blackwell, Julie Myers
**Myers, Katherine**
**Myers, Mary Ruth**
**Myers, Peggy**
Ann Williams
**Myers, Virginia**
Jane Worth Abbott
**Myles, Frances**
**Myles, Sabrina**
Rebecca Ashley, Candice Adams,
Lois A. Walker
**Myles, Sandra**
Sandra Marton
**Myrus, Joyce**

---

*Notes*

Names in *italics* indicate an author's legal name which does not appear on books. She or he uses pseudonym (s) only.

Names <u>underlined</u> indicate that the author uses legal name for works and may or may not use pseudonym (s).

Naismith, Marion
Napier, Priscilla
Napier, Susan
Nash, Jean
   *Jean Sutherland*
Nash, Newlyn
   *Mary Munro,* Doris Howe
Nash, Noreen
<u>Nauman, Eileen</u>
   Beth Brookes, Lindsay McKenna
Neal, Hilary
   Olive Norton, Bess Norton,
   Kate Norway, *T. R. Noon*
Neale, Linda
Neels, Betty
<u>Neggers, Carla</u>
   Amalia James, Anne Harrell
*Neher, Lisa*
   Juli Greene
*Neibor, Elizabeth*
   Angel Milan, Mary Lynn,
   Elizabeth Nelson
Neilan, Sarah
Nel, Stella Frances
Nelson, Elizabeth
   Angel Milan, Mary Lynn,
   *Elizabeth Neibor*
Nelson, Judith
Nelson, Louella
Nelson, Marguerite
   Austin Brett, Maria S. Sterling,
   Grace Lang, Matt Harding,
   Lee Floren, Lisa Franchon,
   Claudia Hall, Len Turner,
   Lee Thomas, Will Watson

Nelson, Valerie K.
Neri, Penelope
*Netzel, Sally*
   Suzanne Jenner
*Neubauer, William*
   Joan Garrison, Rebecca Marsh,
   Norma Newcomb, Jan Hathaway,
   William Arthur, Christine Bennett
*Neukrug, Linda*
   Jill Castle
*Neuman, Margaret*
   Anne Betteridge, Margaret Evans,
   Margaret Potter, Anne Melville
Neville, Anne
   *Jane Viney*
Nevins, Kate
   <u>Margaret Malkind</u>
Newcomb, Kerry
   Shana Carrol, Peter Gentry,
   Christina Savage
Newcomb, Norma
   Joan Garrison, Rebecca Marsh,
   Jan Hathaway, William Arthur,
   *William Neubauer,* Christine Bennett
Newell, Rosemary
Newman, Holly
Newman, Mona
   Barbara Fitzgerald, Jean Stewart
*Nichols, Carolyn*
   Iona Charles
Nichols, Charlotte
   Patricia Knoll & *Barbara Williams,*
   Patricia Forsythe
Nichols, Jane
   *Lisa Scales*

**109**

Nichols, Leigh
  Dean Koontz
Nichols, Mary
Nichols, Sarah
  Lee Hays
Nichols, Suzanne
  *Marlys Staplebrock*
Nicholson, Catherine
Nicholson, Christina
  Daniel Adams, Leslie Arlen,
  Mark Logan, Christopher Nicole,
  Simon McKay, Alison York,
  Peter Grange, Robin Cade,
  Andrew York
Nicholson, Peggy
Nickson, Hilda
Nickson, Jeanne
Nicole, Christopher
  Leslie Arlen, Daniel Adams,
  Simon McKay, Andrew York,
  Mark Logan, Christina Nicholson,
  Peter Grange, Robin Cade,
  Alison York
Nicole, Claudette
  Colleen Moore, Pamela Windsor,
  Jon Messman, Claudia Nicole
Nicole, Claudia
  Claudette Nicole, Colleen Moore,
  Pamela Windsor, Jon Messman
Nicole, Marie
  Marie Charles, Marie Rydzynski,
  Marie Michael, Marie Ferrarella,
Nielsen, Virginia
  Virginia McCall
*Nielson, Ingrid*
  Iris May Bancroft, Andrea Layton
Nigro, Deborah
Nile, Dorothea
  Michael Avallone, Mark Dane,
  Priscilla Dalton, Nick Carton,
  Troy Conway, Steve Michaels,
  Sidney Stuart, Vance Stanton,
  Jean-Anne DePre, Edwina Noone
Nixon, Kathleen
  *V. R. Blundell*
*Nobisso, Joi*
  Nuria Wood, Nadja Bride

*Noble, Judith*
  Judith Baker
Noel, Angela
Nolan, Jenny
  *Mary Jo Young*
*Nollett, Lois*
  Diana Delmore
*Noon, T. R.*
  Hilary Neal, Olive Norton,
  Bess Norton, Kate Norway
Noone, Edwina
  Michael Avallone, Troy Conway,
  Priscilla Dalton, Mark Dane,
  Nick Carton, Steve Michaels,
  Dorothea Nile, Vance Stanton,
  Sidney Stuart, Jean-Anne DePre
Norcross, Lisabet
  Margaret SeBastian, Cilla Whitmore,
  Maggie Gladstone, *Arthur Gladstone*
Norman, Dee
  *Dee Lopez & Norma Williams*,
  Wynn Williams
Norman, Diana
Norman, Elizabeth
Norman, Nicole
  Bettina Montgomery, Edythe Cudlipp,
  Julia Alcott, Maureen Norris,
  Rinalda Roberts, *Edythe Lachlan*
Norman, Yvonne
  Norma Yvonne Seely
Norrell, Marjorie
  Marjorie Ellison, *Marjorie Norton*
Norris, Carol
  Kris Karron
Norris, Maureen
  Julia Alcott, Edythe Lachlan,
  Bettina Montgomery, Nicole Norman,
  Rinalda Roberts, *Edythe Cudlipp*
North, Jessica
  *Robert Somerlott*
North, Miranda
North, Sara (series):
  Barbara Bonham, Jean Hager,
  Marlaine Kyle, Jeanne Stephens,
  Leah Crane, Amanda McAllister
Northan, Irene
Norton, Alice Mary
  Andre Norton, Andrew North

**Norton, Andre**
Andrew North, Alice Mary Norton
**Norton, Bess**
Hilary Neal, Olive Norton,
Kate Norway, *T. R. Noon*
*Norton, Marjorie*
Marjorie Ellison, Marjorie Norrell
**Norton, Olive**
Hilary Neal, Bess Norton,
Kate Norway, *T. R. Noon*
**Nottingham, Poppy**
*Patti Dunaway*
*Novak, Rose*
Marcia Rose
**Nowinson, Marie**
**Noyes, Patricia Ann**
*Nuccio, Marsha*
M. L. Gamble
**Nuelle, Helen**
**Nunn, Rebecca**
**Nye, Valerie**

*Notes*

# Notes

**Oakson, Pat C.**
  Robin Tolivar
**O'Banyon, Constance**
  *Evelyn Gee*, Micah Leigh
**O'Brian, Eve**
  *Judith Bryer & Arnie Heller*
**O'Brian, Gayle**
**O'Brien, Kathleen**
  Kathleen Pynn
**O'Brien, Saliee**
  Francesca Greer, *Frankie-Lee Janas*
**O'Bryan, Sofi**
**O'Caragh, Mary**
**O'Connell, Karen**
  Lynette Morland
**O'Connor, Megan**
**Ocork, Shannon**
**O'Dell, Amanda**
**O'Donnell, Kate**
  *Nancy Garcia*
**O'Donoghue, Maureen**
*Ogan, George & Margaret*
  Rosetta Stowe
**O'Grady, Leslie**
**O'Grady, Rohan**
  *June Skinner*
<u>**O'Green, Jennifer**</u>
  Jay Mitchell, Jennifer Roberson
**O'Hallion, Sheila**
  Sheila R. Allen
**O'Hara, Gerri**
  Michelle Christie, Michelle Michaels
**O'Hara, Kate**
*Ohlrogge, Anne K. S.*
  Anne Stuart

*O'Laimhin, Marti L.*
  Marti Laven
**Oldfield, Elizabeth**
*Oleyar, Rita Balkey*
  Rita Balkey
**Oliver, Amy Roberta**
  Berta Ruck, *Berta Onions*
**Oliver, Jan**
  *Janece Hudson*, Jan Hudson
**Oliver, Marina**
**Oliver, Tess**
  Tess Holloway, *Teri Kovack*,
  Teri Shapiro
**Olshaker, Thelma**
*Oltmann, Vanessa*
  Vanessa Grant
**O'More, Peggy**
  Jeanne Bowman, Betty Blocklinger
**O'Nair, Mairi**
  Jane Gray, Constance M. Evans
**O'Neal, Reagan**
  *James O. Rigney, Jr.*
**O'Neill, Egan**
  Dell Shannon, Anne Blaisdell,
  <u>Elizabeth Linington,</u> Lesley Egan
**O'Neill, Jude**
  *Judy Blundell*
**O'Neill, Noreen**
  *Thomas Armstrong*
**O'Neill, Olivia**
*Onions, Berta*
  Berta Ruck, Amy Roberta Oliver
**Oppenheimer, Joan**
**Ord, Irene**
  Kate Fairfax

*Notes*

Names in *italics* indicate an author's legal name which does not appear on books. She or he uses pseudonym (s) only.

Names <u>underlined</u> indicate that the author uses legal name for works and may or may not use pseudonym (s).

Pace, DeWanna
Pace, Laurel
  *Barbara Wojhoski*
Pacotti, Pamela
Pade, Victoria
Page, Betsy
  Elizabeth August, *Bettie Wilhite*
  Elizabeth Douglas
Page, Vicki
  *Ruby D. Avery*
Paige, Laurie
  *Olivia M. Hall*, Libby Hall
Palencia, Elaine Fowler
  Laurel Blake
*Pall, Ellen*
  Fiona Hill
Palmer, Catherine
Palmer, Diana
  Diana Blayne, Katy Currie
  <u>Susan Kyle</u>
Palmer, Gail
*Palmer, Linda Varner*
  Scotney St. James, Linda Varner
Palmer, Rachel
  *Ruth Potts*
<u>Papazoglou, Orania</u>
  Nicola Andrews, Ann Paris
Pape, Sharon
<u>Pappano, Marilyn</u>
Paquin, Ethel
Paradise, Mary
  Dorothy Eden
Parenteau, Shirley
Pargeter, Margaret

Paris, Ann
  Nicola Andrews,
  <u>Orania Papazoglou</u>
Parker, Beatrice
  Edwina Marlow, Jennifer Wilde,
  <u>Tom E. Huff</u>, Katherine St. Clair
Parker, Cynthia
*Parker, Karen Blair*
  Blair Cameron, Kathryn Blair
Parker, Laura
  *Laura Castoro*
Parker, Norah
  Eleanor Howard, *Eleanor Hodgson*
Parkes, Patricia
Parkin, Bernadette
*Parkinson, Cornelia*
  Day Taylor
<u>Parmett, Doris</u>
<u>Parnell, Andrea</u>
*Parris, Laura*
  Laura Magner
Parrish, Mary
  Margaret Cousins, Avery Johns,
  William Masters
Parrish, Patt
  Patt Bucheister
Parv, Valerie
Pascoe, Irene M.
  Andrea Haley
Patrick, DeAnn
  *Dotti Corcoran & Mary Ann Slojkowski*,
  Mary Ann Hammond
Patrick, Lynn
  *Patricia Pinianski & Linda Sweeney*,
  Patricia Rosemoor, RoseAnne McKenna

**Patrick, Maxine**
  Patricia Maxwell, Jennifer Blake,
  Elizabeth Trehearne,
  Patricia Ponder
**Patten, Darlene**
**Patterson, Betty Ann**
  Vickie York
**Patterson, Morgan**
*Pattison, Nancy*
  Nan Asquith, Susannah Broome
*Pattison, Ruth*
  Ruth Abbey
**Patton, Sarah**
  Genevieve English
**Paul, Barbara**
  Rosalind Laker, Barbara Douglas,
  Barbara Ovstedahl
**Paul, Danielle**
  Ann Cristy, Hayton Monteith,
  Helen Mittermeyer
**Paul, Paula**
**Paul, Wynne**
**Pauley, Barbara Anne**
**Paulos, Sheila**
*Pavlik, E. M.*
  Adora Sheridan
**Paxton, Jean**
  Martha Jean Powers
**Paxton, Lois**
  Dorothy Mackie Low, Lois Low,
  Zoe Cass
**Payes, Rachel Cosgrove**
  Rachel R. Cosgrove, Joanne Kaye,
  E.L. Arch
**Payne, Tiffany**
**Peake, Lilian**
**Peake, Lynsey**
**Peale, Constance F.**
  *Whitney Stine*
**Pearl, Ester E.**
  Jessica Lansing, *David Ritz*
*Pearl, Jack*
  Stephanie Blake
**Peart, Jane**
**Peck, Maggie**
  Margot Prince, Marjorie Price
**Pedersen, Gloria**

*Pelfrey, Judy*
  Judith Daniels, Rhett Daniels
**Pellicane, Patricia**
**Pelton, Sonya T.**
*Peltonen, Carla*
  Lynn Erickson
**Pemberton, Margaret**
**Pemberton, Nan**
  Nina Pykare, Regina Towers,
  Nina Coombs, Natalie Pryor,
  Ann Coombs, Nora Powers
**Pence, Joanne**
**Pender, Laura**
  *Dana Anderson*
**Pepper, Joan**
  Joan Alexander
*Perez-Venero, Mirna*
  Mirna Pierce
**Perkins, Barbara**
**Perry, Anne**
**Perry, Michalann**
  Megan Blythe
**Pershall, Mary**
  Susan Shelley
**Pershing, Karen**
  Kerry Price
**Pershing, Marie**
  *Pearle Henriksen Schultz*
**Peters, Anne**
  *Anne Hansen*
**Peters, Clarice**
  Laureen Kwock
**Peters, Elizabeth**
  Barbara Michaels, *Barbara Mertz*
**Peters, Louise**
**Peters, Maureen**
  Catherine Darby, Maureen Black,
  Veronica Black, Sharon Whitby,
  Judith Rothman, Elizabeth Law,
  Levanah Lloyd
**Peters, Natasha**
  Anastasia Cleaver
**Peters, Sue**
  Angela Carson
*Petratur, Joyce*
  Joyce Verrette
**Phillips, Barbara**

**Phillips, Dorothy**
    Johanna Phillips, Dorothy Glenn,
    <u>Dorothy Garlock</u>
**Phillips, Johanna**
    Dorothy Phillips, Dorothy Glenn,
    <u>Dorothy Garlock</u>
**Phillips, Patricia**
    Sonia Phillips
**Phillips, Susan**
<u>**Phillips, Susan Elizabeth**</u>
    Justine Cole
**Phillips, Susan Leslie**
**Phillipson, Sandra**
<u>**Pianka, Phyllis Taylor**</u>
    Winter Ames
<u>**Pickart, Joan Elliott**</u>
    Robin Elliott
*Picker, Rita*
    Martina Sultan
**Pierce, Georgia**
    Lindsey Hanks
**Pierce, Mirna**
    *Mirna Perez-Venero*
**Pilcher, Rosumunde**
    Jane Fraser
**Pindrus, Nancy Elaine**
*Pinianski, Patricia*
    Patricia Rosemoor, Lynn Patrick,
*Plagakis, Jim*
    Christy Dore
**Plaidy, Jean**
    Victoria Holt, Philippa Carr,
    Eleanor Hibbert, Elbur Ford,
    Kathleen Kellow, Ellalice Tate,
    Eleanor Burford
**Plummer, Clare**
    Clare Ensley
*Pogony, Jean Coulter*
    Catherine Coulter
*Pohle, Robert Warren*
    Devon Lee
**Polk, Dora**
<u>**Polley, Judith Anne**</u>
    Valentina Luellan, Judith Hagar,
    Helen Kent, Judith Stewart
**Pollock, Ida**
    Susan Barrie, Jane Beaufort,
    Rose Burghley, Anita Charles,

Pamela Kent, Barbara Rowan,
    Mary Whistler
**Pollock, Rosemary**
**Ponder, Patricia**
    Jennifer Blake, <u>Patricia Maxwell</u>,
    Elizabeth Trehearne, Maxine Patrick
**Pope, Ann**
    Lee Pope, Ann Zavala
**Pope, Lee**
    Ann Pope, Ann Zavala
**Pope, Pamela**
**Porter, Jessica**
*Porter, Joyce*
    Deborah Joyce
*Porter, Madeline*
    Anna James, Madeline Harper,
    Elizabeth Habersham
**Porter, Margaret Evans**
**Porterfield, Kay**
    Colleen Kimbrough
**Porterfield, Marie**
*Posner, Richard*
    Beatrice Murray
*Poteet, Ardia*
    Georgia McKinney
**Potter, Allison**
**Potter, Jackie**
    Jane Ireland
**Potter, Margaret**
    Anne Betteridge, Margaret Evans,
    *Margaret Neuman*, Anne Melville
**Potter, Patricia**
*Potts, Ruth*
    Rachel Palmer
**Powell, Jan Hamilton**
    Celeste Hamilton, Neely Powell
**Powell, Neely**
    Celeste Hamilton, Jan Hamilton Powell
**Power, Elizabeth**
**Powers, Anne**
    *Anne Schwartz*
<u>**Powers, Martha Jean**</u>
    Jean Paxton
**Powers, Nora**
    Natalie Pryor, Nina Pykare,
    Nan Pemberton, Regina Towers,
    Nina Coombs, Ann Coombs

**Pozzessere, Heather Graham**
Heather Graham, Shannon Drake
**Prate, Kit**
*Dorothy Howell*
**Preble, Amanda**
*Christine B. Tayntor*
**Prentiss, Charlotte**
**Pressley, Hilda**
**Preston, Fayrene**
Jaelyn Conlee
**Preston, Hilary**
**Prewit-Parker, Jolene**
**Price, Ashland**
Laura Ashcroft, Laura Price,
Janice Carlson
**Price, Dianne**
**Price, Kerry**
Karen Pershing
**Price, Laura**
Laura Ashcroft, Ashland Price,
Janice Carlson
**Price, Lynn**
*Cheryl Purviance*, Cheryl Spencer
**Price, Marjorie**
Maggie Peck, Margot Prince
**Prince, Margot**
Maggie Peck, Marjorie Price
**Prior, Mollie**
Janet Roscoe
**Pritchett, Ariadne**
**Proctor, Carol**
**Proctor, Kate**
**Prole, Lozania**
Sheila Burns, Ursula Bloom,
Mary Essex, Rachel Harvey,
Deborah Mann, Ursula Harvey
*Pugh, Dana Rae*
Deanna Linden
*Purviance, Cheryl Lynn*
Lynn Price, Cheryl Spencer
**Pryor, Natalie**
Nora Powers, Nina Pykare,
Nan Pemberton, Regina Towers,
Nina Coombs, Ann Coombs
**Pryor, Pauline**
Pamela D'Arcy, Georgina Grey,
Mary Wilson, Elisabeth Welles,
Mary Linn Roby, Valerie Bradstreet

**Pryor, Vanessa**
Chelsea Quinn Yarbro
**Ptacek, Kathy**
Kathryn Atwood, Anne Mayfield
**Putney, Mary Jo**
*Puyear-Alerding, Kathleen*
Kathy Alerding
**Pyatt, Rosina**
**Pykare, Nina**
Nan Pemberton, Regina Towers,
Nina Coombs, Nora Powers,
Natalie Pryor, Ann Coombs
**Pynn, Kathleen**
Kathleen O'Brien

*Notes*

Names in *italics* indicate an author's legal name which does not appear on books. She or he uses pseudonym (s) only.

Names <u>underlined</u> indicate that the author uses legal name for works and may or may not use pseudonym (s).

**Quentin, Dorothy**
**Quest, Erica**
    Hilary London, Nancy John,
    Nancy Buckingham, Christina Abbey,
    *Nancy & John Sawyer*
***Quigley, Aileen***
    Erica Lindley, Ruth Fabian,
    Aileen Armitage
**Quinn, Alison**
**Quinn, Colleen**
    *Colleen Bosler*
**Quinn, Samantha**
    *Maureen Bullinger*

*Notes*

*Notes*

Names in *italics* indicate an author's legal name which does not appear on books. She or he uses pseudonym (s) only.

Names <u>underlined</u> indicate that the author uses legal name for works and may or may not use pseudonym (s).

Radcliffe, Janette
  Louisa Bronte, Rebecca Danton,
  <u>Janet Louise Roberts</u>
Rade, Sheila
*Radford, Richard Francis*
  Amy Lyndon
Rae, Doris
*Rae, Hugh C.*
  Jessica Stirling
Rae, Patricia
  Gina Delaney, *Patricia Walls*
<u>Raffel, Elizabeth & Burton</u>
Rafferty, Carin
  Allyson Ryan, *Linda Kichline*
<u>Ragosta, Millie J.</u>
  Melanie Randolph
Raine, Nicole
  <u>Sandi Gelles</u>
Rainone, Christopher
  Violet Hawthorne
Raintree, Lee
  Con Sellers
<u>Rainville, Rita</u>
*Ramin, Terey daly*
  Terese Ramin
Ramin, Terese
  *Terey daly Ramin*
*Ramirez, Alice*
  Candice Arkham, Serena Alexander
Ramsay, Fay
  Helen Eastwood, Olive Baxter
Ramsey, Eileen Ainsworth
Rand, Suzanne
  Debra Brand

Randall, Diana
  W.E.D. Ross, Clarissa Ross,
  Marilyn Ross, <u>Dan Ross</u>,
  Dana Ross, Rose Williams,
  Jane Rossiter, Ellen Randolph,
  Leslie Ames, Ann Gilmor,
  Rose Dana, Ruth Dorset,
  Miriam Leslie, Marilyn Carter
Randall, Lindsay
  *Susan M. Anderson*
Randall, Rona
  Virginia Standage, *Rona Shambrook*
Randolph, Elise
  Andrea Davidson, *Susan Lowe*
Randolph, Ellen
  Leslie Ames, Rose Dana,
  Ruth Dorset, Ann Gilmor,
  Miriam Leslie, W. E. D. Ross,
  Clarissa Ross, Marilyn Ross,
  Diana Randall, <u>Dan Ross,</u>
  Jane Rossiter, Marilyn Carter
Randolph, Ellen
Randolph, Melanie
  <u>Millie J. Ragosta</u>
Rangel, Doris
Ransom, Dana
  Lauren Giddings, *Nancy Gideon*
Ransom, Katherine
  Katherine Granger, *Mary Sederquest*
*Rasley, Alicia Todd*
  Michelle Venet, Elizabeth Todd
Rasmussen, Alysse S.
  Alysse Lemery
Rather, Deborah
  Arlene James

**121**

**R**

**Richards-Akers, Nancy**
Mary Alice Kirk
**Richards, Ann**
*Frankie Merkt*
**Richards, Celia Gardner**
**Richards, Cinda**
Cheryl Reavis
**Richards, Clare**
Louise Titchener & Carolyn Males,
Alyssa Howard, Alexis Hill Jordan,
Alexis Hill, Jane Silverwood,
Anne Silverlock, Tess Marlowe,
Clare Richmond
**Richards, Emilie**
Emilie McGee
**Richards, Jessica**
**Richards, Leigh**
*Richards, Penny*
Sandi Shane, Bay Matthews
**Richards, Serena**
**Richards, Stephanie**
**Richards, Vanessa**
*Paula Moffett*
**Richardson, Alaine**
Alaine Hawthorne
**Richardson, Evelyn**
**Richardson, Hope**
**Richardson, Mozelle**
**Richardson, Susan**
**Richmond, Clare**
Louise Titchener & *Carolyn Males*,
Alexis Hill, Alexis Hill Jordan,
Alyssa Howard, Clare Richards,
Jane Silverwood, Tess Marlowe,
Anne Silverlock
**Richmond, Emma**
*Ricks, Patricia*
Patricia Wynn
*Rider, Elisie B.*
Isobel Chace, Elizabeth Hunter,
Elizabeth de Guise
*Riefe, Alan*
Barbara Riefe, A. R. Riefe
**Riefe, A. R.**
*Alan Riefe*, Barbara Riefe
**Riefe, Barbara**
*Alan Riefe*, A. R. Riefe

**Rift, Valerie**
Rowena Lee, Marie Bartlett
**Rigg, Jennifer**
Genevieve Scott
**Riggs, Paula Detmer**
*Rigney, James O.*
Reagan O'Neal
**Riker, Leigh**
**Riley, Eugenia**
*Eugenia R. Essenmacher*
*Riley, Stella*
Juliet Blyth
**Rimmer, Christine**
**Rinehold, Connie**
**Ripy, Margaret**
Kathleen Daley, Patti Moore,
Margaret Daley, Kit Daley
**Risku, Cillay**
**Ritchie, Claire**
Nora Gibbs, Lisette Garland,
Nina Shayne, Sara Whittingham,
Noelle Ireland, Lynne Merrill,
Prudence Boyd, Heather Wayne,
Dallas Romaine
**Ritter, Margaret**
*Ritz, David*
Jessica Lansing
**Rivers, Diana**
Faye Ashley, Ashley Summers
**Rivers, Dorothy**
Leonora Starr, *Leonora Mackesy*
**Rivers, Francine**
**Rivers, Georgina**
**Rivers, Kendall**
*Robarchek, Peg*
Katheryn Brett
**Robards, Karen**
**Robb, Christine**
*Christine R. Goold*
**Robb, JoAnn**
JoAnn Robbins, JoAnn Ross
**Robb, Sandra**
**Robbe, Michele**
*Lucy Seaman*
**Robbins, Andrea**
*Peter Albano*
**Robbins, JoAnn**
JoAnn Robb, JoAnn Ross

**R**

Robbins, Kay
  Kay Hooper
Robbins, Serena
Roberson, Jennifer
  Jennifer O'Green, Jay Mitchell
Robert, Adrian
  Elizabeth Bolton, Kate Chambers,
  Catherine Chambers, Pamela Dryden,
  Lavinia Harris, Norma Johnston,
  Nicole St. John
Roberta, Phyllis
Roberts, Desmond
  Breton Amis, Rayleigh Best,
  Leslie Wilde, Leigh Haddow,
  *Ray Bentinck,* Terence Hughes
Roberts, Doreen
Roberts, Irene
  Roberta Carr, Iris Rowland,
  Irene Shaw, Ivor Roberts,
  Elizabeth Harle
Roberts, Ivor
  Roberta Carr, Iris Rowland,
  Irene Roberts, Irene Shaw,
  Elizabeth Harle
Roberts, Jacqueline
Roberts, Janet Louise
  Louisa Bronte, Janette Radcliffe,
  Rebecca Danton
Roberts, Leigh
  *Lora Smith*
Roberts, Nora
Roberts, Paula
  Joan M. Hohl, Amii Lorin
Roberts, Phyllis
Roberts, Rinalda
  Julia Alcott, Maureen Norris,
  *Edythe Lachlan,* Nicole Norman,
  Bettina Montgomery, Edythe Cudlipp
Roberts, Suzanne
  *Laurie Marath*
Roberts, Virginia
  Nell Marr Dean, Anne Marr,
  *Nell Dean Ratzlaff*
*Robertson, Susan E.*
  Susan Haynesworth
Robins, Denise
  Ashley French, Harriet Gray,
  Francesca Wright, Julia Kane

Robins, Eleanor
Robins, Gina
  Carol Finch, Connie Drake,
  *Connie Fedderson*
Robins, Madeleine
Robins, Patricia
  Claire Lorrimer, *Beatrice Coogan*
Robinson, Irene
  Jo Manning
Roby, Mary Linn
  Georgiana Grey, Mary Wilson,
  Valerie Bradstreet, Elisabeth Welles,
  Pauline Pryor, Pamela D'Arcy
Rochester, Jane
*Roddick, Barbara*
  Hilary Mason
Roding, Frances
Rodgers, M.J.
  *Mary Johnson*
*Roe, M. S.*
  Daisy Thomson, Daisy Hicks,
  Jonathon H. Thompson
Roffman, Jan
  Margaret Summerton
Roffman, Sara
  Evelyn Bond, Jan Kavanaugh,
  Janet Templeton, Jessica Wilcox,
  Sara Rothman, Lionel Webb,
  Morris Hershman
Rogers, Betsy
  Rebecca Swan
*Rogers, Eleanor*
  Eleanor Woods
Rogers, Evelyn
  Keller Graves
*Rogers, Lee*
  Jean Barrett
Rogers, Marylyle
  Mary Lisle
Rogers, Patricia
  Rachel Welles, Patricia Welles
Rogers, Rosemary
  *Marina Mayson*
Roland, Michelle
  Robin Francis, Valerie Ferris,
  Rose Marie Ferris
Roland, Paula
Rollins, Helen

**Rolofson, Kristine**
**Romaine, Dallas**
Claire Ritchie, Prudence Boyd,
Sara Whittingham, Nora Gibbs,
Nina Shayne, Lisette Garland,
Noelle Ireland, Lynne Merrill,
Heather Wayne
*Romberg, Nina*
*Nina Andersson*, Jane Archer,
Asa Drake
**Rome, Margaret**
*Roper, Lester*
Samantha Lester
**Roscoe, Janet**
Mollie Prior
**Rose, Hilary**
Vivian Donald, Charles Conte,
Charles Stuart, Rory Macalpin,
Iain Torr, Graham Montrose,
Charles Roy MacKinnon
**Rose, Jennifer**
*Nancy Webber*
**Rose, Marcia**
*Marcia Kamien & Rose Novak*
**Rosemoor, Patricia**
Lynn Patrick, *Patricia Pinianski*,
RoseAnne McKenna
**Ross, Clarissa**
W.E.D. Ross, Marilyn Ross,
Dana Ross, <u>Dan Ross</u>,
Diana Randall, Rose Williams,
Jane Rossiter, Leslie Ames,
Ellen Randolph, Rose Dana,
Ruth Dorset, Ann Gilmor,
Miriam Leslie, Marilyn Carter
<u>Ross, Dan</u>
W.E.D. Ross, Clarissa Ross,
Dana Ross, Marilyn Ross,
Diana Randall, Jane Rossiter,
Leslie Ames, Ellen Randolph,
Rose Dana, Ruth Dorset,
Ann Gilmor, Miriam Leslie,
Marilyn Carter, Rose Williams
**Ross, Dana**
W.E.D. Ross, Dan Ross,
Marilyn Carter, Leslie Ames,
Jane Rossiter, Diana Randall,
Rose Williams, Rose Dana,

Ruth Dorset, Ann Gilmor,
Miriam Leslie, Clarissa Ross,
Marilyn Ross
**Ross, Dana Fuller**
<u>Noel B. Gerson,</u> Phillip Vail,
Samuel Edwards, Carter Vaughn,
Paul Lewis
**Ross, Deborah**
**Ross, Erin**
*Shirley Tallman*
**Ross, Helaine**
Angela Gray, Dorothy Daniels,
Danielle Dorsett, Geraldine Thayer,
Suzanne Somers, Cynthia Kavanaugh,
Helen Gray Weston
<u>Ross, JoAnn</u>
JoAnn Robb, JoAnn Robbin
**Ross, Marilyn**
Dana Ross, Rose Williams,
W.E.D. Ross, Clarissa Ross,
Dan Ross, Diana Randall,
Jane Rossiter, Leslie Ames,
Ellen Randolph, Rose Dana,
Ruth Dorset, Ann Gilmor,
Miriam Leslie, Marilyn Carter
**Ross, Regina**
**Ross, W.E.D.**
Clarissa Ross, Dan Ross,
Dana Ross, Rose Williams,
Marilyn Ross, Diana Randall,
Jane Rossiter, Leslie Ames,
Ellen Randolph, Rose Dana,
Ruth Dorset, Ann Gilmor,
Miriam Leslie, Marilyn Carter
**Rosse, Susanna**
Vivian Connolly
**Rossiter, Clare**
**Rossiter, Jane**
Dana Ross, W. E. D. Ross,
Marilyn Ross, Dan Ross,
Clarissa Ross, Rose Williams,
Diana Randall, Leslie Ames,
Ellen Randolph, Rose Dana,
Ruth Dorset, Ann Gilmor,
Miriam Leslie, Marilyn Carter
**Roszel, Renee**
Renee Wilson

**Roth, Jillian**
  Linda Ladd
**Roth, Pamela**
  Toth, Pamela
**Rothman, Judith**
  Catherine Darby, Maureen Black,
  Veronica Black, Maureen Peters,
  Sharon Whitby, Elizabeth Law,
  Levanah Lloyd
**Rothman, Sara**
  Janet Templeton, Evelyn Bond,
  Jessica Wilcox, Ian Kavanaugh,
  Morris Hershman, Sara Roffman,
  Lionel Webb
**Rothwell, Una**
**Rotter, Elizabeth**
  Laura Matthews,
  Elizabeth Neff Walker
**Rouverol, Jean**
**Rowan, Barbara**
  Susan Barrie, Jane Beaufort,
  Rose Burghley, Anita Charles,
  Pamela Kent, Ida Pollock,
  Mary Whistler
**Rowan, Deirdre**
  Megan Castell, Jeanne Williams,
  Jeanne Crecy, Jeanne Foster,
  Kristin Michaels, Megan Stuart
**Rowan, Hester**
**Rowe, Melanie**
  Pamela Browning, *Pam Ketter*
**Rowe, Myra**
*Rowland, Donald S.*
  Edna Murray, Vera Craig
**Rowland, Iris**
  Irene Roberts, Roberta Carr,
  Ivor Roberts, Irene Shaw,
  Elizabeth Harle
**Rowland, Susannah**
**Rowlands, V.M.D.**
**Royal, Diane**
**Royal, Rosamond**
  Jeanne Hines, Valerie Sherwood
**Royall, Vanessa**
  Michael T. Hinkemeyer
**Ruck, Berta**
  *Berta Onions*, Amy Roberta Oliver

*Rudeen, Anne & Louisa*
  Leigh Ellis
**Rudick, Marilynne**
*Rugg, Leslie*
  Louisa Gillette, Madeline Hale
**Rundle, Anne**
  Joanne Marshall, Alexandra
  Manners, Marianne Lamont,
  Jean Sanders
**Rush, Alison**
**Russell, Nelle**
**Russell, Renee**
  Jessica Jeffries, Samantha Scott,
  Nancy Hermann
**Russell, Sybil**
  Janet Gray
*Rutherford, Pat*
  Taria Hayford
**Rutland, Eva**
**Ryan, Allyson**
  *Linda Kichline*, Carin Rafferty
**Ryan, Courtney**
  *Tonya Wood*
**Ryan, Jenna**
  *Jacqueline Goff*
**Ryan, Nan**
  Nancy Henderson Ryan
**Ryan, Nancy Henderson**
  Nan Ryan
**Ryan, Rachel**
  Sandra Brown, Laura Jordan,
  Erin St. Claire
**Ryan, Sabrina**
  Elisabeth MacDonald
**Rydzynski, Marie**
  Marie Charles, Marie Michael,

---

*Notes*

126

Names in *italics* indicate an author's legal name which does not appear on books. She or he uses pseudonym (s) only.

Names <u>underlined</u> indicate that the author uses legal name for works and may or may not use pseudonym (s).

*Sachs, Judith*
　　Petra Diamond
**Sackett, Susan**
　　Suzanne Savoy, *Susan Stern*
*Safford, Leslie A.*
　　Caroline Campbell
**Sage, Jessie Belle**
　　F. Rosanne Bittner
**Sager, Esther**
**St. Clair, Elizabeth**
　　*Susan Cohen*
**St. Clair, Joy**
**St. Clair, Katherine**
　　<u>Tom E. Huff,</u> Beatrice Parker,
　　Jennifer Wilde, Edwina Marlow
**St. Clair, Stephanie**
　　*Donald Maas*
**St. Claire, Erin**
　　<u>Sandra Brown,</u> Laura Jordan,
　　Rachel Ryan
**St. Claire, Jessica**
**St. David, Joy**
　　Ellen Dupont
**St. George, Edith**
　　<u>Edith Delatush,</u> Alyssa Morgan,
　　Edith De Paul
**St. George, Margaret**
　　<u>Maggie Osborne</u>
**St. James, Emma**
**St. James, Jessica**
**St. James, Scotney**
　　*Linda Varner Palmer & Charlotte Hoy,*
　　Linda Varner
**St. John, Andrea**
　　Don M. Howard

**St. John, Gail**
　　Alicia Grace, Anita Grace,
　　Riva Carles, <u>Irving Greenfield</u>
**St. John, Lisa**
　　Anne Shore, Meg Dominique,
　　Anne Starr, Mary Carroll,
　　<u>Annette Sanford</u>
**St. John, Nicole**
　　Elizabeth Bolton, Kate Chambers,
　　Catherine Chambers, Pamela Dryden,
　　Lavinia Harris, Norma Johnston,
　　Adrian Robert
**St. Pierre, Lisann**
　　*Lisa Ann Verge*
**St. Thomas, Robin**
　　*Tom Bade & Robin Stevenson*
*Salerno, Ann*
　　Ann Hurley
**Salisbury, Carola**
　　*Isobel Julien*
**Sallis, Susan**
**Salvato, Sharon Anne**
　　Day Taylor
**Sanders, Dorothy**
　　Lucy Walker
**Sanders, Glenda**
　　Genda Sands,
　　*Glenda S. Kachelmeier*
**Sanders, Jean**
　　Joanne Marshall, Alexandra
　　Manners, <u>Marianne Lamont,</u>
　　Anne Rundle
**Sanders, Lia**
　　*Angela & Sandra Jackson*

# S

**Sanderson, Jill**
  Helen Beaumont, Anna Stanton,
  Jill Eckersley, Denise Emery
**Sanderson, Nora**
**Sandifer, Linda P.**
**Sands, Glenda**
  *Glenda S. Kachelmeier,* Glenda Sanders
**Sands, Leslie**
*Sandstrom, Eve K.*
  Elizabeth Storm
**Sandys, Elspeth**
**Sanford, Annette**
  Anne Starr, Lisa St. John,
  Mary Carroll, Anne Shore
**Sans, Martha**
  Jenny Loring, Lee Sawyer
**Santore, Sue**
**Santori, Helen**
  Helen Erskine
**Sargent, Joan**
  Sara L. Jenkins
**Sargent, Katherine**
**Sargent, Nancy**
**Satran, Pamela Redmond**
**Sattler, Veronica**
**Saucier, Donna**
  *Donna Schomberg*
**Saunders, Anne**
  *Margaret Alred*
**Saunders, Diana**
  Virginia Coffman, Kay Cameron
  Jeanne Duval, Victor Cross,
  Ann Stanfield
**Saunders, Irene**
**Saunders, Jean**
  Jean Innes, Rowena Summers,
  Sally Blake
**Saunders, Jaroldine**
**Savage, Christina**
  Shana Carrol, Peter Gentry,
  *Frank Schaefer & Kerry Newcomb*
**Savoy, Suzanne**
  Susan Sackett, *Susan Stern*
**Saxon, Antonia**
**Sawyer, Lee**
  Jane Loring, Martha Sans
**Sawyer, Meryl**
  *Martha Unickel*

*Sawyer, Nancy & John*
  Nancy John, Nancy Buckingham,
  Erica Quest, Hilary London,
  Christina Abbey
**Sayers, Jessica**
**Saxe, Coral Smith**
*Scales, Lisa*
  Jane Nichols
*Scamehorn, Mary Kathryn*
  Blair Cameron, Kathryn Blair
*Scantlin, Bea*
  Ruth Stewart
**Scariano, Margaret M.**
*Schaal, Elizabeth*
  Elizabeth Shelley
*Schaefer, Frank*
  Shana Carrol, Peter Gentry,
  Christina Savage
*Scharf, Marian*
  Malissa Carroll, Marissa Carroll
*Schattner, E.*
  Emma Church, Elizabeth Graham
*Scheirman, Marian*
  Lucinda Day
*Schenck, Barbara*
  Anne McAllister
**Schere, Jean K.**
  Jessica Howard, Abigail Winter,
  *Schere Monroe*
*Schimek, Gayle Malon*
  Joleen Daniels
*Schmidt, Anna*
  Anne Shorr
**Schneider, Rosemary**
*Schoder, Judith*
  Lacey Shay
*Schomberg, Donna*
  Donna Saucier
*Schrempp, Elizabeth K.*
  Katherine Court
**Schuler, Candace**
  Jeanette Darwin
*Schultz, Janet*
  Jan Stuart, Tracy Sinclair
**Schultz, Marion**
  Marion Clarke
*Schultze, Pearle Henriksen*
  Marie Pershing

**Schulze, Dallas**
  Dallas Hamlin
**Schulze, Hertha**
  Kate Wellington
**Schwartz, Anne**
  Anne Powers
**Schwartz, Paula**
  Elizabeth Mansfield, *Paula Reibel*
**Scofield, Carin**
**Scott, Adrienne**
  Laurie Williams
**Scott, Alexandra**
**Scott, Amanda**
  Lynne Scott-Drennan
**Scott, Araby**
  Abra Taylor, *Barbara Brouse*
**Scott, Celia**
**Scott, DeLoras**
**Scott, Fela Dawson**
**Scott, Genevieve**
  Jennifer Rigg
**Scott, Grace**
  Gail Clark, Grace South,
  Maggie MacKeever
**Scott, Isobel**
**Scott, Jane**
  Adeline McElfresh, Jennifer Blair,
  Elizabeth Wesley
**Scott, Janey**
  Roberta Leigh, Rachel Lindsay,
  Rozella Lake, Roumelia Lane
**Scott, Joanna**
**Scott, Melissa**
  Janet Joyce, Jenna Lee Joyce,
  Joyce Thies
**Scott, Rachel**
  Celina Mullan, Marisa de Zavala,
  *Ana Lisa de Leon*
**Scott, Samantha**
  Jessie Jeffries, Renee Russell,
  Nancy Hermann
**Scott, Therese**
**Scott-Drennan, Lynne**
  Amanda Scott
**Scott-Gibbons, Marion**
  Marion Chesney, Helen Crampton,
  Ann Fairfax, Jennie Tremain,
  Charlotte Ward, Sarah Chester

**Scotti, Lita**
  Angelica Aimes
**Seabaugh, Carolyn**
  Carolyn Matthews
**Seale, Sara**
  A. D. L. MacPherson
**Seaman, Lucy**
  Michele Robbe
**Searight, Ellen**
  Dee Stuart, Doris Stuart,
  Joan Darling
**Searle, Julia**
**SeBastian, Margaret**
  Maggie Gladstone, Cilla Whitmore,
  Lisabet Norcross, *Arthur Gladstone*
**Sederquest, Mary**
  Katherine Granger, Katherine Ransom
**Seely, Norma Yvonne**
  Yvonne Norman
**Sefton, Juliet**
**Seger, Maura**
  Jenny Bates, Laurel Winslow,
  Sara Jennings, Anne MacNeill,
  Maeve Fitzgerald
**Seibert, Catherine**
  Alexandra Lord
**Seidel, Kathleen Gilles**
**Seidick, Kathie**
  Kasey Michaels, Michelle Kasey
**Seifert, Elizabeth**
  *Elizabeth Gasparotti*
**Selby, Robin Anne**
**Sellers, Alexandra**
**Sellers, Con**
  Lee Raintree
**Sellers, Lorraine**
**Service, Pamela E.**
**Severson, K. D.**
  Robin Gideon
**Seymour, Arabella**
**Seymour, Janette**
**Seymour, Samantha**
  Barbara South, Barbara Stephens
**Shah, Diane K,**
*Shaheen, Leigh*
  Valerie Zayne, Harriet L. Hudson
*Shakarjian, Victoria*
  Veronica Gregory

**Shallenberger, Sharon**
Sharon McCaffree
**Shambrook, Rona**
Rona Randall, Virginia Standage
**Shane, Sandi**
Sandra Canfield & Penny Richards,
Karen Keast, Christy Charles,
Bay Matthews
**Shann, Renee**
Carol Gage
**Shannon, Colleen**
*Colleen Jeske*
**Shannon, Dell**
Elizabeth Linington, Lesley Egan,
Egan O'Neill, Anne Blaisdell
**Shannon, Doris**
**Shannon, Evelyn**
Francine Shore, Cynthia Sinclair,
Sharon Francis, Maureen Wartski
**Shapiro, Teri**
Tess Oliver, Tess Holloway,
*Teri Kovack*
*Shaver, Pat*
Pepper Adams, JoAnn Stacey,
Dianne Thomas, Joanna Jordan
**Shaw, Gabrielle**
**Shaw, Heather**
**Shaw, Irene**
Irene Roberts, Roberta Carr,
Iris Rowland, Ivor Roberts,
Elizabeth Harle
**Shaw, Laura**
*Nancy Motheral*
**Shaw, Linda**
**Shay, Lacey**
Sharon S. Shebar & Judith Schoder
**Shayne, Nina**
Claire Ritchie, Prudence Boyd,
Nora Gibbs, Sara Whittingham,
Lisette Garland, Noelle Ireland,
Lynne Merrill, Heather Wayne,
Dallas Romaine

*Shebar, Sharon Sigmond*
Lacey Shay
**Shelbourne, Cecily**
**Shelley, Elizabeth**
Elizabeth Schaal & Elaine Cichanth

**Shelley, Lillian**
*Lillian & Shelley Koppel*
**Shelley, Susan**
Mary Pershall
**Shepherd, Perdita**
*Mary Lee Grisanti*
**Sheridan, Adora**
*E. M. Pavlik & J. F. Hong*
**Sheridan, Anne-Marie**
**Sheridan, Elsie**
Elsie Lee, Elsie Cromwell,
Lee Sheridan, Jane Gordon
**Sheridan, Jane**
**Sheridan, Lee**
Elsie Cromwell, Elsie Lee,
Jane Gordon, Elsie Sheridan
**Sheridan, Theresa**
**Sherman, Joan**
Peggy Gaddis, Peggy Dern,
*Erolie P. Dern*, Perry Lindsay,
Roberta Courtland, Gail Jordan,
James Clayford, Georgia Craig
**Sherrell, Carl**
**Sherrill, Suzanne**
Alexandra Kirk, Sherry Woods,
Sherryl Ann Woods
**Sherrod, Barbara**
**Sherwood, Deborah**
**Sherwood, Valerie**
Jeanne Hines, Rosamond Royal
**Shields, Dinah**
Jane Clare
*Shiffman, Janis Laden*
Janis Laden
**Shimer, Ruth H.**
**Shiplett, June Lund**
**Shock, Marianne**
**Shoebridge, Marjorie**
**Shore, Anne**
Mary Carroll, Lisa St. John,
Anne Starr, Meg Dominique,
Annette Sanford
**Shore, Edwina**
**Shore, Francine**
Sharon Francis, Cynthia Sinclair,
Evelyn Shannon, *Maureen Wartski*
**Shore, Juliet**
Jan Haye, Anne Vinton

Shorr, Anne
  *Anna Schmidt*
**Shulman, Sandra Dawn**
  Lisa Montague
Siddon, Barbara
  *Barbara Bradford & Sally Siddon,*
  Sally Bradford
*Siddon, Sally*
  Sally Bradford, Barbara Siddon
Siebond, Valerie
  Valerie Greyland
Silverlock, Anne
  Alyssa Howard, Alexis Hill,
  Clare Richards, Jane Silverwood,
  Alexis Hill Jordan, Tess Marlowe,
  Clare Richmond, Louise Titchener
Silverwood, Jane
  Louise Titchener, Alexis Hill,
  Anne Silverlock, Clare Richards,
  Alyssa Howard, Clare Richmond,
  Tess Marlowe, Alexis Hill Jordan,
  Samantha Chase
*Sima, Elaine*
  Leslie Lynn, Lynn Leslie
Simak, Clifford
Simmons, Deborah
Simmons, Mary Kay
  *Mary Kay Freed*
Simmons, Suzanne
  Suzanne Simms, Suzanne Guntrum
Simms, Suzanne
  Suzanne Simmons, Suzanne Guntrum
Simon, Angela
  Irene Mahoney
Simon, Jo Ann
  Joanna Campbell
Simon, Laura
Simons, Renee
Simonson, Sheila
Simpson, Carla
*Simpson, Judith*
  Judy Baxter, Rosalind Foxx,
  Sara Logan
Simpson, Rosemary
Sims, Lavonne
Sinclair, Alberta
  Theresa Grazia, Theresa Alderton

Sinclair, Cynthia
  Sharon Francis, Francine Shore,
  Evelyn Shannon, *Maureen Wartski*
Sinclair, Heather
Sinclair, Helene
  Helene Lehr
Sinclair, Joanne
Sinclair, Katherine
  Katherine Kent, Joan Dial,
  Alexandra Devon, Amanda York
Sinclair, Olga
  Olga Daniels, Ellen Clare
Sinclair, Olivia
  Sandra Langford
Sinclair, Tracy
  *Janet Schultz*, Jan Stuart
Sinclaire, Francesca
*Singer, Ron*
  Margaret Hunter, Delphine Marlowe
Singer, Sally M.
  Amelia Jamison
*Sizer, Mona*
  Deana James
Skillern, Christine
Skinner, June
  Rohan O'Grady
Sky, Kathleen
Slack, Claudia
*Slattery, Sheila*
  Roseanne Williams
Slide, Dorothy
*Slojkowski, Mary Ann*
  DeAnn Patrick, Mary Ann Hammond
**Small, Bertrice**
**Small, Lass**
  Cally Hughes
Smiley, Virginia K.
  *Tess Ewing*
Smith, Alana
  Eileen Bryan, Ruth Alana Smith
*Smith, Barbara Cameron*
  Barbara Cameron
Smith, Barbara Dawson
Smith, Bobbi
  *Bobbi Smith Walton*
Smith, Carol Sturm
Smith, Christine

Smith, Dana Warren
**Smith, Deborah**
Jackie Leigh, Jacqueline Lennox
Smith, Elaine C.
Kami Lane
*Smith, Genell Dellin*
Gena Dalton
*Smith, George*
Diana Summers
Smith, Hazel
**Smith, Joan**
Jennie Gallant
*Smith, Lois*
Cleo Chadwick
*Smith, Lora*
Leigh Roberts
*Smith, Lynne*
Lynn Michaels, Paula Christopher
Smith, Marcine
Smith, Marion
Marion Collin
*Smith, Nancy*
Amber Fitzgerald
**Smith, Ruth Alana**
Alana Smith, Eileen Bryan
Smith, Sandra Lee
Sandra Lee
Smith, Veronica
*Smith-Ware, Sandra*
Gabrielle DuPre
Smith, Wynne
**Snodgrass, Melinda**
Melinda Harris, Melinda McKenzie
Snow, Ashley
Maryhelen Clague
Snow, Lucy
*Rosemary Aubert*
Snow, Lyndon
Hebe Elsna, Vicky Lancaster,
Laura Conway, Dorothy P. Ansle,
Margaret Campbell Barnes
**Sohl, Jerry**
Roberta Mountjoy
*Somerlott, Robert*
Jessica North
Somers, Suzanne
Dorothy Daniels, Angela Gray,
Cynthia Kavanaugh, Danielle Dorsett,

Geraldine Thayer, Helen Gray Weston,
Helaine Ross
Somerset, Rose
Sommars, Colette
Sommerfield, Sylvie F.
Sommers, Beverly
Sommers, Jeanne
Barrie Meyers
Sommers, Justine
Sommers, Lilah
Sommerset, Judith
*Sorel, Marilyn Meeske*
Nina Lansdale
*Sorrels, Roy*
Anna McClure
Soule, Maris
**South, Barbara**
Barbara Stephens, Samantha Seymour
South, Grace
Gail Clark, Grace Scott,
Maggie MacKeever
Spark, Natalie
Sparks, Christine
Lucy Gordon
Sparrow, Laura
Jocelyn Griffin, *Laura Halford*
Spearman, Stephanie L.
Speas, Jan Cox
Speer, Flora
*Speicher, Helen Ross*
Alice Abbott
Spencer, Anne
Spencer, Catherine
*Kathleen Orr,* Kathy Orr,
Kathleen Garner
Spencer, Cheryl
Lynn Price, *Cheryl Purviance*
Spencer, Emma Jane
Spencer, LaVyrle
Spenser, Emily
*Charlotte Elkins*
Spindler, Erica
Spring, Marianne
Springer, Lacey
Stables, Mira
Stacey, JoAnn
*Debrah Morris & Pat Shaver,*
Pepper Adams, Dianne Thomas,

Joanna Jordan
**Stadler, Jillian**
**Staff, Adrienne**
Natalie Stone
**Stafford, Caroline**
**Stafford, Jayne**
**Stafford, Lee**
**Stamford, Sarah**
**Stancliffe, Elaine**
Elisa Stone
**Standage, Virginia**
Rona Randall, *Rona Shambrook*
**Standard, Patti**
**Standish, Carole**
Maggi Charles, Meg Hudson,
Russell Mead, Margaret Koehler
**Standish, Caroline**
Lorna Read
**Stanfield, Ann**
Virginia Coffman, Kay Cameron,
Jeanne Duval, Victor Cross
**Stanford, Sondra**
**Stanley, Beth**
Elizabeth Anderson, *Beth Amerski*
**Stanley, Mary Lee**
**Stanton, Anna**
Helen Beaumont, Jill Eckersley,
Jill Sanderson, Denise Emery
**Stanton, Cathy**
Cathryn Clare
**Stanton, Elinor**
**Stanton, Vance**
Michael Avellone, Edwina Noone,
Priscilla Dalton, Mark Dane,
Troy Conway, Dorothea Nile,
Sidney Stuart, Steve Michaels,
Jean-Anne DePre
*Staplebrock, Marlys*
Suzanne Nichols
**Starr, Anne**
Anne Shore, Meg Dominique,
Mary Carroll, Lisa St. John,
Annette Sanford
**Starr, Cynthia**
**Starr, Kate**
Joyce Dingwell
**Starr, Leonora**
Dorothy Rivers, *Leonora Mackesy*

**Starr, Martha**
Martha Gordon
**Starr, Morgana**
Alice H. Orr, Elizabeth Allison
**Statham, Frances Patton**
**Staub, Molly**
**Steel, Judith**
**Steele, Jessica**
**Steele, Marianne**
**Steen, Sandy**
**Steiner, Irene Hunter**
**Steiner, Susan**
*Steinke, Ann E.*
Anne Reynolds, Ann Williams,
Elizabeth Reynolds
**Stephens, Barbara**
Barbara South, Samantha Seymour
**Stephens, Casey**
Sharon Wagner
**Stephens, Doreen**
Kay Stephens, Rachel Benedict,
Jane Beverley
**Stephens, Jeanne**
Jean Hager, Leah Crane,
Marlaine Kyle, Sarah North,
Amanda McAllister
**Stephens, Kay**
Rachel Benedict, Jane Beverley,
Doreen Stephens
**Stephens, Sharon**
Lisa Gregory, Kristin James,
Candace Camp
**Sterling, Maria S.**
Lee Floren, Marguerite Nelson,
Grace Lang, Lisa Franchon,
Austin Brett, Claudia Hall,
Matt Harding, Lee Thomas,
Len Turner, Will Watson
*Stern, Susan*
Susan Sackett, Suzanne Savoy
**Stevens, Amanda**
Marilyn Medlock, *Marilyn M. Amman*
**Stevens, Blaine**
Ashley Carter, Suzanne Stephens,
Harry Whittington
**Stevens, Diane**
**Stevens, Janice**
Kay Kirby, Janice Kay Johnson,

Janice Baczewski, *Kay Bartlett*
**Stevens, Kimberly**
**Stevens, Linda**
  *Melinda & Steve Hamilton,* Linda Vail
**Stevens, Lucille**
**Stevens, Lynsey**
  *Lynette Howard,* Lynde Howard
**Stevens, Serita**
  Megan MacDonnell, Shira Stevens
**Stevens, Shira**
  Serita Stevens, Megan MacDonnell
**Stevens, Susan**
  Mary Mackie, Mary Christopher,
  Cathy Christopher, Alex Andrews,
  Caroline Charles
**Stevenson, Anne**
**Stevenson, Florence**
  Lucia Curzon, Zabrina Faire,
  Zandra Colt, Pamela Frazier,
  Ellen Fitzgerald
**Stevenson, Robin**
  Robin St. Thomas
**Steward, Ada**
  *Adah Rhome,* Ada Sumner
**Stewardson, Dawn**
**Stewart, Florence**
  Mary Stewart
**Stewart, Isobel**
**Stewart, Jean**
  Barbara Fitzgerald, Mona Newman
**Stewart, Judith**
  Judith Hagar, Judith Anne Polley,
  Valentina Luellan, Helen Kent
**Stewart, Leigh**
**Stewart, Lucy Phillips**
**Stewart, Mary**
  Florence Stewart
**Stewart, Rosalind**
**Stewart, Ruth**
  *Bea Scantlin*
**Stewart, Sally**
**Stine, Whitney**
  Constance F. Peale
**Stirling, Elaine K.**
**Stirling, Jessica**
  Pat Coghlan & Hugh C. Rae
**Stirling, Jocelyn**

**Stockenberg, Antoinette**
  Antoinette Hale, Antoinette Hardy
**Stone, Charlotte**
**Stone, Elisa**
  Elaine Stancliffe
**Stone, Gillian**
**Stone, Karen**
  Karen Young
**Stone, Katherine**
**Stone, Natalie**
  Adrienne Staff & Sally Goldenbaum
**Stone, Sharon**
**Storm, Elizabeth**
  *Eva K. Sandstrom*
**Storm, Virginia**
  Fay Chandos, Theresa Charles,
  Leslie Lance, Jan Tempest,
  *Irene Mossop, Charles &*
  *Irene Swatridge*
**Stowe, Rosetta**
  *George & Margaret Ogan*
**Strasser, Heidi**
  *Ilse Dallmayr*
**Stratton, Rebecca**
  Lucy Gillen
**Street, Octavia**
  *Kaa Byington,* Sybil LeGrand
**Streib, Daniel**
  Louise Grandville
**Stribling, Jean**
  Ruth Jean Dale
**Strickland, Laura**
**Stromeyer, Carolyn**
  Carolyn Thornton
**Strother, Pat Wallace**
  Pat Wallace, Pat West,
  Vivian Lord, Patricia Cloud
**Strutt, Sheila**
**Stuart, Alex**
  Vivian Stuart, William Stuart Long,
  Robyn Stuart, Barbara Allen,
  *Violet V. Mann*
**Stuart, Anne**
  Anne Kristine Stuart Ohlrogge
**Stuart, Becky**
  *Stuart Buchan,* Pamela Foxe
**Stuart, Casey**
  *Ann E. Bullard*

S

**Stuart, Charles**
  Vivian Donald, Hilary Rose,
  Iain Torr, Graham Montrose,
  Charles Conte, Rory Macalpin,
  Charles Roy MacKinnon
**Stuart, Dee**
  Ellen Searight, Doris Stuart,
  Joan Darling
**Stuart, Diana**
  Jane Toombs
**Stuart, Doris**
  Dee Stuart, Ellen Searight,
  Joan Darling
**Stuart, Elizabeth**
  Elizabeth Awbrey, *Elizabeth Beach*
**Stuart, Jan**
  Janet Schultz, Tracy Sinclair
**Stuart, Megan**
  Deirdre Rowan, Megan Castell,
  Kristin Michaels, Jeanne Crecy,
  Jeanne Foster, Jeanne Williams
**Stuart, Penelope**
  Penelope Wisdom
**Stuart, Robyn**
  Barbara Allen, Vivian Stuart,
  Alex Stuart, *Violet V. Mann,*
  William Stuart Long
**Stuart, Sheila**
  *Mary Gladys Baker*
**Stuart, Sherry**
**Stuart, Sidney**
  Michael Avellone,
  Edwina Noone, Priscilla Dalton,
  Mark Dane, Nick Carton,
  Troy Conway, Vance Stanton,
  Steve Michaels, Jean-Anne DePre
**Stuart, Vivian**
  Alex Stuart, Robyn Stuart,
  *Violet V. Mann*, Barbara Allen,
  William Stuart Long
**Sullivan, Jo**
**Sultan, Martina**
  *Rita Picker*
**Summers, Ashley**
  Faye Ashley
**Summers, Diana**
  George Smith
**Summer, Essie**

**Summers, Iris**
  *Mary Kuczir & Joan Giezey Knight*,
  Fern Michaels
**Summers, Jessica**
**Summers, Rowena**
  Jean Innes, Sally Blake, Jean Saunders
**Summers, True**
  *Hope Campbell*
**Summerskill, Shirley**
**Summerton, Margaret**
  Jan Roffman
**Summerville, Margaret**
  Barbara & Pamela Wilson
**Sumner, Ada**
  *Adah Rhome,* Ada Steward
**Sunshine, Linda**
**Surrey, Kathryn**
  Phyllis Matthewman
**Suson, Marlene**
**Sutcliffe, Katherine**
**Sutherland, Jean**
  Jean Nash
***Svee, Sally***
  Irene LeRoy
**Swan, Rebecca**
  Betsy Rogers
**Swan, Rose**
**Swann, Lois**
***Swanton, Molly***
  Lynn Erickson
***Swatridge, Charles & Irene***
  Fay Chandos, Theresa Charles,
  Leslie Lance, Jan Tempest,
  *Irene Mossop,* Virginia Storm
**Sweeney, Linda**
  Lynn Patrick
**Swinford, Katherine**
**Synge, Ursula**
**Syril, Binnie**
  *Binnie Syril Braunstein*

135

*Notes*

Names in *italics* indicate an author's legal name which does not appear on books. She or he uses pseudonym (s) only.

Names <u>underlined</u> indicate that the author uses legal name for works and may or may not use pseudonym (s).

Tahourdin, Jill
Talbot, Charlene
   Elizabeth Alden, Lucy Lee
*Talbot, Katherine*
   Katherine Ashton
*Talias, Angela*
   Angela Alexie
*Tallman, Shirley*
   Erin Ross
Tarling, Moyra
*Tatara, Ellen M.*
   Lee Magner
Tate, Ellalice
   Victoria Holt, Jean Plaidy,
   Philippa Carr, Elbur Ford,
   Eleanor Hibbert, Eleanor Burford,
   Kathleen Kellow
Tate, Mary
   Arlene Hale, Mary Hale,
   Gail Everett, Tracy Adams,
   Lynn Williams
Tattersall, Jill
Tavare, Gwendoline
Taylor, Abra
   Araby Scott, *Barbara Brouse*
Taylor, Allison
Taylor, Beatrice
Taylor, Day
   Sharon Salvato & Cornelia Parkinson
Taylor, Dorothy E.
Taylor, Edwina
Taylor, Georgia Elizabeth
Taylor, Janelle

Taylor, Jayne
   Jayne Bentley, Jayne Castle,
   Amanda Glass, <u>Jayne Krentz</u>,
   Stephanie James
Taylor, Jennifer
<u>Taylor, Laura</u>
*Taylor, Lois Cole*
   Caroline Arnett, Lynn Avery,
   Nancy Dudley, Allan Dwight,
   Anne Lattin
*Taylor, Lynn*
   Karen Lynn
<u>Taylor, Mary Ann</u>
   Kate Bowe, Cass McAndrew
Taylor, Sally Ann
Taylor, Susan
   Mary Cummins
*Tayntor, Christine*
   Amanda Preble
*Teer, Barbara*
   Barbara Allister
Tegler, Leta
Teller, Lee Stewart
Tempest, Jan
   Theresa Charles, Fay Chandos,
   Leslie Lance, Virginia Storm,
   *Irene Mossop, Charles &*
   *Irene Swatridge*
Templeton, Janet
   Evelyn Bond, <u>Morris Hershman</u>,
   Sara Rothman, Jessica Wilcox,
   Ian Kavanaugh, Sara Roffman,
   Lionel Webb
<u>Temte, Myrna</u>
   Molly Thomas

Tichenor, Vivian H.
  Vivian Harris
*Tidd, Diane*
  Catherine Hart
Tierney, Ariel
Tilbury, Quenna
  Pauline Ash, Kathleen Ash,
  Emily Walker, Eileen Barry,
  Sara Devon, Delia Foster,
  Jane Lester, Christine Lawson,
  Cora Mayne, Kay Winchester,
  Jill Murray, Kathleen Treves,
  Honor Vincent, Heather Vincent
Timson, Keith
  Danielle de Winter
<u>Titchener, Louise</u>
  Alyssa Howard, Alexis Hill,
  Clare Richards, Jane Silverwood,
  Clare Richmond, Anne Silverlock,
  Tess Marlowe, Alexis Hill Jordan
<u>Title, Elise</u>
  Alison Tyler
*Titus, Coral Hoyle*
  Coral Hoyle
Tobias, Katherine
  Kathleen Fuller, Ted Mark,
  Harry Gregory, *Theodore Mark Gottfried*
Todd, Elizabeth
  Michelle Venet, *Alicia Todd Rasley*
Tolivar, Robin
  Pat C. Oakson & Leslie Bishop
Tone, Teona
<u>Toombs, Jane</u>
  Diana Stuart
<u>Toombs, John</u>
  Fortune Kent, Jocelyn Wilde
Topaz, Jacqueline
  Jacqueline Diamond, Jacqueline Jade,
  <u>Jackie Hyman</u>
*Torday, Ursula*
  Charlotte Keppel, Paula Allardyce,
  Charity Blackstock
Torr, Iain
  Vivian Donald, Hilary Rose,
  Graham Montrose, Charles Conte,
  Charles Stuart, Rory Macalpin,
  Charles R. MacKinnon
Toth, Emily Jane

<u>Toth, Pamela</u>
  Pamela Roth
Towers, Regina
  Nina Pykare, Nan Pemberton,
  Nina Coombs, Nora Powers,
  Natalie Pryor, Ann Coombs
Tracey, Ann
  Iris Bromige
*Tracey, Marie*
  Audra Adams
Tracey, Susan
Tracy, Marilyn
Tracy, Pat
*Tracy, Marie*
  Audra Adams
Trainer, Dixie Dean
*Traynor, Pixie & Anthony*
  Page Anthony
Trehearne, Elizabeth
  *Patricia Ponder & Carol Albritton,*
  Maxine Patrick, <u>Patricia Maxwell</u>,
  Jennifer Blake
Tremain, Jennie
  Marion Chesney, Helen Crampton,
  Ann Fairfax, *Marion Scott-Gibbons,*
  Sarah Chester
Trench, Caroline
Trent, Brenda
  Megan Lane, *Brenda Himrod*
Trent, Dan & Lynda
  <u>Lynda Trent</u>, Danielle Trent
Trent, Danielle
  Lynda Trent, *Dan & Lynda Trent*
Trent, Jessica
<u>Trent, Lynda</u>
  Danielle Trent, Dan & Lynda Trent
Treves, Kathleen
  Kathleen Ash, Pauline Ash,
  Emily Walker, Eileen Barry,
  Sara Devon, Delia Foster,
  Cora Mayne, Kay Winchester,
  Jill Murray, Christine Lawson,
  Jane Lester, Quenna Tilbury,
  Honor Vincent, Heather Vincent
Trevor, June
  Casey Douglas, *June E. Casey,*
  Constance Ravenlock, Melissa Ash
Trevor, Meriol

**T**

**Triegel, Linda**
   Elisabeth Kidd
**Triner, Jeanne**
   Jeanne Kaye Triner, Caylin Jennings
**Triner, Jeanne Kaye**
   Jeanne Triner & *Kaye L. Clements*,
   Caylin Jennings
**Troke, Molly**
   Hester Bourne
**Troy, Amanda**
   Miranda Cameron, *Mary Kahn*
**Troy, Katherine**
   Anne Maybury, *Anne Buxton*
**Tucker, Delaine**
   Elaine Camp, Deborah Benet,
   Deborah Camp, Elaine Tucker,
   Delayne Camp
**Tucker, Elaine**
   Elaine Camp, Deborah Benet,
   Deborah Camp, Delaine Tucker,
   Delayne Camp
**Tucker, Helen**
**Tucker, Ruth B.**
   Hope McIntyre
**Turner, Barbara**
**Turner, Elizabeth**
   *Gail Oust*
**Turner, Judy**
**Turner, Len**
   Lee Floren, Austin Brett,
   Grace Lang, Marguerite Nelson,
   Lisa Franchon, Maria S. Sterling,
   Claudia Hall, Matt Harding,
   Lee Thomas, Will Watson
**Turner, Linda Ray**
   Linda Raye
**Turner, Lynn**
   *Mary Watson*
**Turner, Mary**
*Turner, Sue Long*
   Kristin Michaels
**Turney, Catherine**
*Twaddle, Susan B.*
   Elizabeth Barron, Susan Bowden
**Tyler, Alison**
   Elise Title
**Tyler, Antonia**
   *Susan Whittlesey Wolf*

Names in *italics* indicate an author's legal name which does not appear on books. She or he uses pseudonym (s) only.

Names <u>underlined</u> indicate that the author uses legal name for works and may or may not use pseudonym (s).

*Unickel, Martha*
 Meryl Sawyer
**Upper, Gloria**
 Gloria Douglas
**Upshall, Helen**
 Susannah Curtis
**Ure, Jean**
 Sara McCulloch
**Uzquiano, Linda Steele**
 Linda Steele

*Notes*

141

*Notes*

Names in *italics* indicate an author's legal name which does not appear on books. She or he uses pseudonym (s) only.

Names <u>underlined</u> indicate that the author uses legal name for works and may or may not use pseudonym (s).

**Vail, Linda**
  *Melinda & Steve Hamilton,*
  Linda Stevens
**Vail, Phillip**
  <u>Noel Gerson</u>, Dana Fuller Ross,
  Samuel Edwards, Carter Vaughan,
  Paul Lewis
**Valcour, Vanessa**
  Leila Lyons, *James Conaway*
**Valenti, Justine**
  Barbara Max, Vanessa Victor
**Valentine, Jo**
  Charlotte Armstrong
**Valentine, Terri**
**Valley, Lorraine**
<u>**Vandergriff, Aola**</u>
  Kitt Brown
**Van Der Zee, Karen**
  *Wendela Kilmer,* Mona Van Wieren
**Vandervelde, Isabel**
**Vandresha, Vita**
**Van Kirk, Elleen**
**Van-Loon, Antonia**
  Janine French
**Vanner, Lynn**
*Van Nuys, Joan*
  Marianna Essex
**Van Slyke, Helen**
  Sharon Ashton
**Van Wieren, Mona**
  *Wandela Kilmer,* Karen Van der Zee
**Varley, John**
**Varlinsky, Deborah**
  Deborah Le Varre

<u>**Varner, Linda**</u>
  Scotney St. James, *Linda Varner Palmer*
*Vasilopoulos, Freda*
  Tina Vasilos, Freda Vasilos
**Vasilos, Freda**
  Tina Vasilos, *Freda Vasilopoulos*
**Vasilos, Tina**
  Freda Vasilos, *Freda Vasilopoulos*
**Vaughan, Carter**
  <u>Noel Gerson</u>, Samuel Edwards,
  Phillip Vail, Dana Fuller Ross,
  Paul Lewis
**Vaughan, Louise**
**Vaughan, Robert**
  Paula Moore, Paula Fairman
**Vaughan, Vivian**
  *Jane Vaughn*
**Vaughn, Jane**
  Vivian Vaughn
**Vaughter, Carolyn**
**Vayle, Valerie**
  Anne Merton Abbey,
  *Jean Brooks-Janowiak,*
  <u>Janet Brooks</u>, Jill Churchill
**Vendresha, Vita**
**Venet, Michelle**
  Elizabeth Todd, *Alicia Todd Rasley*
*Verge, Lisa Ann*
  Lisann St. Pierre
**Vermandel, Janet Gregory**
**Vernon, Claire**
  August Boon, *Clare Breton-Smith,*
  Elinor Caldwell, Hilary Wilde
**Vernon, Dorothy**

**143**

## V

**Vernon, Kathleen**
  Kay Vernon, Lesley Dixon
**Vernon, Kay R.**
  Kathleen Vernon, Lesley Dixon
**Verrette, Joyce**
  *Joyce Petratur*
**Veryan, Patricia**
  *Patricia Bannister*, Gwyneth Moore
**Vickery, Katherine**
  Katherine Kramer
**Victor, Cindy**
**Victor, Kathleen**
**Victor, Vanessa**
  Barbara Max, Justin Valenti
*Viens, Carol*
  Carol Daniels
**Vincent, Claire**
  Moira Lord, Miriam Lynch,
  Dolores Craig
**Vincent, Heather**
  Pauline Ash, Kathleen Ash,
  Emily Walker, Eileen Barry,
  Kathleen Treves, Jill Murray,
  Cora Mayne, Kay Winchester,
  Sara Devon, Christine Lawson,
  Jane Lester, Quenna Tilbury,
  Delia Foster, Honor Vincent
**Vincent, Honor**
  Kathleen Ash, Pauline Ash,
  Emily Walker, Eileen Barry,
  Kathleen Treves, Cora Mayne,
  Kay Winchester, Sara Devon,
  Christine Lawson, Jill Murray,
  Quenna Tilbury, Jane Lester,
  Heather Vincent, Delia Foster
**Vincent, Joan**
  *Joan Wesolowsky*
*Vincentnathan, Lyn*
  Sally DuBois
**Vine, Kerry**
  Gillian Oxley
*Vines-Haines, Beverly*
  Becca Cassidy, Jamie West
**Vinet, Lynette**
**Viney, Jane**
  Anne Neville
**Vinton, Anne**
  Juliet Shore, Jan Haye

**Vitek, Donna Kimel**
  Donna Alexander
**Vivian, Angela**
**Vivian, Daisy**
  Meredith Leigh, Bruce Kenyon
**Vosbein, Barbara**
  Nikki Benjamin

---

*Notes*

Names in *italics* indicate an author's legal name which does not appear on books. She or he uses pseudonym (s) only.

Names <u>underlined</u> indicate that the author uses legal name for works and may or may not use pseudonym (s).

**Wade, Elizabeth Evelyn**
**Wade, Jennifer**
**Wadsworth, Mary Rebecca**
    Rebecca Brandewyne
**Wagner, Carol**
    Joellyn Carroll, Marissa Carroll,
    Malissa Carroll
**Wagner, Kimberli**
**Wagner, Sharon**
    Casey Stephens
**Wake, Vivien Fiske**
**Wakefield, Maureen**
**Wakeley, Dorothy**
**Walden, Luanne**
**Walford, Christian**
    Jill Christian, Norrey Ford,
    *Noreen Dilcock*
***Walker, Barbara***
    Barbara Kaye
**Walker, Dorothy**
<u>**Walker, Elizabeth Neff**</u>
    Laura Matthews,
    Elizabeth Rotter
**Walker, Emily**
    Pauline Ash, Kathleen Ash,
    Kay Winchester, Cora Mayne,
    Jill Murray, Quenna Tilbury,
    Kathleen Treves, Sara Devon,
    Christine Lawson, Eileen Barry,
    Heather Vincent, Honor Vincent,
    Jane Lester, Delia Foster
<u>**Walker, Irma**</u>
    Andrea Harris, Ruth Walker
**Walker, Joan**
**Walker, Kate**

<u>**Walker, Lois A.**</u>
    Rebecca Ashley, Candice Adams,
    Sabrina Myles
**Walker, Lucy**
    Dorothy Sanders
**Walker, Margaret**
    Margaret Alexander
**Walker, Ruth**
    <u>Irma Walker</u>, Andrea Harris
***Wall, Judith***
    Anne Henry
**Wallace, Claire**
<u>**Wallace, Pamela**</u>
    Dianne King
**Wallace, Pat**
    Patricia Cloud, Vivian Lord,
    Pat West, <u>Pat Wallace Strother</u>
***Wallerich, Linda H.***
    Linda Benjamin, Jessica Douglass
***Walls, Patricia***
    Patricia Rae, Gina Delaney
**Walsh, Alida**
**Walsh, Kelly**
    V. P. Walsh
**Walsh, Sheila**
    *Sophie Leyton*
**Walsh, V. P.**
    Kelly Walsh
**Walters, Jade**
**Walters, Linda**
    *Linda & Walter Rice*
**Walters, Shelly**
***Walton, Bobbi S.***
    Bobbi Smith

**Ward, Kate**
Barbara Cust, Caroline Fanshawe
**Ward, Lynda**
Julia Jeffries
**Ward, Rebecca**
**Ware, Ciji**
*Warre, Mary D.*
Jennifer Ames, Maysie Greig,
Ann Barclay
**Warren, Betsy**
**Warren, Beverly C.**
*Warren, Linda*
Frances West
**Warren, Norma**
**Warren, Pat**
Patricia Cox
**Warren, Paulette**
*Paul Fairman*, Paula Fairman,
Janet Lovesmith
*Wartski, Maureen*
Sharon Francis, Cynthia Sinclair,
Evelyn Shannon, Francine Shore
*Washington, Elsie*
Rosalind Welles
**Watson, Julia**
Jane De Vere, Julia Hamilton,
Julia Fitzgerald
*Watson, Mary*
Lynn Turner
**Watson, Will**
Austin Brett, Matt Harding,
Lee Floren, Marguerite Nelson,
Maria S. Sterling, Grace Lang,
Lee Thomas, Len Turner,
Claudia Hall, Lisa Franchon
**Waugh, Hillary**
Elissa Grandower
**Way, Margaret**
**Wayne, Heather**
Nora Gibbs, Sara Whittingham,
Prudence Boyd, Noelle Ireland,
Lisette Garland, Claire Ritchie,
Lynne Merrill, Nina Shayne,
Dallas Romaine
**Wayne, Marcia**
Susan Ashe, Carol Ann Best,
Con Darlington, Ann Martin
**Wayne, Rachel**

**Wayne, Rochelle**
*Rochelle A. Mulvihill*
**Weale, Anne**
Andrea Blake, Anne Wilson
**Weaver, Judith**
Ashley Chapel, Harper McBride
**Webb, Jean Francis**
Roberta Morrison
**Webb, Lionel**
Evelyn Bond, Ian Kavanaugh,
Janet Templeton, Sara Rothman,
Sara Roffman, Lionel Webb,
Jessica Wilcox, Morris Hershman
**Webb, Peggy**
**Webber, Nancy**
Jennifer Rose
**Webster, Elizabeth**
**Weger, Jackie**
**Weir, Theresa**
*Weller, Dorothy*
Dorothy Bernard, Dorothea Hale
**Welles, Alyssa**
Nomi Berger
**Welles, Caron**
Jan Jones
**Welles, Elisabeth**
Pamela D'Arcy, Georgina Grey,
Mary Wilson, Valerie Bradstreet,
Pauline Pryor, Mary Linn Roby
**Welles, Patricia**
Rachel Welles, Patricia Rogers
**Welles, Rachel**
Patricia Rogers
**Welles, Rosalind**
Elsie Washington
**Wellington, Kate**
Hertha Schulze
**Wells, Angela**
*Angela Bostwick*
**Wells, Angela**
**Welsh, Jeanette**
**Wendt, Jo Ann**
**Wentworth, Julia**
**Wentworth, Sally**
**Werner, Hazeldell**
*Werner, Herma*
Roxanne Jarrett, Eve Gladstone
**Werner, Pat**

**Wert, Lynette**
Lynn LeMon
**Wesley, Elizabeth**
Adeline McElfresh, Jane Scott,
Jennifer Blair
*Wesolowsky, Joan*
Joan Vincent
**West, Anna**
Ann Edward
West, Cara
**West, Christine**
Christine Baker
**West, Eugenia Lovett**
**West, Frances**
*Linda Warren*
**West, Jamie**
Becca Cassidy, *Beverly Vines-Haines*
**West, Jennifer**
Jennifer Justin
**West, Nicola**
**West, Pat**
Pat Wallace, Patricia Cloud,
Vivian Lord, Pat Wallace Strother
**West, Sara Ann**
**Westcott, Jan**
**Westcott, Kathleen**
Cristabel, *Christine Abrahamsen*
**Westhaven, Margaret**
Peggy M. Hansen
**Weston, Helen Gray**
Dorothy Daniels, Angela Gray,
Suzanne Somers, Cynthia Kavanaugh,
Danielle Dorsett, Geraldine Thayer,
Helaine Ross
**Weston, Nigella**
Veronica Mixon
**Weston, Sophie**
**Westwood, Gwen**
**Westwood, Hillary**
**Weyrick, Becky Lee**
**Whaley, Frances**
*Whearley, Bob*
Fran Earley
*Wheat, Carolyn*
Corintha Bennet
**Wherlock, Julia**
**Whindham, Eleanor**

Whisenand, Valerie
Kasey Adams
**Whistler, Mary**
Susan Barrie, Jane Beaufort,
Rose Burghley, Anita Charles,
Pamela Kent, Ida Pollock,
Barbara Rowan
**Whitby, Sharon**
Catherine Darby, Maureen Black,
Veronica Black, Maureen Peters,
Judith Rothman, Elizabeth Law,
Levanah Lloyd
White, Charlotte
Jennifer Dale, Marianne Cole
**White, Frances**
*White, Jude Gilliam*
Jude Deveraux
**White, Linda**
**White, Patricia**
**Whitehead, Barbara**
**Whitmee, Jeanne**
**Whitmore, Cilla**
Margaret SeBastian, Maggie Gladstone,
*Arthur Gladstone,* Lisabet Norcross
**Whitmore, Loretta**
**Whitney, Jamisan**
Noreen Brownlie
**Whitney, Diana**
*Diana Hinz*
**Whitney, Phyllis**
*Phyllis A. Garner*
**Whittaker, Charlotte Amalie**
**Whittal, Yvonne**
**Whittenburg, Karen**
**Whittington, Harry**
Ashley Carter, Blaine Stevens
**Whittingham, Sara**
Nora Gibbs, Prudence Boyd,
Lisette Garland, Noelle Ireland,
Lynne Merrill, Nina Shayne,
Claire Ritchie, Heather Wayne,
Dallas Romaine
**Whitworth, Karen**
*Wiath, Linda C.*
Laurel Collins
**Wibberley, Anna**
**Wibberley, Mary**
**Widmer, Mary Lou**

**Wieselberg, Helen**
**Wiete, Robin LeAnne**
**Wiggs, Susan**
  Susan Childress
**Wilby, Jane**
  Anne Hampson
**Wilcox, Jessica**
  Janet Templeton, Evelyn Bond,
  Sara Rothman, Morris Hershman,
  Ian Kavanaugh, Sara Roffman,
  Lionel Webb
**Wilde, Hilary**
  *August Boon*, Clare Breton-Smith,
  Claire Vernon, Elinor Caldwell
**Wilde, Jennifer**
  Tom E. Huff, Katherine St. Clair,
  Beatrice Parker, Edwina Marlow
**Wilde, Jocelyn**
  Fortune Kent, John Toombs
**Wilde, Lauren**
  Joanne Redd
**Wilde, Leslie**
  Breton Amis, Rayleigh Best,
  Ray Bentinck, Terence Hughes,
  Leigh Haddow, Desmond Roberts
**Wilder, Joan**
  Catherine Lanigan
**Wilder, Quinn**
*Wildman, Corinna*
  Corinna Cunliffe
**Wildman, Faye**
  Jillian Fayre, *Jillian Dagg,*
  Marilyn Brian
**Wiley, Laura**
  Patricia Matthews, Patty Brisco
*Wilhite, Bettie*
  Betsy Page, Elizabeth August,
  Elizabeth Douglas
**Wilkins, Gina**
  Gina Ferris
**Wilkinson, Lee**
**Williams, Ann**
  Peggy Myers
**Williams, Anne**
  Elizabeth Reynolds, Anne
  Reynolds, *Ann E. Steinke*
**Williams, Barbara**
  Charlotte Nichols

**Williams, Bronwyn**
  Dixie Browning & Mary Williams
**Williams, Claudette**
  Melanie Davis
**Williams, Frances**
  *Frances Hardter*
**Williams, Jeanne**
  Megan Castell, Kristin Michaels,
  Jeanne Foster, Jeanne Crecy,
  Deirdre Rowan, Megan Stuart
**Williams, Jennifer**
**Williams, Laurie**
  Adrienne Scott
**Williams, Lee**
  Leigh Anne Williams, William Mernit
**Williams, Leigh Anne**
  Lee Williams, William Mernit
**Williams, Lynn**
  Arlene Hale, Gail Everrett,
  Mary Tate, Tracy Adams,
  Mary Hale
**Williams, Mary**
  Bronwyn Williams
**Williams, Mary**
  Marianne Harvey
**Williams, Norma**
  Dee Norman, Wynn Williams
**Williams, Patricia**
  Alexandra Lord
**Williams, Paula**
  *Paula Darrington*
**Williams, Roseanne**
  *Sheila Slattery*
**Williamson, Penelope**
**Willman, Marianne**
  Sabina Clark, Marianne Clark
**Wills, Ann Meredith**
  *Maralys Wills*
*Wills, Maralys*
  Ann Meredith Wills
**Wilroy, Jan**
**Wilsen, Marolyn**
**Wilson, Abigail**
  Sandra Harris, Brittany Young,
  *Sandra Young*
**Wilson, Alanna**
**Wilson, Anne**
  Anne Weale, Andrea Blake

**Wilson, Barbara & Pamela**
  Margaret Summerville
**Wilson, Christine**
  *Christine Geach*, Anne Lowing
*Wilson, Ellen*
  Laurel Evans
**Wilson, Fran**
**Wilson, Joyce**
  Sally James
**Wilson, Mary**
  Elisabeth Welles, Georgina Grey,
  Pauline Pryor, Valerie Bradstreet,
  Pamela D'Arcy, Mary Linn Roby
**Wilson, Mary Anne**
**Wilson, Patricia**
*Wilson, Renee*
  Renee Roszel
**Wilson, Rowena**
**Wilson, Sandra**
  Sandra Heath
**Winchester, Kay**
  Kathleen Ash, Pauline Ash,
  Emily Walker, Quenna Tilbury,
  Cora Mayne, Kathleen Treves,
  Heather Vincent, Honor Vincent,
  Sara Devon, Delia Foster,
  Christine Lawson, Jill Murray,
  Eileen Barry, Jane Lester
<u>**Wind, David**</u>
  Monica Barrie, Jenifer Dalton,
  Marilyn Davids
**Wind, Ruth**
**Windham, Kit**
  *Joan Wilson Hicks*
**Windham, Susannah**
**Windsor, Pamela**
  Colleen Moore, Claudette Nicole,
  <u>Jon Messman</u>, Claudia Nicole
**Wing, Janet**
  Lenora Barber
**Winslow, Ellie**
  Winslow Eliot
**Winslow, Laurel**
  <u>Maura Seger</u>, Jenny Bates,
  Sara Jennings, Anne MacNeill,
  Maeve Fitzgerald
**Winspear, Violet**
**Winston, Donna**

**Winter, Abigail**
  Jessica Howard, *Schere Monroe,*
  Jean K. Schere
**Winter, Pat**
**Winters, Malori**
  *Lisa M. Renshaw*
**Winters, Rebecca**
  *Rebecca Burton*
**Wisdom, Linda**
**Wisdom, Penelope**
  Penelope Stuart
*Wisely, Charlotte*
  Charlotte Hastings
**Witmer-Gow, Karyn**
  Elizabeth Kary
**Witton, Eileen**
  Janice Bennett
*Wojhoski, Barbara*
  Laurel Pace
**Wolf, Bernice**
<u>**Wolf, Joan**</u>
*Wolf, Susan Whittlesey*
  Antonia Tyler
**Wolfe, Gene**
*Wolfe, Lois*
  Gillian Wyeth
**Wood, Barbara**
**Wood, Nuria**
  *Joi Nobisso*, Nadja Bride
**Wood, Sara**
*Wood, Tonya*
  Courtney Ryan
**Woodbury, Leonora**
  *Ellen Kelman*
*Woodcock, Maureen*
  Maureen Bronson
**Woodhouse, Sarah**
**Woodiwiss, Kathleen**
**Woodland, Eva**
  Nicole De Lyn, Nicole Lindsay
**Woods, Eleanor**
  *Eleanor Rogers*
*Woods, Margery*
  Margery Hilton, Rebecca Caine
<u>**Woods, Sherryl Ann**</u>
  Suzanne Sherrill, Alexandra Kirk
**Woodward, Daphne**

**Woolf, Victoria**
Charlotte Lamb, Laura Hardy,
Sheila Lancaster, Sheila Coates,
Sheila Holland
**Worboys, Anne**
Vicky Maxwell, Annette Eyre
**Worth, Margaret**
Helen Arvonen
**Worthington, Avis**
**Wright, Cynthia**
Devon Lindsay
**Wright, Francesca**
Ashley French, Harriet Gray,
Julia Kane, Denise Robins
**Wright, Lucretia**
Alicia Knight
**Wright, Patricia**
**Wyatt, Stephanie**
**Wyeth, Gillian**
*Lois Wolfe*
**Wyland, Amanda**
**Wyndham, Esther**
*Mary Lutyens*
**Wynn, Patricia**
*Patricia Ricks*
**Wynne, Annabel**

*Notes*

Names in *italics* indicate an author's legal name which does not appear on books. She or he uses pseudonym (s) only.

Names <u>underlined</u> indicate that the author uses legal name for works and may or may not use pseudonym (s).

*Yansick, Susan*
  Erin Yorke
**Yarbro, Chelsea Quinn**
  Vanessa Pryor
*Yarde, Jeanne*
  Joan Hunter, Jeanne Montague
**Yates, Judith**
  *Judith Yoder*
*Yoder, Judith*
  Judith Yates
**York, Alison**
  Leslie Arlen, Daniel Adams,
  Peter Grange, Simon McKay,
  Christopher Nicole, Mark Logan,
  Christina Nicholson, Robin
  Cade, Andrew York
**York, Amanda**
  <u>Joan Dial,</u> Katherine Kent,
  Alexandra Devon, Katherine Sinclair
**York, Andrew**
  Leslie Arlen, Daniels Adams,
  Robin Cade, Peter Grange,
  Mark Logan, Simon McKay,
  Chistopher Nicole, Christina
  Nicholson, Alison York
**York, Elizabeth**
  Margaret E. York, Joanna Makepeace,
  Margaret Abbey
**York, Georgia**
**York, Helen**
**York, Margaret E.**
  Margaret Abbey, Elizabeth York,
  Joanna Makepeace
**York, Pauline**
  Johanna Hailey, *Marcia Y. Howl*

**York, Rebecca**
  <u>*Ruth Glick*</u> & *Eileen Buckholtz,*
  <u>Alyssa Howard, Alexis Hill,</u>
  Tess Marlowe, Alexis Hill Jordan,
  Samantha Chase
**York, Vickie**
  Betty Ann Patterson
**Yorke, Erin**
  *Christine Healy & Susan Yansick*
**Yorke, Katherine**
  Rosemary Ellerbeck, Nicola Thorne,
  Anna L'Estrange
**Young, Brittany**
  Sandra Harris, *Sandra Young,*
  Abigail Wilson
**Young, Ena**
  Kerry Carr, Jane Joyce
**Young, Karen**
  *Karen Stone*
*Young, Mary Jo*
  Jenny Nolan
**Young, Maryann**
**Young, Rena**
*Young, Sandra*
  Brittany Young, Sandra Harris,
  Abigail Wilson
**Young, Selwyn Marie**
**Youngblood, Ila Dell**

# Notes

Names in *italics* indicate an author's legal name which does not appear on books. She or he uses pseudonym (s) only.

Names <u>underlined</u> indicate that the author uses legal name for works and may or may not use pseudonym (s).

**Zach, Cheryl**
  Jennifer Cole
**Zachary, Elizabeth**
**Zavala, Ann**
  Ann Pope, Lee Pope
**Zayne, Valerie**
  *Leigh Shaheen*, Harriet L. Hudson
*Zeig, Joan*
  Alicia Meadowes
**Zide, Donna Comeaux**
**Ziobro, Marie**
**Zumwalt, Eva**

*Notes*

# Recommended
# Reads

# To Be
# The Best

by Melinda Helfer

*T*he fierce competition in the romance genre has given rise to some of the best young writers of fiction to be found anywhere today. These authors have whisked us away from the cares of our everyday lives into worlds of magic, sharing with us all the hopes and fears of their wonderful characters.

When I encounter such a special book, one that makes me oblivious to everything except the author's reality, I rate it as a 4+. And for those rare books transcending even that high plateau, I have marked them with a rating of 5 to signify a totally unique reading experience, a true classic of the genre.

That does not happen very often. Out of the 10,000 plus books I have reviewed for *Romantic Times*, only the following have received the classic 5 ♥ rating:

LIGHTNING THAT LINGERS
**Sharon & Tom Curtis**
*Loveswept*

A SPECIAL MAN
**Billie Green**
*Silhouette Special Edition*

SARAH'S CHILD
**Linda Howard**
*Silhouette Special Edition*

THE TRUSTWORTHY REDHEAD
**Iris Johansen**
*Loveswept*

ONE LAVENDER EVENING
**Karen Keast**
*Silhouette Special Edition*

DANGER ZONE
**Doreen Owens Malek**
*Silhouette Intimate Moments*

A CRIME OF THE HEART
**Cheryl Reavis**
*Silhouette Special Edition*

ONE SUMMER
**Nora Roberts**
*Silhouette Special Edition*

**Also rated as 5 ❤, although not series books themselves, are:**

SUNSHINE AND SHADOW
**Sharon & Tom Curtis**
*Bantam*

SWEET STARFIRE
**Jayne Ann Krentz**
*Warner/Popular Library*

CRYSTAL FLAME
**Jayne Ann Krentz**
*Warner/Popular Library*

THE WINDFLOWER
**Laura London**
*Dell*

TELL ME NO LIES
**Elizabeth Lowell**
*Worldwide*

EYE OF THE STORM
**Maura Seger**
*Worldwide*

EDGE OF DAWN
**Maura Seger**
*Worldwide*

THE DEDICATED VILLAIN
**Patricia Veryan**
*St. Martin's*

487

*Silhouette Special Edition*

CHERYL
REAVIS

A Crime
of the Heart

JayneAnnKrentz
author of
*Sweet Starfire*

Crystal
Flame

Dark passion drew them
toward bursting ecstasy in
an adventure that would change their world.

306

*Silhouette Special Edition*

NORA
ROBERTS
One
Summer

469

*Silhouette Special Edition*

KAREN
KEAST
One Lavender
Evening

# Series Romances 1987—1989

### by Melinda Helfer

*H*ere is a list of all the series romance books that have received 4+ ratings between 1987 and 1989. Hasten thee to the nearest used book store and get thyself at least one of these pearls beyond price. ♥

# 1987

**Kelly Adams**
#395—Devin's Promise
*Second Chance*

**Judith Arnold**
#225—Comfort and Joy
*Harlequin American*

**Linda Barlow**
#379—Midnight Rambler
*Silhouette Desire*

**Parris Afton Bonds**
#189—Wanted Woman
*Silhouette Intimate Moments*

**Barbara Boswell**
#194—Not a Marrying Man
*Loveswept*

**Barbara Bretton**
#193—Playing for Time
*Harlequin American*

**Barbara Bretton**
#211—Second Harmony
*Harlequin American*

**Annette Broadrick**
#336—Made in Heaven
*Silhouette Desire*

**Annette Broadrick**
#533—Mystery Lover
*Silhouette Romance*

**Annette Broadrick**
#501—Strange Enchantment
*Silhouette Romance*

**Annette Broadrick**
#544—That's What Friends Are For
*Silhouette Romance*

**Sandra Brown**
#185—Sunny Chandler's Return
*Loveswept*

**Patt Bucheister**
#202—Touch the Stars
*Loveswept*

# *Lass Small*

## Reviewer's Choice Award Winner
*Goldilocks And The Behr\**
Best Silhouette Desire
1987—1988

Born and raised in San Antonio, Texas, I'm a Hoosier by osmosis. I was always told that I should write, but I studied at the School of Fine Arts.
I attended a writers' workshop with a friend who didn't want to go alone. We were told that if we wanted to write, write. So, I did.

---

### AS CALLY HUGHES

❤ **Second Chance At Love**

*A Lasting Treasure*
Waldenbooks bestseller '84
*Innocent Seduction*
*Cupid's Revenge*

❤ **To Have And To Hold**

*Whatever It Takes*
*Treasure To Share*
(Sequel to *A Lasting Treasure,* Second Chance)
*Never Too Late*

### AS LASS SMALL

❤ **Candlelight Ecstasy**
*The Dedicated Man*
Waldenbooks bestseller '83

**Harlequin Temptation**
Collaboration:
*Marry Me Not*

❤ **Silhouette Romance**
*An Irritating Man*
*Snow Bird*
Aug. '87, RWA finalist '88

❤ **Silhouette Desire**
*Tangled Web*
*To Meet Again*
*Stolen Day*
Spotlighted in RT
*Possibles*
*Intrusive Man*
*To Love Again*

❤ **Silhouette Desire**
*Lambert Sisters Series*

*Blindman's Bluff*
March '88 (Intro. to Series)
*Goldilocks and the Behr*
July '88\* (Book 2 of 6)
*Hide And Seek*
Oct. '88 (Book 3 of 6)
*Red Rover*
April '89 (Book 4 of 6)
*Odd Man Out*
July '89 (Book 5 of 6)
Silhouette Man of the Month
*Tagged*
October '89 (Book 6 of 6)

*A Silhouette Christmas Story—1989*
**...and more books to come.**

---

**Carole Buck**
#424—All That Jazz
*Second Chance*

**Linda Cajio**
#224—Double Dealing
*Loveswept*

**Sandra Canfield**
#278—Night Into Day
*Harlequin Superromance*

**Suzanne Carey**
#368—Any Pirate in a Storm
*Silhouette Desire*

**Rosalind Carson**
#156—The Marrying Kind
*Harlequin Temptation*

**Susanna Christie**
#203—Close Encounter
*Silhouette Intimate Moments*

**Marion Smith Collins**
#179—Another Chance
*Silhouette Intimate Moments*

**Evelyn Crowe**
#262—Twice Shy
*Harlequin Superromance*

**Saranne Dawson**
#222—Summer's Witness
*Harlequin American*

**Barbara Delinsky**
#164—Cardinal Rules
*Harlequin Temptation*

**Judith Duncan**
#251—All That Matters
*Harlequin Superromance*

**Kathleen Eagle**
#396—Carved in Stone
*Silhouette Special Edition*

**Kathleen Eagle**
#359—Something Worth Keeping
*Silhouette Special Edition*

**Barbara Faith**
#173—Desert Song
*Silhouette Intimate Moments*

**Barbara Faith**
#193—Kiss of the Dragon
*Silhouette Intimate Moments*

**Sibylle Garrett**
#211—Surrender to a Stranger
*Silhouette Intimate Moments*

**Lucy Gordon**
#380—Eagle's Prey
*Silhouette Desire*

**Lucy Gordon**
#363—Just Good Friends
*Silhouette Desire*

**Jeanne Grant**
#390—Tender Loving Care
*Second Chance*

**Ginna Gray**
#416—Fools Rush In
*Silhouette Special Edition*

**Ginna Gray**
Season of Miracles
*Silhouette Christmas*

**Billie Green**
#415—Time After Time
*Silhouette Special Edition*

**Billie Green**
#379—Voyage of the Nightingale
*Silhouette Special Edition*

**Jennifer Greene**
#350—Dear Reader
*Silhouette Desire*

**Jennifer Greene**
#366—Minx
*Silhouette Desire*

**Phyllis Haldorson**
#515—To Choose a Wife
*Silhouette Romance*

**Steffie Hall**
#409—Hero at Large
*Second Chance*

**Brooke Hastings**
#385—Forbidden Fruit
*Silhouette Special Edition*

**Joan Hohl**
#390—Falcon's Flight
*Silhouette Desire*

**Joan Hohl**
#354—Lady Ice
*Silhouette Desire*

**Joan Hohl**
#372—One Tough Hombre
*Silhouette Desire*

**Kay Hooper**
#189—In Serena's Web
*Loveswept*

**Kay Hooper**
#193—Raven on the Wing
*Loveswept*

**Kay Hooper**
#225—Zach's Law
*Loveswept*

**Naomi Horton**
#386—Pure Chemistry
*Silhouette Desire*

**Linda Howard**
Bluebird Winter
*Silhouette Christmas*

**Linda Howard**
#177—Diamond Bay
*Silhouette Intimate Moments*

**Linda Howard**
#201—Heartbreaker
*Silhouette Intimate Moments*

**BJ James**
#396—Twice in a Lifetime
*Silhouette Desire*

**Stephanie James**
#342—The Challoner Bride
*Silhouette Desire*

**Iris Johansen**
#191—Across River of Yesterday
*Loveswept*

**Iris Johansen**
#187—Last Bridge Home
*Loveswept*

**Iris Johansen**
#221—The Spellbinder
*Loveswept*

**Kathleen Korbel**
#389—A Prince of a Guy
*Silhouette Desire*

**Kathleen Korbel**
#191—Worth Any Risk
*Silhouette Intimate Moments*

**Jackie Leigh**
#428—Angel on My Shoulder
*Second Chance*

**Elizabeth Lowell**
#355—Love Songs for a Raven
*Silhouette Desire*

**Lee Magner**
#169—Night of the Matador
*Ecstasy Supreme*

# Anne & Ed Kolaczyk

*As a couple, Anne and Ed
were not rare.
Married with dogs, cats
and kids in their hair.
But then a book
Anne did write,
From IBM Ed did quit,
Now Happily Ever Afters
they write as a pair.*

*I*t's not that long since Anne (as Anne Hillary and Anne Benson) wrote that first Regency, but a lot has changed for us. Our sons have left for college and the Army and the little girls that tormented *Captain Wonder* (Loveswept) are about to trod the hallowed halls of high school. Aging a bit also, we've stopped playing soccer (*Rose In Bloom*—Silhouette Special Edition) and stick to coaching it (*Some Kind Of Wonderful*—Second Chance At Love). We escaped from Chicago's urban sprawl in 1987 and settled in a quiet, tree-lined neighborhood just south of Notre Dame's golden dome (*Ghost of a Chance*—Silhouette Special Edition).

*J*ust as our forty-some books have reflected our lives, they also reflect our fascination with multi-generational family units and our need for roots and a sense of belonging. Let us know if you've enjoyed reading them as much as we've enjoyed writing them.

**P.O. Box 164
Notre Dame, IN 46556-0164**

**Doreen Owens Malek**
#343—Bright River
*Silhouette Desire*

**Anne McAllister**
#186—Body and Soul
*Harlequin American*

**Lindsay McKenna**
#377—A Measure of Love
*Silhouette Special Edition*

**Lindsay McKenna**
#397—Solitaire
*Silhouette Special Edition*

**Judith McWilliams**
#184—Honorable Intentions
*Harlequin Temptation*

**Jan Milella**
#175—Night Heat
*Silhouette Intimate Moments*

**Hayton Monteith**
#178—Sapphire Heart
*Ecstasy Supreme*

**Nancy Morse**
#181—Sacred Places
*Silhouette Intimate Moments*

**Diana Palmer**
The Humbug Man
*Silhouette Christmas*

**Marilyn Pappano**
#214—The Lights of Home
*Silhouette Intimate Moments*

**Marilyn Pappano**
#182—Within Reach
*Silhouette Intimate Moments*

**Heather Graham Pozzessere**
#174—A Matter of Circumstance
*Silhouette Intimate Moments*

**Heather Graham Pozzessere**
#220—King of the Castle
*Silhouette Intimate Moments*

**Rita Rainville**
#478—Family Affair
*Silhouette Romance*

**Rita Rainville**
#502—It Takes a Thief
*Silhouette Romance*

**Cinda Richards**
#382—Fire Under Heaven
*Second Chance*

**Emilie Richards**
#520—Aloha Always
*Silhouette Romance*

**Emilie Richards**
#188—Bayou Midnight
*Silhouette Intimate Moments*

**Suzanne Richardson**
#186—Fiddlin' Fool
*Loveswept*

**Nora Roberts**
#198—Command Performance
*Silhouette Intimate Moments*

**Nora Roberts**
#361—For Now, Forever
*Silhouette Special Edition*

**Nora Roberts**
#185—Mind Over Matter
*Silhouette Intimate Moments*

**Nora Roberts**
#212—The Playboy Prince
*Silhouette Intimate Moments*

**JoAnn Ross**
#153—Tempting Fate
*Harlequin Temptation*

**165**

**Dallas Schulze**
#185—Stormwalker
*Harlequin American*

**Maura Seger**
#176— Happily Ever After
*Silhouette Intimate Moments*

**Maura Seger**
#194—Legacy
*Silhouette Intimate Moments*

**Maura Seger**
#209—Sea Gate
*Silhouette Intimate Moments*

**Renee Simons**
#187—Colton's Folly
*Silhouette Intimate Moments*

**Sandy Steen**
#202—Past Perfect
*Silhouette Intimate Moments*

**Anne Stuart**
#59—Hand in Glove
*Harlequin Intrigue*

**Jeanne Triner**
#267—By Any Other Name
*Harlequin Superromance*

**Alison Tyler**
#174—Double Masquerade
*Ecstasy Supreme*

**Linda Vail**
#171—A Secret Arrangement
*Ecstasy Supreme*

**Linda Vail**
#179—Loving Charade
*Ecstasy Supreme*

**Linda Randall Wisdom**
#173—A Perilous Affair
*Ecstasy Supreme*

**Eleanor Woods**
#154—Breathless Temptation
*Ecstasy Supreme*

**Sherryl Woods**
#425—Safe Harbor
*Silhouette Special Edition*

# 1988

**Kelly Adams**
#440—Released Into Dawn
*Second Chance*

**Laine Allen**
#445—Friendly Persuasion
*Second Chance*

**Stella Bagwell**
#560—The Outsider
*Silhouette Romance*

**Barbara Boswell**
#272—And Tara, Too
*Loveswept*

**Barbara Boswell**
#242—Intimate Details
*Loveswept*

**Barbara Boswell**
#236—Sharing Secrets
*Loveswept*

**Deana Brauer**
#599—Simply Sam
*Silhouette Romance*

**Barbara Bretton**
#251—Honeymoon Hotel
*Harlequin American*

**Annette Broadrick**
#609—Come Be My Love
*Silhouette Romance*

# Sally Garrett

# DESERT STAR

Harlequin Superromance #344—February 1989

Caroline Noble and hero Granville Kane are lovers who get the wish made on their own wishing star from long ago.

As supporting players, meet again David and Sammy McCormack from SR #90 UNTIL FOREVER as they encounter new obstacles to love. Can love last forever?

*P.O. Box 212, Dillon MT 59725*   *Include SASE*

**Annette Broadrick**
#414—Momentary Marriage
*Silhouette Desire*

**Sandra Brown**
#263—Hawk O'Toole's Hostage
*Loveswept*

**Carole Buck**
#448—The Real Thing
*Second Chance*

**Marion Smith Collins**
#252—Better Than Ever
*Silhouette Intimate Moments*

**Kathleen Creighton**
#240—Rogue's Valley
*Silhouette Intimate Moments*

**Kathleen Creighton**
#239—The Prince and the Patriot
*Loveswept*

**Kathleen Creighton**
#299—The Sorceror's Keeper
*Loveswept*

**Kathleen Creighton**
#279—Winter's Daughter
*Loveswept*

**Sharon DeVita**
#610—Italian Knights
*Silhouette Romance*

**Sharon DeVita**
#593—Sherlock's Home
*Silhouette Romance*

**Judith Duncan**
#291—Beginnings
*Harlequin Superromance*

**Kathleen Eagle**
#257—But That Was Yesterday
*Silhouette Intimate Moments*

**Kathleen Eagle**
#437—Candles in the Night
*Silhouette Special Edition*

**Kathleen Eagle**
#242—More Than a Miracle
*Silhouette Intimate Moments*

**Patricia Gardner Evans**
#243—Summer of the Wolf
*Silhouette Intimate Moments*

**Patricia Gardner Evans**
#228—Whatever It Takes
*Silhouette Intimate Moments*

**Barbara Faith**
#262—Flower of the Desert
*Silhouette Intimate Moments*

**Marie Ferrarella**
#588—The Gift
*Silhouette Romance*

**Gina Ferris**
#496—Healing Sympathy
*Silhouette Special Edition*

**Judy Gill**
#282—Renegade
*Loveswept*

**Sally Goldenbaum**
#233—The Baron
*Loveswept*

**Lucy Gordon**
#596—A Night of Passion
*Silhouette Romance*

**Lucy Gordon**
#611—A Woman of Spirit
*Silhouette Romance*

**Ginna Gray**
#468—Where Angels Fear
*Silhouette Special Edition*

**Jennifer Greene**
#463—Lady of the Island
*Silhouette Desire*

**Jennifer Greene**
#439—The Castle Keep
*Silhouette Desire*

**Brooke Hastings**
#486—Both Sides Now
*Silhouette Special Edition*

**Joan Hohl**
#444—Forever Spring
*Silhouette Special Edition*

**Kay Hooper**
#296—Captain's Paradise
*Loveswept*

**Kay Hooper**
#256—Outlaw Derek
*Loveswept*

**Kay Hooper**
#286—Shades of Gray
*Loveswept*

**Linda Howard**
#452—White Lies
*Silhouette Special Edition*

**Sandra James**
#306—Guardian Angel
*Harlequin Superromance*

**Iris Johansen**
#274—Blue Skies and Shining Promises
*Loveswept*

**Iris Johansen**
#257—Man from Half Moon Bay
*Loveswept*

**Iris Johansen**
#232—Star Light, Star Bright
*Loveswept*

**Iris Johansen**
#280—Strong Hot Winds
*Loveswept*

**Mary Alice Kirk**
#462—Promises
*Silhouette Special Edition*

**Kathleen Korbel**
#222—Edge of the World
*Silhouette Intimate Moments*

**Kathleen Korbel**
#455—The Princess and the Pea
*Silhouette Desire*

**Jayne Ann Krentz**
#229—Dreams, Part One
*Harlequin Temptation*

**Jayne Ann Krentz**
#230—Dreams, Part Two
*Harlequin Temptation*

**Jayne Ann Krentz**
#219—Montclair Emeralds: Joy
*Harlequin Temptation*

**Shirley Larson**
#214—Building on Dreams
*Harlequin Temptation*

**Elizabeth Lowell**
#256—Chain Lightning
*Silhouette Intimate Moments*

**Elizabeth Lowell**
#415—Fever
*Silhouette Desire*

**Debbie Macomber**
#567—Some Kind of Wonderful
*Silhouette Romance*

**Lee Magner**
#246—Mustang Man
*Silhouette Intimate Moments*

# MARGARET CHITTENDEN a.k.a. ROSALIND CARSON

*loves to answer letters....*
P.O. Box 1225
Ocean Shores, WA 98569
(An SASE helps!)

***Dear Readers***: My thanks for all your great letters about FOREVER LOVE, my reincarnation novel.

As *Margaret Chittenden,* I've also published articles, short stories, children's books, occult suspense and romantic suspense novels. I do like variety!

As *Rosalind Carson* (my middle name and my husband's middle name), I've published nine romance novels. #10 will be a Harlequin Superromance, which has a chiropractor as the hero. (By a strange coincidence, my son is a chiropractor.)

| | | |
|---|---|---|
| **Harlequin** | *Dark Enchantment* | 1982 |
| **Superromance** | *Song of Desire* | 1982 |
| | *Such Sweet Magic* | 1983 |
| | *Love Me Tomorrow* | 1984 |
| | *To Touch The Moon* | 1985 |
| | *Close to Home* | 1986 |
| | *The Moon Gate* | 1988 |
| **Temptation** | *Lovespell* | 1984 |
| | *The Marrying Kind* | 1987 |
| **Worldwide** | *Beyond the Rainbow* | 1986 |
| **Library** | *Forever Love* | 1988 |

**Ann Major**
#457—Night Child
*Silhouette Desire*

**Jan Mathews**
#434—Surrender the Dawn
*Second Chance*

**Anne McAllister**
#275—Gifts of the Spirit
*Harlequin American*

**Anne McAllister**
#234—Marry Sunshine
*Harlequin American*

**Mary Kay McComas**
#287—Obsession
*Loveswept*

**Lindsay McKenna**
#434—Heart of the Tiger
*Silhouette Special Edition*

**Jackie Merritt**
#466—Big Sky Country
*Silhouette Desire*

**Carla Neggers**
#208—All in a Name
*Harlequin Temptation*

**Carla Neggers**
#190—Family Matters
*Harlequin Temptation*

**Diana Palmer**
#580—Long Tall Texans: Calhoun
*Silhouette Romance*

**Marilyn Pappano**
#258—Cody Daniels' Return
*Silhouette Intimate Moments*

**Marilyn Pappano**
#233—Guilt by Association
*Silhouette Intimate Moments*

**Joan Elliott Pickart**
#291—Man of the Night
*Loveswept*

**Heather Graham Pozzessere**
#225—Strangers in Paradise
*Silhouette Intimate Moments*

**Heather Graham Pozzessere**
#260—This Rough Magic
*Silhouette Intimate Moments*

**Linda Raye**
#437—Temptress
*Second Chance*

**Emilie Richards**
#261—Smoke Screen
*Silhouette Intimate Moments*

**Paula Detmer Riggs**
#226—Fantasy Man
*Silhouette Intimate Moments*

**Paula Detmer Riggs**
#250—Suspicious Minds
*Silhouette Intimate Moments*

**Doreen Roberts**
#239—Willing Accomplice
*Silhouette Intimate Moments*

**Nora Roberts**
#463—Dance to the Piper
*Silhouette Special Edition*

**Nora Roberts**
#232—Irish Rose
*Silhouette Intimate Moments*

**Nora Roberts**
#427—Local Hero
*Silhouette Special Edition*

**Nora Roberts**
#475—Skin Deep
*Silhouette Special Edition*

**Nora Roberts**
#451—The Last Honest Woman
*Silhouette Special Edition*

**Patricia Rosemoor**
# 95—Ambushed
*Harlequin Intrigue*

**JoAnn Ross**
#221—Eve's Choice
*Harlequin Temptation*

**Courtney Ryan**
#438—Cody's Gypsy
*Second Chance*

**Lass Small**
#437—Goldilocks and the Behr
*Silhouette Desire*

**Deborah Smith**
#290—Caught by Surprise
*Loveswept*

**Deborah Smith**
#255—Hold on Tight
*Loveswept*

**Deborah Smith**
#245—Jed's Sweet Revenge
*Loveswept*

**Sondra Stanford**
#586—Heart of Gold
*Silhouette Romance*

**Anne Stuart**
#260—Cry for the Moon
*Harlequin American*

**Anne Stuart**
#246—Partners in Crime
*Silhouette Intimate Moments*

**Joyce Theis**
#432—Moon of the Raven
*Silhouette Desire*

**Linda Turner**
#238—The Echo of Thunder
*Silhouette Intimate Moments*

**Lynda Ward**
#321—Leap the Moon
*Harlequin Superromance*

**Lynda Ward**
#317—Race the Sun
*Harlequin Superromance*

**Lynda Ward**
#325—Touch the Stars
*Harlequin Superromance*

**Sherryl Woods**
#484—Edge of Forever
*Silhouette Special Edition*

**Brittany Young**
#550—A Matter of Honor
*Silhouette Romance*

# 1989

**Lynn Bartlett**
#290—The Price of Glory
*Silhouette Intimate Moments*

**Nikki Benjamin**
#539—Emily's House
*Silhouette Special Edition*

**Barbara Boswell**
#334 — Simply Irresistible
*Loveswept*

**Annette Broadrick**
#499 — Irresistible
*Silhouette Desire*

**Sandra Brown**
#300—Long Time Coming
*Loveswept*

**Patt Bucheister**
#311 — Near the Edge
*Loveswept*

**Bethany Campbell**
#116—Roses of Constant
*Harlequin Intrigue*

**Sandra Canfield**
#338—Calloway Corners: Mariah
*Harlequin Superromance*

**Sara Chance**
#500—Eye of the Storm
*Silhouette Desire*

**Kathy Clark**
#282 — Kissed by an Angel
*Harlequin American*

**Evelyn Crowe**
#362—Word of Honor
*Harlequin Superromance*

**Carol Duncan**
#270—Stranger on the Shore
*Silhouette Intimate Moments*

**Barbara Faith**
#277 — In a Rebel's Arms
*Silhouette Intimate Moments*

**Sibylle Garrett**
#271—Rebel's Return
*Silhouette Intimate Moments*

**Ginna Gray**
#528 — If There Be Love
*Silhouette Special Edition*

**Jennifer Greene**
#498 — Dancing in the Dark
*Silhouette Desire*

**Steffie Hall**
#456 — Foul Play
*Second Chance*

**Steffie Hall**
#466—Full House
*Second Chance*

**Tami Hoag**
#315 — Mismatch
*Loveswept*

**Tami Hoag**
#304—Rumour Has It
*Loveswept*

**Joan Hohl**
#458 — Window on Tomorrow
*Second Chance*

**Kay Hooper**
#312 — It Takes a Thief
*Loveswept*

**Naomi Horton**
#487 — A Dangerous Kind of Man
*Silhouette Desire*

**Linda Howard**
#281 — Mackenzie's Mountain
*Silhouette Intimate Moments*

**Tracy Hughes**
#342 — Calloway Corners: Jo
*Harlequin Superromance*

**Karen Keast**
#536—A Tender Silence
*Silhouette Special Edition*

**Mary Kirk**
#524 — Phoenix Rising
*Silhouette Special Edition*

**Jayne Ann Krentz**
#241 — A Woman's Touch
*Harlequin Temptation*

**Lindsay McKenna**
#535—No Surrender
*Silhouette Special Edition*

# MIDNIGHT BLUE

June 1989

Harlequin
Superromance

by

## Nancy
## Landon

After reading an advance copy of MIDNIGHT BLUE, citizens of Granbury, Texas turned their town inside out for the Oklahoma author who had set her first book in their restored town on the Brazos River.

MIDNIGHT BLUE begins with a bed race scene straight from Granbury's Fourth of July celebration that draws thousand of tourists, so townsfolk scheduled Landon to ride in the Independence Day parade, planned a riverboat gala in her honor and auctioned her off as "Have Dinner with Famous Author."

Look for more fireworks from Landon, who pursued successful careers in public relations and newspaper journalism in Texas, Virginia, North Carolina and Washington, D.C. before returning to her home state to write fiction. A finalist in the 1988 RWA Golden Heart Contest, she writes a fast-paced book and swims and water skis in her spare time.

---

*Nancy welcomes letters from readers, booksellers*
*and librarians, with SASE please:*
**Post Office Box 720662**
**Oklahoma City, OK 73172-0662**

**Judith McWilliams**
#253—The Royal Treatment
*Harlequin Temptation*

**Jan Milella**
#269—Once Forgotten
*Silhouette Intimate Moments*

**Helen Mittermeyer**
#341—White Heat
*Loveswept*

**Diana Palmer**
#469—Reluctant Father
*Silhouette Desire*

**Marilyn Pappano**
#294—Something of Heaven
*Silhouette Intimate Moments*

**Heather Graham Pozzessere**
#293—Borrowed Angel
*Silhouette Intimate Moments*

**Rita Rainville**
#663—No Way To Treat a Lady
*Silhouette Romance*

**Emilie Richards**
#285 — Out of the Ashes
*Silhouette Intimate Moments*

**Emilie Richards**
#273 — Rainbow Fire
*Silhouette Intimate Moments*

**Penny Richards**
#350 — Calloway Corners: Eden
*Harlequin Superromance*

**Paula Detmer Riggs**
#284 — Desperate Measures
*Silhouette Intimate Moments*

**Doreen Roberts**
#295—Threat of Exposure
*Silhouette Intimate Moments*

**Nora Roberts**
#511 — Best Laid Plans
*Silhouette Special Editions*

**Nora Roberts**
#499—Loving Jack
*Silhouette Special Edition*

**Courtney Ryan**
#462 — Absolute Beginners
*Second Chance*

**Dallas Schulze**
#291 — Together Always
*Harlequin American*

**Lass Small**
#505—Odd Man Out
*Silhouette Desire*

**Deborah Smith**
#326 — Sundance and the Princess
*Loveswept*

**Pat Tracy**
#654 — His Kind of Woman
*Silhouette Romance*

**Jackie Weger**
#289 — Full House
*Harlequin American*

**Frances Williams**
#287 — Night Secrets
*Silhouette Intimate Moments*

**Brittany Young**
#640 — The White Rose
*Silhouette Romance*

# Recommended Non-Series Contemporary Romances

DOUBLE DEALING
**Jayne Castle**
*Dell*

GUINEVERE JONES Series
**Jayne Castle**
*Dell*

TRADING SECRETS
**Jayne Castle**
*Dell*

WILD PARADISE
**Pat Coughlin**
*Warner/Popular Library*

SUNSHINE AND SHADOW
**Sharon & Tom Curtis**
*Bantam*

RIDE THE THUNDER
**Janet Dailey**
*Pocket*

AGAIN THE MAGIC
**Lee Damon**
*Gallen*

HUSTLE, SWEET LOVE
**Maggie Davis**
*PaperJacks*

WILD MIDNIGHT
**Maggie Davis**
*Bantam*

COMMITMENTS
**Barbara Delinsky**
*Warner/Popular Library*

FINGER PRINTS
**Barbara Delinsky**
*Worldwide*

HEART OF THE NIGHT
**Barbara Delinsky**
*Warner*

THE GOLDEN SKY
**Kristin James**
*Gallen*

THE FOREVER DREAM
**Iris Johansen**
*Bantam*

JESSIE'S SONG
**Nancy Jones**
*NAL*

THE SILKEN WEB
**Laura Jordan**
*Gallen*

GIFT OF FIRE
**Jayne Ann Krentz**
*Warner/Popular Library*

GIFT OF GOLD
**Jayne Ann Krentz**
*Warner/Popular Library*

# *Theresa Weir*

## 1988 Romantic Times Award Winner

*"An exceptional new talent...Ms. Weir has written a splendid adventure that will delight readers with its realistic background and outstanding sensual tension."*                    *Rave Reviews*

*"...completely off the Richter scale in tremors of the heart. Amazon Lily has the one magic ingredient that puts Theresa Weir on the genius level of romance writers...reality."*                    *A. E. Ferguson*
                                                                      *Alberta's Reader Service*

*"I guarantee Amazon Lily will touch your heart in ways you could never imagine and you'll never be the same again."* *Amy R. Mitchell*
                                                                      *Reader*

**and for Silhouette Romance...**

### THE FOREVER MAN      LOVING JENNY
#### April 1988                    May 1989
### IGUANA BAY
#### Intimate Moments
#### coming in 1990

*Dear Readers,*
*Thank you for taking the time to write to me. The letters I've received in response to Amazon Lily are wonderful. If you're having trouble finding copies of Lily, ask your bookseller to order it for you or contact me for ordering information.. And please keep writing. I really enjoy hearing from you!*                    *Theresa Weir*
*RR1, Box 24    Gladstone, Illinois 61437*

MIDNIGHT JEWELS
**Jayne Ann Krentz**
*Warner/Popular Library*

TELL ME NO LIES
**Elizabeth Lowell**
*Worldwide*

CLASH BY NIGHT
**Doreen Owens Malek**
*Worldwide*

FAIR GAME
**Doreen Owens Malek**
*Warner/Popular Library*

NIGHT MAGIC
**Karen Robards**
*Warner*

TO LOVE A MAN
**Karen Robards**
*Warner*

WILD ORCHIDS
**Karen Robards**
*Warner*

HOT ICE
**Nora Roberts**
*Bantam*

SACRED SINS
**Nora Roberts**
*Bantam*

SWEET REVENGE
**Nora Roberts**
*Bantam*

ONLY 'TIL DAWN
**Esther Sager**
*Berkley*

ECHO OF THUNDER
**Maura Seger**
*Worldwide*

EDGE OF DAWN
**Maura Seger**
*Worldwide*

EYE OF THE STORM
**Maura Seger**
*Worldwide*

SEPARATE BEDS
**LaVyrle Spencer**
*Jove*

MAGGIE BENNETT Series
**Anne Stuart**
*Dell*

SEEN AND NOT HEARD
**Anne Stuart**
*Pocket*

HONOR BOUND
**Laura Taylor**
*Berkley*

AMAZON LILY
**Theresa Weir**
*Pocket*

PEREGRINE CONNECTION
Series
**Rebecca York**
*Dell*

# Kathleen Gilles Seidel

## writes only as

# Kathleen Gilles Seidel

*...although perhaps not as often as you would wish.*

# Golden Oldies
# of Series
# Romance

### by Melinda Helfer

*I*t's hard to believe that it's almost 10,000 books since I started reviewing for *Romantic Times* in 1982.

That's a staggering number, one that is even more impressive since it represents on the average of 1500 books in a single year. Is it any surprise to learn that the romance genre accounts for around 25% of all paperback sales?

This is no passing fancy. Year in, year out, romance accounts for the largest sales of any genre.

Series romance in particular has blossomed in the last decade with the advent of American publishers into the marketing arena. At one time or another, almost every major publishing house has introduced its own line in an attempt to capitalize on this lucrative market.

From Dell's Candlelight Ecstasy and Supreme, Berkley's Second Chance, NAL's Rapture, Bantam's Loveswept, Avon's Velvet Glove, Ballantine's Love & Life through the powerhouse Silhouette and Harlequin groups, each line has offered memorable reading.

It wasn't easy, but I have managed to come up with a relatively small list of some of my all-time favorites. Fortunately, there are many excellent used book stores and book search services specializing in romance, so with diligent searching a determined reader still has a good chance to secure their own copies of these "golden oldies."❤

Diana
Palmer

Terri
Herrington

# Jackie Casto

"Writers talk about what a lonely profession writing is, and it is, until someone reads what we've written. And then, a private daydream somehow turns into communication. That's why I never feel the process of creating a book is complete until at least one reader lets me know that what I had to say affected him or her. Whether the effect was negative or positive isn't the point. The point is that I initiated a conversation, and he or she responded."

## Dell Books by Jackie Black

*Candlelight Ecstasy*

*Winter Winds*
*Crimson Morning*
*Autumn Fires*
*Promises in the Night*
*A Time to Love*
*Romantic Roulette*
*Catch of the Season*
*Island of Illusions*
*The Vixen's Kiss*
*Charlie's Chance*

*Ecstasy Supreme*

*Payment in Full*
*Fascination*
*For All Time*
*From This Day Forward*
*A Little Bit of Warmth*
*Dark Paradise*

*Single Title*
*Wayfaring Stranger*

## Harlequin American Books by Jacqueline Ashley

*Love's Revenge*
*Hunting Season*
*The Other Half of Love*
*In the Name of Love*
*Spring's Awakening*

*The Long Journey Home*
*A Question of Honor*
*The Gift*
*Love Thy Neighbor*
*Secrets of the Heart (Intrigue)*

**I love to hear from readers & booksellers:**
**11100 Gilliam Avenue, Oklahoma City, OK 73170.**
**(Send SASE for bookmark.)**

## Bantam Loveswept

INTIMATE DETAILS
LANDSLIDE VICTORY
SHARING SECRETS
**Barbara Boswell**

ALL IS FAIR
DOUBLE DEALING
**Linda Cajio**

LIGHTNING THAT LINGERS
**Sharon & Tom Curtis**

PHARR LAKE AFFAIR
**Joan Domning**

TO SEE THE DAISIES FIRST
TOUGH ACT TO FOLLOW
**Billie Green**

MISMATCH
**Tami Hoag**

CJ'S FATE
SHADES OF GRAY
TIME AFTER TIME
**Kay Hooper**

SHAMROCK TRINITY
**Hooper, Johansen, Preston**

STRANGER CALLED ADAM
**BJ James**

ALWAYS
GOLDEN VALKYRIE
RELUCTANT LARK
TOUCH THE HORIZON
TRUSTWORTHY REDHEAD
**Iris Johansen**

GOODIES CASE
**Sara Orwig**

LOOK FOR THE SEA GULLS
**Joan E. Pickart**

SILVER MIRACLES
**Fayrene Preston**

INHERITED
**Marianne Shock**

CAUGHT BY SURPRISE
**Deborah Smith**

DUPLICITY
**Peggy Webb**

## Berkley Second Chance

DEVIN'S PROMISE
**Kelly Adams**

FRIENDLY PERSUASION
**Laine Allen**

SIREN'S SONG
**Linda Barlow**

CODY'S HONOR
**Carole Buck**

TORN ASUNDER
**Ann Cristy**

LAUGH WITH ME, LOVE
WITH ME
**Lee Damon**

HEART OF THE HUNTER
**Liz Grady**

AIN'T MISBEHAVIN'
NO MORE MR. NICE GUY
SILVER AND SPICE
TENDER LOVING CARE
**Jeanne Grant**

WINDOW ON TOMORROW
**Joan Hohl**

# Sherryl Woods

## *Bringing you romance, laughter and suspense since 1982*

**From Dell Candlelight Ecstasy**
*written as Suzanne Sherrill:*
Restoring Love, 1982
Desirable Compromise, 1984

**From Bantam Circle of Love**
*written as Alexandra Kirk:*
Sand Castles, 1982
Images Of Love, 1982

**From NAL Signet:**
Thrown For A Loss, 1984

**From Avon Velvet Glove:**
Jamaican Midnight, 1984

**From Golden Apple,**
*written as Alexandra Kirk:*
Shadow On The Hill, 1985

**From Berkley Second Chance at Love:**
#326  A Kiss Away, 1986
#342  A Prince Among Men, 1986

#375  All For Love, 1986
#398  Best Intentions, 1987
#412  Two's Company, 1987
#430  Prince Charming Replies, '88

**From Silhouette Desire:**
#309  Not At Eight, Darling, 1986
#329  Yesterday's Love, 1987
#345  Come Fly With Me, 1987
#371  A Gift Of Love, 1987
#431  Can't Say No, 1988
#472  Heartland, 1989
# 521  One Touch of Moondust, Sept. '89

**From Silhouette Special Edition:**
#425  Safe Harbor, 1987
#446  Never Let Go, 1988
#484  Edge Of Forever, 1988
#522  In Too Deep, 1989
       Miss Liz's Passion, Jan. 1990

**From Popular Library:**
Reckless,1989
Body And Soul (August) 1989
Stolen Moments (April) 1990

*For a free bookmark, send S.A.S.E. to:*
**Sherryl Woods**
**P.O. Box 490326**
**Key Biscayne, FL  33149**

ANYTHING GOES
**Diana Morgan**

FOUL PLAY
HERO AT LARGE
**Steffie Hall**

BLITHE SPIRIT
**Mary Haskell**

SLIGHTLY SCANDALOUS
**Jan Mathews**

DILLON'S PROMISE
FIRE UNDER HEAVEN
**Cinda Richards**

CODY'S GYPSY
**Courtney Ryan**

PRINCE CHARMING REPLIES
**Sherryl Woods**

# Dell Candlelight Ecstasy

CRIMSON MORNING
**Jackie Black**

LOVING ARRANGEMENT
**Diana Blayne**

OUT OF THIS WORLD
**Lori Copeland**

SENSUOUS BURGUNDY
**Bonnie Drake**

ON WINGS OF MAGIC
**Kay Hooper**

STAR-CROSSED
**Sara Jennings**

MORGAN WADE'S WOMAN
**Amii Lorin**

BEGUILING PRETENDER
**Lee Magner**

ALL'S FAIR
**Anne Reisser**

MAGIC TOUCH
**Linda Vail**

# Dell Candlelight Supreme

PAYMENT IN FULL
**Jackie Black**

FOREVER AFTER
**Lori Copeland**

SEASON OF ENCHANTMENT
**Emily Elliott**

QUEEN OF HEARTS
**Heather Graham**

NIGHT STRIKER
**Amii Lorin**

SAPPHIRE HEART
**Hayton Monteith**

ANOTHER DAY OF LOVING
**Rebecca Nunn**

AGAINST THE WIND
**Anne Stuart**

PERILOUS AFFAIR
**Linda Wisdom**

# Harlequin American

COMFORT AND JOY
**Judith Arnold**

PLAYING FOR TIME
Barbara Bretton

RISK WORTH TAKING
Kathleen G. Seidel

INTIMATE STRANGERS
SUMMER'S WITNESS
Saranne Dawson

BODY AND SOUL
QUICKSILVER SEASON
STARSTRUCK
Anne McAllister

STORMWALKER
TOGETHER ALWAYS
Dallas Schulze

BLUE SAGE
PARTNERS IN CRIME
Anne Stuart

# Harlequin Intrigue

ROSES OF CONSTANT
Bethany Campbell

A SIREN'S LURE
Andrea Davidson

CALL AFTER MIDNIGHT
Tess Gerritsen

AMBUSHED
Patricia Rosemoor

CATSPAW
HAND IN GLOVE
Anne Stuart

MYSTERY TRAIN
Lynn Turner

# Harlequin Superromance

TOUCH THE SKY
Debbi Bedford

CALLOWAY CORNERS Series
Katherine Burton
Sandra Canfield
Tracy Hughes
Penny Richards

NIGHT INTO DAY
Sandra Canfield

CHARADE
MOMENT OF MADNESS
TWICE SHY
Evelyn Crowe

BEGINNINGS
INTO THE LIGHT
WHEN MORNING COMES
Judith Duncan

SHADOWS IN THE SUN
Jocelyn Haley

GUARDIAN ANGEL
Sandra James

TENDER TRIUMPH
Judith McNaught

SEASON OF MIRACLES
Emilie Richards

FIRE IN THE WIND
SEASON OF STORM
Alexandra Sellers

BY ANY OTHER NAME
Jeanne Triner

# Harlequin Temptation

BRONZE MYSTIQUE
CARDINAL RULES
**Barbara Delinsky**

GHOST OF A CHANCE
WOMAN'S TOUCH
**Jayne Ann Krentz**

DOUBLE STANDARDS
**Judith McNaught**

HONORABLE INTENTIONS
IN GOOD FAITH
**Judith McWilliams**

TOUCH THE HEAVENS
**Eileen Nauman**

ALL IN A NAME
**Carla Neggers**

EVE'S CHOICE
**JoAnn Ross**

# NAL Rapture

SHADES OF MOONLIGHT
**Laurel Chandler**

GENTLE DIPLOMACY
ROMANTIC CAPER
**Melinda MacKenzie**

WOLFE'S PREY
**JoAnn Robb**

# Silhouette Desire

MIDNIGHT RAMBLER
**Linda Barlow**

HEAT OF THE NIGHT
IRRESISTIBLE
**Annette Broadrick**

LOVE MEDICINE
**Suzanne Carey**

EYE OF THE STORM
**Sara Chance**

JUDGEMENT OF PARIS
**Lucy Gordon**

DEAR READER
**Jennifer Greene**

TEXAS GOLD
**Joan Hohl**

LADY LIBERTY
**Naomi Horton**

FABULOUS BEAST
NIGHTWALKER
**Stephanie James**

MAN OF THE HOUSE
**Janet Joyce**

PRINCE OF A GUY
PRINCESS AND THE PEA
**Kathleen Korbel**

TEXAS WILDCAT
**Lindsay McKenna**

BIG SKY COUNTRY
**Jackie Merritt**

LADY LOVE
TENDER STRANGER
**Diana Palmer**

OF PASSION BORN
**Suzanne Simms**

GOLDILOCKS AND THE
BEHR
**Lass Small**

# Angela Wells

*Writes regularly
for*
**HARLEQUIN ROMANCES**

*USA Publications:*

**SWEET POISON—1986
MOROCCAN MADNESS—1987
DESPERATE REMEDY—1988**

***Dear Reader,***

I'm delighted to have the opportunity of saying 'hello' to you, and thanking you for your support.

As I'm English, living just outside London with my husband and teenage son, this is the first time I've been able to introduce myself to my North American readers.

All my novels are Contemporary Series Romances with locations in many different countries, and I've been thrilled with the response I've received from my readers in the USA.

As my books are published in the UK first, there is a time lag before they appear over here. So keep a look out for them, won't you? On the way over the Atlantic: ***Fortune's Fool; Love's Wrongs; Errant Daughter; Still Temptation; Rash Contract; Brash Intruder*** and others!

I do enjoy writing for you—and I hope you continue to enjoy reading me!

**9 Emerson Drive, Hornchurch, Essex RM11 1XH England**

For response, I'd appreciate an international postal coupon.

## Silhouette Intimate Moments

AFTERSHOCKS
Catherine Coulter

DEMON LOVER
DOUBLE DEALINGS
Kathleen Creighton

SUMMER OF THE WOLF
WHATEVER IT TAKES
Patricia Gardner Evans

BEDOUIN BRIDE
DESERT SONG
Barbara Faith

REBEL'S RETURN
Sibylle Garrett

DIAMOND BAY
MACKENZIE'S MOUNTAIN
MIDNIGHT RAINBOW
TEARS OF THE RENEGADE
Linda Howard

RAVEN'S PREY
SERPENT IN PARADISE
Stephanie James

WORTH ANY RISK
Kathleen Korbel

LOVER IN THE ROUGH
Elizabeth Lowell

DANGER ZONE
MONTEGA'S MISTRESS
Doreen Owens Malek

PART OF THE BARGAIN
Linda Lael Miller

SOMETHING OF HEAVEN
Marilyn Pappano

BORROWED ANGEL
NIGHT MOVES
Heather Graham Pozzessere

SMOKE SCREEN
Emilie Richards

DESPERATE MEASURES
Paula Detmer Riggs

THREAT OF EXPOSURE
Doreen Roberts

AFFAIRE ROYALE
TONIGHT AND ALWAYS
Nora Roberts

QUEST OF THE EAGLE
SEA GATE
Maura Seger

KILLING MOON
Amanda Stevens

ECHO OF THUNDER
Linda Turner

## Silhouette Romance

MYSTERY LOVER
Annette Broadrick

SHERLOCK'S HOME
Sharon De Vita

ISLAND OF DREAMS
WOMAN OF SPIRIT
Lucy Gordon

PERFECT MATCH
Ginna Gray

BEHIND CLOSED DOORS
Diana Morgan

NOTHING LOST
Laurie Paige

SOLDIER OF FORTUNE
**Diana Palmer**

GALLAGHER'S LADY
WHITE ROSE
**Brittany Young**

# Silhouette
## Special Edition

EMILY'S HOUSE
**Nikki Benjamin**

ARISTOCRAT
**Catherine Coulter**

KNIGHTLY LOVE
**Billie Douglass**

GEORGIA NIGHTS
**Kathleen Eagle**

SWEET PROMISE
WHERE ANGELS FEAR
**Ginna Gray**

SPECIAL MAN
VOYAGE OF THE NIGHTINGALE
**Billie Green**

FORWARD PASS
**Brooke Hastings**

SARAH'S CHILD
WHITE LIES
**Linda Howard**

A TENDER SILENCE
ONE LAVENDER EVENING
**Karen Keast**

PHOENIX RISING
**Mary Kirk**

PROMISES
**Mary Alice Kirk**

CAPTIVE OF FATE
NO SURRENDER
SOLITAIRE
**Lindsay McKenna**

CRIME OF THE HEART
**Cheryl Reavis**

LOCAL HERO
LOVING JACK
MACGREGOR Series
ONE SUMMER
REFLECTIONS
WILL AND WAY
**Nora Roberts**

SHADOWS IN THE NIGHT
**Linda Turner**

SAFE HARBOR
**Sherryl Woods**

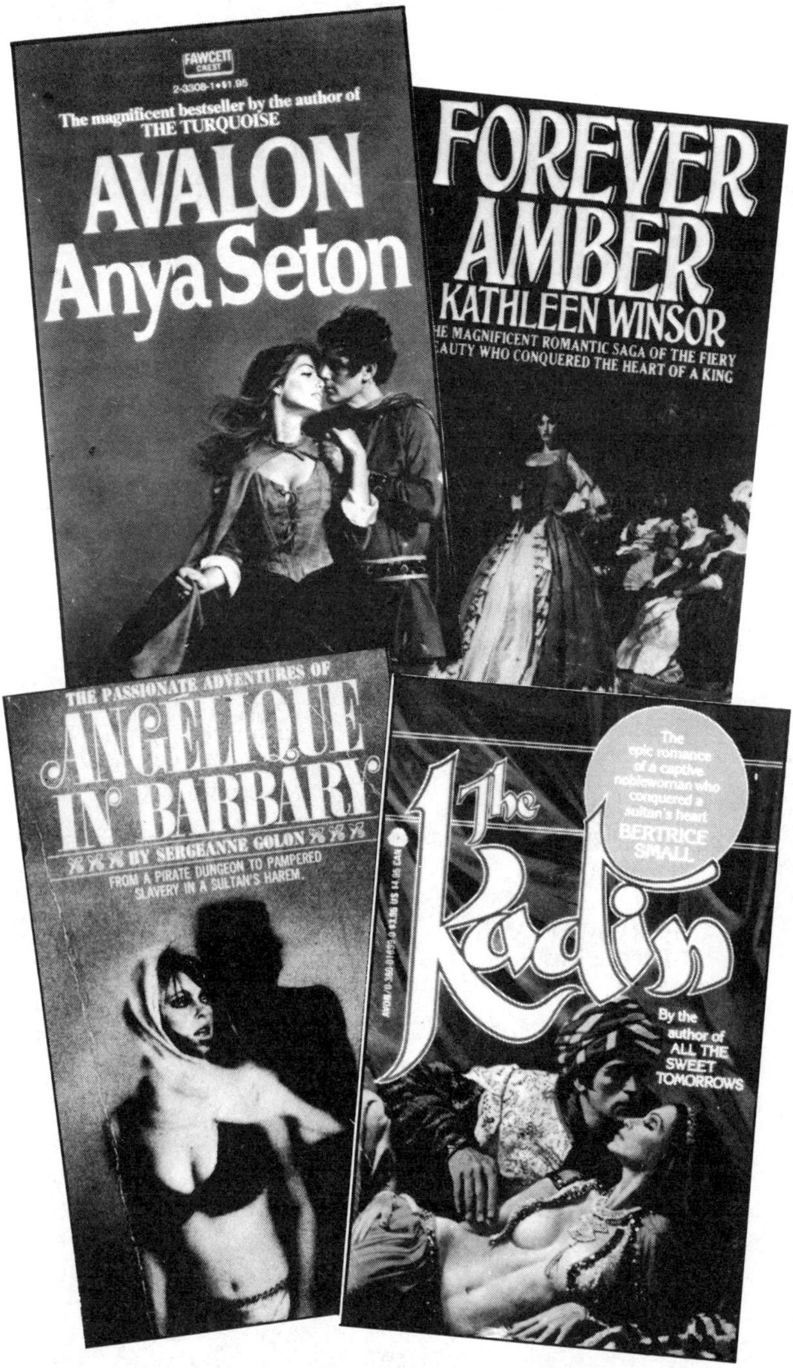
FAWCETT CREST
2-3308-1 • $1.95
The magnificent bestseller by the author of
THE TURQUOISE
AVALON
Anya Seton
FOREVER
AMBER
KATHLEEN WINSOR
HE MAGNIFICENT ROMANTIC SAGA OF THE FIERY
EAUTY WHO CONQUERED THE HEART OF A KING
THE PASSIONATE ADVENTURES OF
ANGELIQUE
IN BARBARY
BY SERGEANNE GOLON
FROM A PIRATE DUNGEON TO PAMPERED
SLAVERY IN A SULTAN'S HAREM.
The epic romance of a captive noblewoman who conquered a sultan's heart
BERTRICE SMALL
The Kadin
By the author of
ALL THE SWEET TOMORROWS

# Classics of Historical Romance

### by Kathe Robin

*L*ong before I became a *Romantic Times* book reviewer, I spent years accumulating a personal collection of my very favorite historical romances. In the early days, the stars on my shelves included Rafael Sabatini, Gwen Bristow, Kenneth Roberts, Frank Yerby, and most of the luminaries on the following list.

These were the books that came along with me on business trips, vacations, and every time I moved. They were always with me.

When avid historical romance readers treasure certain old favorites, we dub them "the Classics."

With this list, I gathered together my own special favorites and came up with these titles, arranged here in alphabetical order by author, as the classics of historical romance.

TAI PAN
**James Clavell**

REBECCA
JAMAICA INN
**Daphne Du Maurier**

ANGELIQUE Series
**Sergeanne Golon**

THE BRIDE OF PENDORIC
**Victoria Holt**

WORLD FROM
ROUGH STONES
**Malcolm Macdonald**

THE THORNBIRDS
**Coleen McCullough**

THE SOURCE
**James Michener**

GONE WITH THE WIND
**Margaret Mitchell**

KATHERINE
GREEN DARKNESS
**Anya Seton**

NINE COACHES WAITING
**Mary Stewart**

EXODUS
**Leon Uris**

FOREVER AMBER
**Kathleen Winsor**

## CONVENTION MEMORIES
### Bermuda, 1988

**ABOVE:** *Romance readers in breathtaking costumes at the 6th annual Booklovers Convention aboard the Nordic Prince, en route to Bermuda.*
*(L to R) Maria Ferrer, Janet Streeter, Jennifer McKnight, Margaret Dear, and Melinda Rommel.*

**RIGHT:** *Sylvie and John Sommerfield as Josephine and Napoleon at the Costume Ball.*

# Historical Romances & Sagas 1987-1989

### by Kathe Robin

*O*ver the past eight years, I have read and reviewed thousands of wonderful books, but only on a select few have I bestowed my highest rating, a 4+. These romances are the best and the brightest of the genre. They are the "keepers"—books that remain a vital and permanent part of a romance reader's library.

It's quite an accomplishment just to get published in today's market. It's an *extraordinary* achievement to write a novel that readers will read, reread and treasure for years to come.

A 4+ historical romance is a rare and special book that not only touches your heart, but tells an uplifting story which brings you a vicarious happiness and joy akin to falling in love for the very first time, but in another era and another place.

The story can be set in prehistoric times, in the years from the Norman conquest to WWII, on the high seas, in an American Indian camp, or on the mountain tops of Tibet.

In a memorable historical romance, you are able to put yourself in the enviable place of the heroine—experience her adventures, see life (and history) through her eyes. Best of all, you fall in love with an unforgettable hero.

This is what makes a book special to this *RT* reviewer. Read on to see the list of some of the romances I have loved, and I hope you will cherish them, too.❤

*Rebecca Brandewyne*

*Judith McNaught*

# Sara Orwig

## ❤ MILLS & BOON
*Camilla* 1981
*Savannah Wedding* 1983

## ❤ MAJOR BOOKS
### Regency
*Runaway Desire* 1978
*Flight to Paradise* 1978

## ❤ HARLEQUIN
### Regency
*The Fairfax Brew* 1983
*Revenge for a Duchess* 1984

## ❤ SUPERROMANCE
#57 *Magic Obsession* 1983
#212 *A Chance in Time* 1986
#241 *Gypsy Fire* 1986

## ❤ NAL
### Historical
*Tides of Passion* 1987
*Sweet Desire* 1988
*San Antonio* 1989
*Albuquerque* 1990
*Denver* 1990

## ❤ WARNER
### Contemporary
*Family Fortunes* 1989
*Favors of the Rich* 1990

## ❤ WALKER
### Hardcover Regency
*A Spy for Love* 1983

## ❤ LOVESWEPT
#18 *Autumn Flames* 1983
#42 *Heat Wave* 1984
#48 *Beware the Wizard* 1984
#58 *Oregon Brown* 1984
#70 *The Midnight Special* 1984
#91 *Calhoun and Kid* 1985
#100 *The Goodies Case* '85
#111 *Dear Mit* 1985
#123 *Under the Ginko Tree* 1986
#132 *The Grass Is Always Greener* 1986
#150 *Hot Tamales* 1986
#171 *Finnegan's Hideaway* 1986
#195 *Wind Warning* 1986
#209 *Visions of Jasmine* 1987
#226 *Out of a Mist* 1987
#248 *Object of His Affection* 1988

---

## ᴬˢ DAISY LOGAN

## ❤ SECOND CHANCE AT LOVE
#50 *Reckless Longing* '82
#138 *Southern Pleasures* 1983
#163 *Sweet Bliss* 1983

For Bookmark send SASE to:
Sara Orwig, P.O. Box 780258, Oklahoma City, OK 73178

# Historical Romances 1987—1989

## 1987

**Elaine Barbieri**
Ecstasy's Trail
*Zebra*

**Lynn Bartlett**
Defy the Eagle
*Worldwide*

**F. Rosanne Bittner**
Frontier Fires
*Popular Library*

**F. Rosanne Bittner**
Prairie Embrace
*Zebra*

**Jennifer Blake**
Louisiana Dawn
*Fawcett*

**Jennifer Blake**
Southern Rapture
*Fawcett*

**Rebecca Brandewyne**
Desire in Disguise
*Warner*

**Joyce Brandon**
The Lady and the Outlaw
*Ballantine*

**Madeline Brent**
The Golden Urchin
*Doubleday*

**Leigh Bristol**
Scarlet Sunrise
*Warner/Popular Library*

**Diana Browning**
All the Golden Promises
*Fawcett*

**Cordia Byers**
Star of the West
*Fawcett*

**Beverly Byrne**
Come Sunrise
*Fawcett*

**Deborah Camp**
Belle Starr
*Crown*

**Virginia Coffman**
Dark Desire
*Warner/Popular Library*

**Catherine Cookson**
Bannaman's Legacy
*Doubleday*

**Susan Coppula**
Winterbourne
*Fawcett*

| | |
|---|---|
| **Celeste De Blasis**<br>The Tiger's Woman<br>*Dell* | **Lisa Gregory**<br>Before the Dawn<br>*Warner* |
| **Jude Deveraux**<br>The Raider<br>*Pocket* | **Pamela Haines**<br>The Golden Lion<br>*Warner* |
| **Shannon Drake**<br>Ondine<br>*Berkley* | **Catherine Hart**<br>Summer Storm<br>*Leisure* |
| **Sandra DuBay**<br>Scarlet Surrender<br>*Leisure* | **Sandra Heath**<br>The Absent Wife<br>*NAL* |
| **Constance O'Day-Flannery**<br>Time-Swept Lovers<br>*Zebra* | **Shirl Henke**<br>Love Unwilling<br>*Warner* |
| **Judith French**<br>Starfire<br>*Avon* | **Victoria Holt**<br>The Silk Vendetta<br>*Doubleday* |
| **Patricia Gallagher**<br>A Perfect Love<br>*Berkley* | **Pamela Jekel**<br>Columbia<br>*Berkley* |
| **Dorothy Garlock**<br>Lonesome River<br>*Warner* | **Carol Jerina**<br>Embrace an Angel<br>*Pocket* |
| **Roberta Gellis**<br>The Fires of Winter<br>*Berkley* | **Laura Kinsale**<br>Uncertain Magic<br>*Avon* |
| **Roberta Gellis**<br>The Rope Dancer<br>*Berkley* | **Ruth Ryan Langan**<br>Destiny's Daughter<br>*Pocket* |
| **Jill Gregory**<br>Moonlit Obsession<br>*Berkley* | **Edith Layton**<br>Love in Disguise<br>*NAL* |
| **Jill Gregory**<br>The Looking Glass Years<br>*Berkley* | **Johanna Lindsey**<br>Hearts Aflame<br>*Avon* |

# LINDA SHAW

*author of*

## Ballad In Blue

*& Award-Winning* **Songbird**

With a decade of romances to her credit, beginning with *Ballad In Blue*, one of the few classic historicals whose charm increases with age, Linda Shaw claims to be one of the best-kept secrets in the history of romance publishing.

Three full-length historicals are under her belt, however: *Ballad In Blue* (Ballantine '79); *The Satin Vixen* (Gallen '81); and *Songbird* (Pocket '87). *Songbird* was voted the Best Post-Civil War Historical of the year by *Romantic Times*, and Best Historical Romance by *Affaire de Coeur*. *An Innocent Deception* is a long contemporary (Gallen '81). Her fifteen Special Editions for Silhouette include *After The Rain*, the popular *Thistle In The Spring, Santiago Heat* and *Thunder High*.

Linda Shaw's determination to build her own career despite successive setbacks resulted in her being the first to ever receive a TRUMP award from *Romantic Times* for outstanding and inspirational achievement in self-promotion.

Being an author isn't the only hat Linda wears. She holds a Bachelor's degree in Music, is the mother of three, grandmother of two, and has been married to her husband, Bennett, for thirty-one years.

*Ballad In Blue*—1979
**Historical, Ballantine**
*The Satin Vixen*—1981
**Historical, Gallen**
*An Innocent Deception*—1981
**Contemporary, Gallen**
*December's Wine*—1982
**Silhouette Special Edition**
*All She Ever Wanted*—1982
**Silhouette Special Edition**
*After The Rain*—1983
**Silhouette Special Edition**
*Way Of The Willow*—1983
**Silhouette Special Edition**
*A Thistle In The Spring*—1983
**Silhouette Special Edition**
*A Love Song And You*—1984
**Silhouette Special Edition**
*The Sweet Rush Of April*—1985
**Silhouette Intl. Moments**
*One Pale, Fawn Glove*—1985
**Silhouette Special Edition**
*Kisses Don't Count*—1985
**Silhouette Special Edition**
*Something About Summer*—1986
**Silhouette Special Edition**
*Fire At Dawn*—1987
**Silhouette Special Edition**
*Santiago Heat*—1987
**Silhouette Special Edition**
*Songbird*—1987
**Historical, Pocket;
Hardcover, Severn House**
*Disarray*—1988
**Silhouette Special Edition**
*Thunder High*—1988
**Silhouette Special Edition**
*Love This Stranger*—July 1989
**Silhouette Special Edition**
*Case Dismissed*—Feb. 1990
**Silhouette Intl. Moments**

I enjoy hearing from readers, booksellers, librarians: 500 Pecan St., Keene, TX 76059. (Include SASE)

**Jacqueline Marten**
Dream Walker
*Pocket*

**Patricia Matthews**
Enchanted
*Worldwide*

**Patricia Matthews**
Tame the Restless Heart
*Bantam*

**Colleen McCullough**
Ladies of Missalonghi
*Harper and Row*

**Megan McKinney**
No Choice But Surrender
*Dell*

**Judith McNaught**
Once and Always
*Pocket*

**Fern Michaels**
To Taste the Wine
*Ballantine*

**Linda Lael Miller**
Wanton Angel
*Pocket*

**Christine Monson**
Surrender the Night
*Avon*

**Constance O'Banyon**
Moontide
*Zebra*

**Leslie O'Grady**
Wildwinds
*NAL*

**Jennifer O'Green**
Royal Captive
*Dell*

**Sheila O'Hallion**
Masquerade of Hearts
*Pocket*

**Sharon Kay Penman**
Here Be Dragons
*Avon*

**Mary Pershall**
Roses of Glory
*Berkley*

**Colleen Quinn**
Daring Desire
*Zebra*

**Alexandra Ripley**
New Orleans Legacy
*Macmillan*

**Francine Rivers**
A Fire in the Heart
*Berkley*

**Karen Robards**
Loving Julia
*Warner*

**Janet Louise Roberts**
My Lady Mischief
*Dell*

**Gina Robins**
Diamond Fire
*Zebra*

**Myra Rowe**
Treasure's Golden Dream
*Warner*

**Nan Ryan**
Desert Storm
*Worldwide*

**Linda Shaw**
Songbird
*Pocket*

**Bertrice Small**
A Love For All Time
*NAL*

**Sylvie Sommerfield**
Catalina's Caress
*Zebra*

**Sylvie Sommerfield**
Moonlit Magic
*Zebra*

**Sylvie Sommerfield**
Elusive Swan
*Zebra*

**LaVyrle Spencer**
The Gamble
*Berkley*

**Frances Patton Statham**
The Roswell Women
*Fawcett*

**Katherine Sutcliffe**
Windstorm
*Avon*

**Patricia Veryan**
Give All To Love
*St. Martin's*

# 1988

**Elaine Barbieri**
Tarnished Angel
*Berkley*

**Jennifer Blake**
Perfume of Paradise
*Fawcett*

**Marsha Canham**
The Pride of Lions
*PaperJacks*

**Theresa Conway**
A Passion for Glory
*Berkley*

**Catherine Coulter**
Calypso Magic
*NAL*

**Jude Deveraux**
The Awakening
*Pocket*

**Julia Fitzgerald**
Taboo
*Bart*

**Constance O'Day Flannery**
Time-Kept Promises
*Zebra*

**Constance O'Day Flannery**
Time-Kissed Destiny
*Zebra*

**Jessie Ford**
A Different Breed
*Ballantine*

**Dorothy Garlock**
Dream River
*Warner*

**Georgina Gentry**
Comanche Cowboy
*Zebra*

**Heather Graham**
Every Time I Love You
*Dell*

**Catherine Hart**
Forever Gold
*Leisure*

**Shirl Henke**
Cactus Flower
*Warner*

**Shirl Henke**
Capture the Sun
*Warner*

**Iris Johansen**
This Fierce Splendor
*Bantam*

**Joan Johnston**
Frontier Woman
*Pocket*

**Joanna Jordan**
Temptation's Darling
*Avon*

**Brenda Joyce**
Firestorm
*Avon*

**Laura Kinsale**
Midsummer Moon
*Avon*

**Lisa Kleypas**
Love, Come to Me
*NAL*

**Jill Marie Landis**
Sun Flower
*Berkley*

**Johanna Lindsey**
Secret Fire
*Avon*

**Johanna Lindsey**
Tender Rebel
*Avon*

**Elizabeth MacDonald**
Falling Star
*Pocket*

**Aileen Malcolm**
Devlyn Tremayne
*Berkley*

**Ellen Tanner Marsh**
Tame the Wild Heart
*Avon*

**Jacqueline Marten**
Forevermore
*Pocket*

**Judith McNaught**
Something Wonderful
*Pocket*

**Linda Lael Miller**
Moonfire
*Pocket*

**Anita Mills**
Fire and Steel
*NAL*

**Christine Monson**
A Flame Run Wild
*Avon*

**Eileen Nauman**
Hostage Heart
*Avon*

**Patricia Potter**
Swampfire
*Harlequin*

**Heather Graham Pozzessere**
Dark Stranger
*Harlequin*

**Maureen Reynolds**
One Golden Hour
*Pageant*

**Eugenia Riley**
Sweet Reckoning
*Warner*

**Karen Robards**
Dark of the Moon
*Avon*

# _Phoebe Conn_

## The name I use is my own

## From Zebra Books:

| | | |
|---|---|---|
| LOVE'S ELUSIVE FLAME | Oct. | '83 |
| SAVAGE FIRE | June | '84 |
| ECSTASY'S PARADISE | Oct. | '84 |
| CAPTIVE HEART | April | '85 |
| SAVAGE STORM | Nov. | '85 |
| LOVING FURY | May | '86 |
| EMERALD FIRE | Jan. | '87 |
| STARLIT ECSTASY | Aug. | '87 |
| ARIZONA ANGEL | April | '88 |
| TENDER SAVAGE | Feb. | '89 |

## From Warner/Popular Library:

| | | |
|---|---|---|
| BEYOND THE STARS | Feb. | '88 |
| HEARTS OF GOLD | Oct. | '88 |
| BY LOVE ENSLAVED | Nov. | '89 |
| IN PASSION'S WAKE | Nov. | '90 |

Correspondence Welcomed. _(SASE Please.)_
P.O. Box 3001
South Pasadena, CA 91030

**Nora Roberts**
Rebellion
*Harlequin*

**Nan Ryan**
Cloudcastle
*Dell*

**Carla Simpson**
Memory and Desire
*Zebra*

**Bertrice Small**
Blaze Wyndham
*NAL*

**Flora Speer**
By Honor Bound
*Leisure*

**LaVyrle Spencer**
Vows
*Berkley*

**Katherine Sutcliffe**
A Heart Possessed
*NAL*

**Katherine Sutcliffe**
Renegade Love
*Avon*

**Becky Lee Weyrich**
The Thistle and the Rose
*Bantam*

# 1989

**F. Rosanne Bittner**
This Time Forever
*Warner*

**Leigh Bristol**
Hearts of Fire
*Warner*

**Janet Young Brooks**
Cinnamon Wharf
*NAL*

**Phoebe Conn**
Tender Savage
*Zebra*

**Lori Copeland**
Sweet Talkin' Stranger
*Dell*

**Susan Coppula**
Shades of Winter
*Fawcett*

**Shannon Drake**
Princess of Fire
*Berkley*

**Dorothy Garlock**
Midnight Blue
*Warner*

**Julie Garwood**
The Bride
*Pocket*

**Georgina Gentry**
Bandit's Embrace
*Zebra*

**Georgina Gentry**
Nevada Nights
*Zebra*

**Heather Graham**
A Pirate's Pleasure
*Dell*

**Karen Harper**
Tame the Wind
*Berkley*

**Deanna James**
Angel's Caress
*Zebra*

**Joan Johnston**
Comanche Woman
*Pocket*

**Brenda Joyce**
Violet Fire
*Avon*

**Elizabeth Kary**
From This Day Onward
*Berkley*

**Betina Krahn**
Passion's Ransom
Passion's Treasure
*Zebra*

**Johanna Lindsey**
Defy Not the Heart
*Avon*

**Ellen Tanner Marsh**
In My Wildest Dreams
*Warner*

**Jan McGowan**
Heart of the Storm
*Pocket*

**Judith McNaught**
A Kingdom of Dreams
*Pocket*

**Linda Lael Miller**
Angel Fire
*Pocket*

**Anita Mills**
Hearts of Fire
*NAL*

**Michalann Perry**
Savage Rogue
*Zebra*

**Patricia Potter**
Seize the Fire
*Harlequin*

**Bertrice Small**
Lost Love Found
*Ballantine*

**Elizabeth Stuart**
Heartstorm
*St. Martin's*

**Katherine Sutcliffe**
Love's Illusion
*NAL*

**Jeanne Williams**
Lady of No Man's Land
*St. Martin's*

*Notes*

# KAREN HARPER

"Karen Harper has the rare talent of creating vivid history and characters, and bringing both to life."

*—Romantic Times*

## Historicals

### Karen Harper
**Berkley/Charter**

The Firelands, October 1990
Eden's Gate, December 1990
Tame the Wind, January 1989
One Fervent Fire, April 1987

**Zebra Books • 1982—1986**

Midnight Mirage, 1985
Rapture's Crown, 1985
Sweet Passion's Pain, 1984
Passion's Reign, 1983
Island Ecstasy, 1982

### As Caryn Cameron
**Harlequin Historicals**

Liberty's Lady, February 1990
Silver Swords, August 1989
Dawn's Early Light, December 1988

*And more to come...*

## Mainstream

Almost Forever, August 1991, Berkley/Charter
1940's glitz, adventure, and romance

---

*Dear Readers and Booksellers,*

Both Karen Harper and Caryn Cameron
would love to hear from you! Write me at my publishers:

The Berkley Publishing Group
200 Madison Avenue
New York, NY 10016

Harlequin Historicals
300 42nd St.
New York, NY 10017

# Golden Oldies of Historical Romance

by Kathe Robin

*O*n the following pages are many of my current "Golden Oldies". The majority are still in print and will be for years to come. I have included some romantic suspense titles, also known as Gothics.

Although the definition of a historical romance is that there is more romance than history, I know that many of you also enjoy the "straight" historicals (those with more history than romance). Therefore, I have also included a list of historical sagas and novels for your perusal.

CAPTIVE ECSTASY
**Elaine Barbieri**

FIRES OF DESTINY
**Linda Barlow**

GENTLE FURY
**Monica Barrie**

COURTLY LOVE
**Lynn Bartlett**

CATHERINE
**Juliette Benzoni**

THE SAVAGE DESTINY
Series
**F. Rosanne Bittner**

FIERCE EDEN
EMBRACE AND CONQUER
LOVE'S WILD DESIRE
SURRENDER IN MOONLIGHT
**Jennifer Blake**

BLUE BAYOU
**Parris Afton Bonds**

LOVE, CHERISH ME
UPON A MOON-DARK MOOR
**Rebecca Brandewyne**

THE LADY AND THE LAWMAN
AFTER EDEN
**Joyce Brandon**

MOONRAKER'S BRIDE
**Madeline Brent**

SUNSET EMBRACE
**Sandra Brown**

GYPSY LADY
LADY VIXEN
WHILE PASSION SLEEPS
THE SPANISH ROSE
**Shirlee Busbee**

SILK AND STEEL
Cordia Byers

NIGHTWYLDE
Kimberleigh Caitlin

THE WIND AND THE SEA
THE PRIDE OF LIONS
Marsha Canham

SURRENDER
Emily Carmichael

THE BELLEROSE BARGAIN
Robyn Carr

PAXTON PRIDE
Shana Carrol

CROWN OF MISTS
Kimberley Cates

MY ENEMY, MY LOVE
Elaine Coffman

VERONIQUE
DARK DESIRES
Virginia Coffman

THE COPELAND BRIDE
Justine Cole

TENDER SAVAGE
CAPTIVE HEART
Phoebe Conn

A PASSION FOR GLORY
Theresa Conway

WINTERBOURNE
Susan Coppula

THE DEVIL'S EMBRACE
THE DEVIL'S DAUGHTER
SWEET SURRENDER
Catherine Coulter

THE CALDER Series
Janet Dailey

THE TIGER'S WOMAN
Celeste De Blasis

THE BLACK LYON
THE ENCHANTED LAND
THE VELVET Series
Jude Deveraux

ONDINE
Shannon Drake

BURN ON SWEET FIRE
Sandra DuBay

REBECCA
JAMAICA INN
Daphne Du Maurier

DESERT HOSTAGE
Diane Dunaway

THE FRENCH PASSION
Diane DuPont

SAVAGE Series
Cassie Edwards

SWEET NEMESIS
Lynn Ericson

CAPTIVE BRIDE
Carol Finch

ROYAL SLAVE
Julia Fitzgerald

TIMELESS PASSION
Constance O'Day Flannery

A DIFFERENT BREED
Jessie Ford

# Dorothy Garlock

*"The undisputed Grand Mistress of the frontier novel"*
—Kathe Robin, *Romantic Times*

## AS **DOROTHY GARLOCK**

**Warner/Popular Library (Historicals)**

Midnight Blue, June 1989
River of Tomorrow
Dream River
Lonesome River
Restless Wind
Wayward Wind
Wind of Promise
Annie Lash
Wild Sweet Wilderness
Forever, Victoria
Glorious Dawn
The Searching Hearts
This Loving Land
Love and Cherish

**Bantam/Loveswept**

A Love for All Time #6
Planting Season #33

## AS **JOHANNA PHILLIPS**

**Berkley/Second Chance at Love**

Gentle Torment  #20
Amber-Eyed Man  #30
Strange Possessions  #43
Hidden Dreams  #125
Passion's Song  #88

## AS **DOROTHY PHILLIPS**

**Dell/Candlelight Ecstasy**

Marriage to a Stranger  #71
Sing Together Softly  #411
She Wanted Red Velvet  #458

## AS **DOROTHY GLENN**

**Silhouette Special Edition**

Sunshine Every Morning  #242

## To My Reader Friends:

*I send you my love, and wish you health, happiness and good eyesight so that you may enjoy many years of good reading.*

*Join in your community's effort to eliminate illiteracy. Help someone to know the joy of reading.*

**Dorothy Garlock
c/o Warner Books
666 Fifth Ave.
New York, NY
10103**

WINDS OF FURY, WINDS OF
FIRE
Rosalind Foxx

CASTLES IN THE AIR
Patricia Gallagher

THIS LOVING LAND
THE COLORADO Series
Dorothy Garlock

HONOR'S SPLENDOR
LYON'S LADY
Julie Garwood

FIONA
SUMMER OF THE
SPANISH WOMAN
Catherine Gaskin

THE ROSELYNDE
Chronicles
BOND OF BLOOD
Roberta Gellis

CHEYENNE CAPTIVE
Georgina Gentry

THE KING'S BRAT
MY LADY BENBROOK
Constance Gluyas

ANGELIQUE Series
Sergeanne Golon

THE CHILD FROM THE SEA
Elizabeth Goudge

GOLDEN SURRENDER
SWEET SAVAGE EDEN
Heather Graham

THE LOOKING GLASS YEARS
WAYWARD HEART
Jill Gregory

BITTERLEAF
THE RAINBOW SEASON
Lisa Gregory

SATAN'S ANGEL
Kristin James

LOVE AND GLORY
Patricia Hagan

PASSION'S REIGN
ONE FERVENT FIRE
Karen Harper

SUMMER STORM
ASHES AND ECSTASY
SILKEN SAVAGE
Catherine Hart

JASMINE ON THE WIND
Mallory Dorn Hart

PASSION'S GAMBLE
Robin Lee Hatcher

SAVAGE DESTINY
Suzanne Hay

CAPTURE THE SUN
TEXAS Trilogy
Shirl Henke

THE CONQUEROR
THE SPANISH BRIDE
Georgette Heyer

MARRY IN HASTE
Jane Aiken Hodge

HUNTER'S MOON
THE DEMON LOVER
Victoria Holt

LOVESTONE
CRIMSON OBSESSION
Deana James

FOX HUNT
Carol Jerina

THIS FIERCE SPLENDOR
Iris Johansen

BLAZE
SILVER FLAME
Susan Johnson

COLTER'S WIFE
DAUGHTERS OF TEXAS
Trilogy
Joan Johnston

HIDDEN FIRES
Laura Jordan

CONQUER THE MEMORIES
SECRETS OF THE HEART
Janet Joyce

A LOVE SO BOLD
BANNER RED AND GOLD
Annelise Kamada

LOVE, HONOR AND BETRAY
Elizabeth Kary

SHIELD OF THREE LIONS
Pamela Kaufman

THE HIDDEN HEART
Laura Kinsale

WHERE PASSION LEADS
Lisa Kleypas

THROUGH A GLASS DARKLY
Karleen Koen

AMBROSIA
Roseanne Kohake

PASSION'S TREASURE
Betina Krahn

SILVERSWEPT
FIREGLOW
Linda Ladd

THE PASSION AND THE GLORY
Lydia Lancaster

SUN FLOWER
Jill Marie Landis

DESTINY'S DAUGHTER
Ruth Ryan Langan

GLYNDA
Susannah Leigh

A ROYAL QUEST
ISOBELLE
Mary Lide

HEART OF THUNDER
A PIRATE'S LOVE
SO SPEAKS THE HEART
CAPTIVE BRIDE
TENDER REBEL
Johanna Lindsey

THE WINDFLOWER
Laura London

THE TAMING
Aileen Malcolm

WRAP ME IN SPLENDOR
TAME THE WILD HEART
SABLE
Ellen Tanner Marsh

DREAM WALKER
Jacqueline Marten

LOVE'S AVENGING HEART
EMBERS OF THE DAWN
TIDES OF LOVE
ENCHANTED
Patricia Matthews

# Myra Rowe

## Pair of Hearts
### Warner Books    August 1989

also from Warner Books:

### *A Splendid Yearning*
### *Treasure's Golden Dream*
### *Cajun Rose*
#### 1987 Reviewer's Choice Award
#### co-author Margie Jordan

#### Zebra Hologram Historicals
### *River Temptress*
### *Louisiana Lady*
### *Wild Embrace*

Hello, readers and booksellers! You're wonderful to write and
send SASE for reply and bookmark. Your letters inspire me,
keep me spinning romances. Thank you--and keep 'em coming!

428 Eastlake, Route #4, Monroe, Louisiana 71203

DEVIL'S DESIRE
TEARS OF GOLD
WHEN THE SPLENDOR FALLS
**Laurie McBain**

BY LOVE DIVIDED
**Jan McKee**

MY WICKED ENCHANTRESS
**Meagan McKinney**

WHITNEY, MY LOVE
ONCE & ALWAYS
SOMETHING WONDERFUL
A KINGDOM OF DREAMS
**Judith McNaught**

GREY GALLOWS
**Barbara Michaels**

CAPTIVE PASSIONS
VIXEN IN VELVET
**Fern Michaels**

BANNER O'BRIEN
WILLOW
**Linda Lael Miller**

LADY OF FIRE
**Anita Mills**

GONE WITH THE WIND
**Margaret Mitchell**

STORMFIRE
A FLAME RUN WILD
**Christine Monson**

DARK SOLDIER
**Katherine Myers**

HOSTAGE HEART
**Eileen Nauman**

HEARTS ENCHANTED
**Penelope Neri**

LADY JADE
THE SECOND SISTER
**Leslie O'Grady**

ROYAL CAPTIVE
**Jennifer O'Green**

MASQUERADE OF HEARTS
**Sheila O'Hallion**

TIDES OF PASSION
**Sara Orwig**

EMERALD & SAPPHIRE
THE ROSE Trilogy
**Laura Parker**

THE ROSE Quartet
**Mary Pershall**

CROCODILE ON
THE SANDBANK
**Elizabeth Peters**

DARK STRANGER
**Heather Graham Pozzessere**

DARING DESIRE
**Colleen Quinn**

ONE GOLDEN HOUR
**Maureen Reynolds**

REBEL IN HIS ARMS
NOT SO WILD A DREAM
**Francine Rivers**

ISLAND FLAME
SEAFIRE
LOVING JULIA
**Karen Robards**

MY LADY MISCHIEF
**Janet Louise Roberts**

REBELLION
**Nora Roberts**

# Janelle Taylor

Award-winning author of 20 bestselling romance novels, including Historical, Fantasy, Contemporary, and Western. She has contributed to other writers' books and published many non-fiction articles.

Married, with two daughters, she lives in Georgia where she often teaches writing at schools and conferences. One of her most popular works is the Gray Eagle "Ecstasy Saga" about a Sioux Warrior. Published in many foreign languages and countries, her American publishers include Zebra, Bantam, and Harlequin.

WALK IN MY SOUL
RIDE THE WIND
**Lucia St. Clair Robson**

SWEET SAVAGE LOVE
THE WILDEST HEART
WICKED LOVING LIES
**Rosemary Rogers**

TREASURE'S GOLDEN DREAMS
**Myra Rowe**

CLOUDCASTLE
SAVAGE HEAT
**Nan Ryan**

DARK INHERITANCE
**Carola Salisbury**

JESSE'S LADY
THE BARGAIN
**Veronica Sattler**

DEFIANT LOVE
THE FLAME ON THE SUN
FORBIDDEN LOVE
REBELLIOUS LOVE
REBELLIOUS DESIRE
**Maura Seger**

DESIREÉ
**Annmarie Selenko**

GREEN DARKNESS
KATHERINE
**Anya Seton**

BALLAD IN BLUE
SONGBIRD
**Linda Shaw**

CAVARAN OF DESIRE
**Eizabeth Shelley**

TO LOVE A ROGUE
**Valerie Sherwood**

THE WIND Series
**June Lund Shiplett**

HOLD FAST TO LOVE
LOVE ONCE IN PASSING
**Jo Ann Simon**

THE KADIN
LOVE WILD AND FAIR
SKYE O'MALLEY Series
**Bertrice Small**

MOONLIT MAGIC
SAVAGE KISS
THE ELUSIVE SWAN
**Sylvie Sommerfield**

THE FULFILLMENT
HUMMINGBIRD
THE GAMBLE
**LaVyrle Spencer**

FLAME OF NEW ORLEANS
**Frances Patton Statham**

THE BLACK EARL
**Sharon Stephens**

HEARTSTORM
**Elizabeth Stuart**

NINE COACHES WAITING
THE MOONSPINNERS
**Mary Stewart**

LOVE'S ILLUSIONS
RENEGADE LOVE
**Katherine Sutcliffe**

THE ECSTASY Series
**Janelle Taylor**

THE WILLIAMSBURG
Series
**Elswyth Thane**

BENEATH THE TEXAS SKY
**Jodi Thomas**

# CASEY STUART

**Reviewer's Choice
Award Winner**

## Moonlight Angel
*Best Civil War Romance*

**WATCH FOR TWO
NEW HISTORICALS
to be released in 1990
from
Bantam Books.**

**A
Contemporary
is also in the
works!**

I enjoy hearing
from readers,
and booksellers.
Send legal size
SASE for
autographed
bookmark.

## Zebra
Releases

| | |
|---|---|
| *Passion's Dream* | 1982 |
| *Waves Of Passion* | 1984 |
| *Moonlight Angel* | 1985 |
| *Passion's Flame* | 1985 |
| *Midnight Thunder* | 1986 |
| *Velvet Deception* | 1987 |
| *Beloved Pirate* | 1988 |
| *Passion's Prisoner* | 1989 |

## Casey
## Stuart
P.O. Box 691
Great Falls, VA
22066

SHINING NIGHTS
WYNDFELL
**Lynda Trent**

NIGHTFIRE
**Valerie Vayle**

FLAMES OF DESIRE
**Katherine Vickery**

SACAJAWEA
**Anna Lee Waldo**

BLADES OF PASSION
CASSANDRA
PASSION'S PRIDE
**Claudette Williams**

A LADY BOUGHT WITH
RIFLES
**Jeanne Williams**

PIECES OF THE SKY
**Maryanne Willman**

FOREVER AMBER
**Kathleen Winsor**

GYPSY MOON
**Becky Lee Weyrich**

THUNDER HEIGHTS
**Phyllis Whitney**

ANGEL IN SCARLET
MIRANDA
**Jennifer Wilde**

THE FLAME AND THE FLOWER
THE WOLF AND THE DOVE
SHANNA
ASHES IN THE WIND
**Kathleen Woodiwiss**

CAROLINE
SPRING FIRES
**Cynthia Wright**

CARESS AND CONQUER
SAVAGE IN SILK
**Donna Comeaux Zide**

# HISTORICAL SAGAS AND NOVELS

CLAN OF THE CAVE BEAR
**Jean Auel**

PASTORA
**Joanna Barnes**

LIGHT A PENNY CANDLE
**Maeve Binchy**

A WOMAN OF SUBSTANCE
**Barbara Taylor Bradford**

THE CAPTAINS AND
THE KINGS
**Taylor Caldwell**

TAI PAN
**James Clavell**

KATIE MULHOLLAND
**Catherine Cookson**

THE MIDWIFE
**Gay Coulter**

AT THE GOING DOWN OF
THE SUN
**Elizabeth Darnell**

THE PROUD BREED
**Celeste De Blasis**

GOD IS AN ENGLISHMAN
**R.F. Delderfield**

# MALLORY DORN HART

*Jasmine On The Wind*

*Defy the Sun*

**Look For**

# Sparklers
### 1990

**A French Historical Set in the Province of Champagne and Russia.**

THE VINES OF YARABEE
Dorothy Eden

RICH IS BEST
Julie Ellis

THE IMMIGRANT
Howard Fast

THE FRENCH
LIEUTENANT'S WOMAN
John Fowles

PROMISES
Catherine Gaskin

THE CACTUS AND THE
CROWN
Catherine Gavin

WEST TO EDEN
Gloria Goldreich

THE DEAN'S WATCH
GREEN DOLPHIN STREET
Elizabeth Goudge

WIDEACRE
Philippa Gregory

ROOTS
Alex Haley

GREAT MARIA
Cecelia Holland

PENMARRIC
Susan Howatch

VERITY
Brenda Jagger

THE KENT FAMILY
Chronicles
John Jakes

AZTEC
Gary Jennings

THE FAR PAVILLIONS
M.M. Kaye

LEGACY
Susan Kay

THROUGH A GLASS
DARKLY
Karleen Koen

QUEENIE
Michael Korda

MISTRAL'S DAUGHTER
Judith Krantz

LION OF IRELAND
Morgan Llewelyan

MADSELIN
Norah Loft

THE WORLD FROM ROUGH
STONES
Malcolm Macdonald

THE THORNBIRDS
Coleen McCullough

ALWAYS TOMORROW
Elizabeth McDonald

HAWAII
THE SOURCE
James Michener

HEIR TO THE KINGDOM
Zoe Oldenburg

THE SUNNE IN SPLENDOUR
Sharon Kay Penman

THE SHELL SEEKERS
Rosamunde Pilcher

# Jean Nash

## SAND CASTLES
Pageant Books
*Nominated in 1988 for
Best Turn-of-the-Century Romance*

## TIES THAT BIND
*(As Jean Sutherland)*
Ballantine Books
*Winner of the 1986
Historical Glitz & Glamour Award*

| **Avon Books** | **Leisure Books** |
|---|---|
| FOREVER, MY LOVE<br>SURRENDER THE HEART<br>GOLDEN RECKONING | THE LAST OF THE LATTIMERS<br>THE SILVER WEB<br>*Volume I*<br>THE GOLDEN THREAD<br>*Volume II* |

Jean Nash
97 Milton Avenue
Nutley, New Jersey 07110
*(Please send SASE for reply)*

| | |
|---|---|
| EVERGREEN<br>Belva Plain | THE MERLIN Trilogy<br>Mary Stewart |
| THE SAVANNAH Quartet<br>Eugenia Price | THE AGONY AND THE<br>ECSTASY<br>Irving Stone |
| INTERVIEW WITH<br>A VAMPIRE<br>Anne Rice | THE WILLIAMSBURG<br>Series<br>Elswyth Thane |
| CHARLESTON<br>Alexandra Ripley | EXODUS<br>Leon Uris |
| LIONHEART<br>Martha Rofheart | THE ETRUSCAN<br>Mika Waltari |
| SARUM<br>Edward Rutherfurd | THE WALSINGHAM WOMAN<br>Jan Westcott |
| AVALON<br>Anya Seton | DOMINA<br>Barbara Woods |
| THE OTHER SIDE OF<br>MIDNIGHT<br>Sidney Sheldon | WINDS OF WAR<br>Herman Wouk |
| THE STORY OF RUTH<br>Frank Slaughter | THE FOXES OF HARROW<br>Frank Yerby |
| AN EXCESS OF LOVE<br>Cathy Cash Spellman | CALL THE DARKNESS LIGHT<br>Nancy Zaroulis |

*Notes*

Bestselling Author of

## After Eden, 1988
## The Lady and the Lawman, 1987
## The Lady and the Outlaw, 1985

### LOOK FOR
**The Lady and the Robber Baron, 1990**
**Adobe Palace, 1991**

# Joyce Brandon
## The Female Zane Grey

**Dear Joyce Brandon,**
   Well, now that I have read both of your books, I find myself torn between the two of them. They are fantastic—vividly descriptive, romantic, and both books had good, interesting plots. I take your book to bed with me and read till my eyes blur and I fall asleep with the book falling on my face. So I guess that should tell you how interesting I find them. I am waiting to get *After Eden*. Believe me, nobody is going to borrow these books as I will read them over and over again and they shall go on *my bookshelf.* Keep up the good writing, and may I wish you much success with *After Eden*.

Sincerely,
**Lulu Carmody,**
**Chico, California**

**Dear Mrs. Brandon,**
   Hi, my name is Meredith. I am 17. I am writing to tell you that I love your books. Your style of writing appeals to me, because it is not sappy or unrealistic.
   Your characters have character. They don't fall to pieces at the drop of a hat. They grow and strive from every experience. They learn to love, hate, kill and forgive. And most important, they heal. They are like real people.
   My mom and teachers say that I learn nothing from romance novels. That I bury myself in books and life is passing me by. But they are wrong. I remember facts from History, everything from the books I read.
   I have learned a lot from your books. I am finally starting to heal. And I realize that everything that has happened to me has built me into what I am today.
   I thank you personally for the time and effort you have put into research and writing of your books. I am looking forward to your next book.

Sincerely,
**Meredith, 17**
**Pasadena, Maryland**

**Dear Ms. Brandon,**
   I have just finished reading your book, *The Lady and the Lawman,* and also *The Lady and the Outlaw.* I just wanted to write and tell you how very much I enjoyed both books. You are such a talented author. Your characters have so much depth and are so believable, and I fell in love with the heroes in both books—and also the heroines.
   I am eagerly awaiting your next book.

Your fan forever,
**Pat Sawada,**
**Sacramento, California**

**Readers can order Joyce's books direct from Preston House Books and Tapes,**
**P.O. Box 25505, Fresno, CA 93729—5505**
*(For a bookmark, please send #10 SASE)*

# GEORGETTE HEYER

## COTILLION

0-515-06026-7/$2.50/A JOVE BOOK

# A TOUCH OF CLASS
# The Regency Romance

### by Melinda Helfer

*O*f all the past eras that figure prominently in historical romance, none has exercised more fascination and enduring appeal than England's Regency period. The dramatic struggle with Napoleon, the glittery decadence of a sophisticated society and the beginning of the industrial revolution all contributed to the unmatchable color and richness of this remarkable timeframe.

In keeping with the tenor of the times, the Regency novel demands much from both author and reader. The rigorous attention to detail required by this often unforgiving sub-genre is well documented: readers have been known to write to authors disputing such minute matters as the height of a saddle's pommel or the actual address of an imaginary residence.

The rewards are equally great. Each reader's discovery of the incomparable Georgette Heyer usually ranks as one of the great moments of life. Read over and over again, this nonpareil's books set the standard for excellence, one which may never be exceeded but is occasionally matched by a select few.

Perhaps the most amazing aspect of Regency fiction is its continuing viability. Just when it appears that everything has been written that could possibly be written, a fresh new voice is heard, an unusual twist is turned, a doorway is opened. Pioneers like **Jo Ann Simon, Mary Balogh, Barbara Hazard, Kasey Michaels, Jane Morgan, Judith McNaught, Carla Kelly, Mary Jo Putney, Anita Mills, Edith Layton, Sheila Simonson, Loretta Lynn Chase, Laura London, Patricia Veryan,** and **Claudette Williams** have kept the genre evergreen fresh.

Here now is the *crème-de-la-crème* of Regency romance.♥

# Regencies

## Regency Historical Romance

BARGAIN
**Veronica Sattler**
*Worldwide*

BEWITCHING MINX
**Janis Laden**
*Zebra*

BLADES OF PASSION
**Claudette Williams**
*Fawcett*

CALYPSO MAGIC
**Catherine Coulter**
*NAL*

CASSANDRA
**Claudette Williams**
*Fawcett*

COPELAND BRIDE
**Justine Cole**
*Dell*

DARING MASQUERADE
**Mary Balogh**
*NAL*

DUEL OF THE HEART
**Sara Blayne**
*Zebra*

FALLEN ANGEL
**Elizabeth Thornton**
*Zebra*

GAME OF LOVE
**Edith Layton**
*NAL*

GUARDED HEART
**Barbara Hazard**
*NAL*

HIDDEN HEART
**Violet Hamilton**
*Zebra*

HIDDEN HEART
**Laura Kinsale**
*Avon*

INDIGO MOON
**Patricia Rice**
*NAL*

LION'S LADY
**Julie Garwood**
*Pocket*

LOVE IN DISGUISE
**Edith Layton**
*NAL*

LOVE ONCE IN PASSING
**Jo Ann Simon**
*Avon*

**Edith Felber
Writing as:**

# EDITH LAYTON

From Onyx Books, New American Library—
## July 1989, THE FIREFLOWER

From Signet Books
The Super Regency "Love Trilogy":

**March 1989, SURRENDER TO LOVE
July 1988, THE GAME OF LOVE
August 1987, LOVE IN DISGUISE**

And

| | | |
|---|---|---|
| October | 1986 | Lady of Spirit |
| June | 1986 | The Indian Maiden |
| October | 1985 | False Angel |
| May | 1985 | The Abandoned Bride (reissued April 1989) |
| Nov. | 1984 | Lord Of Dishonor |
| May | 1984 | Red Jack's Daughter (re-issued Sept. 1986) |
| January | 1984 | The Mysterious Heir (re-issued March 1989) |
| August | 1983 | The Disdainful Marquis (re-issued Dec. 1988) |
| Feb. | 1983 | The Duke's Wager (re-issued Nov. 1986) |

... please look for the forthcoming

Short story: THE DUKE'S PROGRESSION,
in A REGENCY CHRISTMAS
from New American Library, November 1989

and from Berkley Books in 1990
THE GILDED CAGE

**Best wishes,**

**Edith Layton**
P.O. Box 764, Hicksville, N.Y. 11802
(Include SASE for bookmark)

LOVE ONLY ONCE
**Johanna Lindsey**
*Avon*

LOVE'S CHARADE
**Jane Feather**
*Zebra*

LOVING JULIA
**Karen Robards**
*Warner*

MIDNIGHT MASQUE
**Janice Bennett**
*Zebra*

MIDSUMMER MAGIC
**Catherine Coulter**
*NAL*

MIDSUMMER MOON
**Laura Kinsale**
*Avon*

MOONSPUN MAGIC
**Catherine Coulter**
*NAL*

ONCE AND ALWAYS
**Judith McNaught**
*Pocket*

PASSION'S LADY
**Sara Blayne**
*Zebra*

PASSIONATE PRUDE
**Elizabeth Thornton**
*Zebra*

RAKE AND REFORMER
**Mary Jo Putney**
*NAL*

ROGUE'S BRIDE
**Paula Roland**
*Zebra*

SMUGGLER'S LADY
**Jane Feather**
*Zebra*

SOMETHING WONDERFUL
**Judith McNaught**
*Pocket*

SURRENDER TO LOVE
**Edith Layton**
*NAL*

UNCERTAIN MAGIC
**Laura Kinsale**
*Avon*

WHERE PASSION LEADS
**Lisa Kleypas**
*NAL*

WHISPER OF SCANDAL
**Janis Laden**
Zebra

WHITNEY, MY LOVE
**Judith McNaught**
*Pocket*

WINDFLOWER
**Laura London**
*Dell*


## *Regency Romance*

AFTER THE STORM
**Claudette Williams**
*Fawcett*

AIM OF A LADY
**Laura Matthews**
*Warner*

AMICABLE ARRANGEMENT
**Elizabeth Barron**
*Warner*

ARDENT LADY AMELIA
**Laura Matthews**
*NAL*

ARDENT SUITOR
**Mariane Lorraine**
*Dell*

AUNT SOPHIE'S DIAMONDS
**Joan Smith**
*Fawcett*

BAD BARON'S DAUGHTER
**Laura London**
*Dell*

BAR SINISTER
**Sheila Simonson**
*Zebra*

BATH INTRIGUE
**Sheila Walsh**
*NAL*

BELEAGUERED LORD BOURNE
**Michelle Kasey**
*NAL*

BELLIGERENT MISS BOYNTON
**Kasey Michaels**
*Avon*

BLUESTOCKING BRIDE
**Elizabeth Thornton**
*Zebra*

BORROWED PLUMES
**Rosaleen Milne**
*NAL*

BRIDE OF CHANCE
**Lucy Phillips Stewart**
*Dell*

BRIGHTON INTRIGUE
**Emma Lange**
*NAL*

BRIGHTON ROAD
**Susan Carroll**
*Fawcett*

BROKEN VOWS
**Elizabeth Hewitt**
*NAL*

CAPTIVATED COUNTESS
**Barbara Allister**
*NAL*

CHADWICK RING
**Julia Jeffries**
*NAL*

CHANCE ENCOUNTER
**Mary Balogh**
*NAL*

CLERGYMAN'S DAUGHTER
**Julia Jeffries**
*NAL*

COME BE MY LOVE
**Diana Brown**
*NAL*

COMPANION IN JOY
**Dorothy Mack**
*Dell*

CONTROVERSIAL COUNTESS
**Mary Jo Putney**
*NAL*

COST OF HONOR
**Emma Lange**
*NAL*

COUNTERFEIT MARRIAGE
**Joan Wolf**
*NAL*

# Lydia Lee

## Valentino's Pleasure

Silhouette Romance
April 1989

## The Magnificent Mirabelle

Pageant Regency
August 1988

### and writing as Rose Marie Lima...
### The Homeless Heart

Thomas Nelson  Promise Romance 1985

"I love to hear from my readers."
P.O. Box 9432 Arlington, VA  22209

COUNTRY FLIRT
**Joan Smith**
*Fawcett*

DAUGHTER OF FORTUNE
**Dawn Lindsey**
*Bantam*

DEMON COUNT
**Anne Stuart**
*Dell*

DEMON COUNT'S DAUGHTER
**Anne Stuart**
*Dell*

DEVIL'S MATCH
**Anita Mills**
*NAL*

DISDAINFUL MARQUIS
**Edith Layton**
*NAL*

DREADFUL DUKE
**Barbara Hazard**
*NAL*

DUCHESS OF VIDAL
**Dawn Lindsey**
*Playboy*

DUKE'S DILEMMA
**Elizabeth Chater**
*Fawcett*

DUKE'S DOUBLE
**Anita Mills**
*NAL*

DUKE'S WAGER
**Edith Layton**
*NAL*

EARL'S FANCY
**Charlotte Hines**
*Berkley*

EARL'S INTRIGUE
**Elisabeth Todd**
*NAL*

EMERALD DUCHESS
**Barbara Hazard**
*NAL*

EMERALD NECKLACE
**Diana Brown**
*NAL*

ENGLISH WITCH
**Loretta Chase**
Walker/Avon

ESCAPADE
**Joan Smith**
*Fawcett*

ESCAPADE
**Marian Devon**
*Fawcett*

FALSE FIANCEE
**Emma Lange**
*NAL*

FORTUNE HUNTER
**Elizabeth Hewitt**
*NAL*

FORTUNE HUNTER
**Ira Morris**
*Fawcett*

GOLDEN Chronicles
**Patricia Veryan**
*STMS/Fawcet*

GAMESTER
**Elizabeth Chater**
*Fawcett*

GOLDEN THISTLE
**Janet Louise Roberts**
*Dell*

# Julia
# Jay
# Kendall

*Contemporary Romantic
Fiction
Warner Books*

## Memento

*November 1988*

## Portraits

*April 1988*

## writing as Katherine Kingsley...

*Signet Regency*

### Wild Rose
*January 1988*

### Honor's Way
*August 1988*

### A Dishonorable Proposal
*July 1989*

*4236 Bellyache Ridge Road   Wolcott, CO 81655*

GRAY FOX WAGERS
**Martha Powers**
*Fawcett*

GREAT LADY TONY
**Dawn Lindsey**
*NAL*

GYPSY HEIRESS
**Laura London**
*Dell*

HEART TOO PROUD
**Laura London**
*Dell*

HER LADYSHIP'S COMPANION
**Joanne Watkins Bourne**
*Avon*

HEROINE'S SISTER
**Frances Murray**
*Pocket*

HIS LORDSHIP'S MISTRESS
**Joan Wolf**
*NAL*

HONOR'S WAY
**Katherine Kingsley**
*NAL*

HOUSEPARTY
**Anne Stuart**
*Fawcett*

ICE MAIDEN
**Elizabeth Hewitt**
*NAL*

IMPETUOUS TWIN
**Irene Saunders**
*NAL*

INCORRIGIBLE RAKE
**Sheila Walsh**
*NAL*

INDIAN MAIDEN
**Edith Layton**
*NAL*

INDOMITABLE MISS HARRIS
**Amanda Scott**
*NAL*

INTIMATE DECEPTION
**Catherine Coulter**
*NAL*

KIDNAP CONFUSION
**Judith Nelson**
*Warner*

KIND OF HONOR
**Joan Wolf**
*NAL*

LA CASA DORADA
**Janet Louise Roberts**
*Dell*

LACES FOR A LADY
**Irene Saunders**
*NAL*

LADY BRITTANY'S CHOICE
**Amanda Scott**
*NAL*

LADY ELIZABETH'S COMET
**Sheila Simonson**
*Warner*

LADY ESCAPADE
**Amanda Scott**
*NAL*

LADY HAWK'S FOLLY
**Amanda Scott**
*NAL*

LADY JANE
**Norma Lee Clark**
*NAL*

LADY JANE'S RIBBONS
**Sandra Heath**
*NAL*

LADY OF FORTUNE
**Mary Jo Putney**
*NAL*

LADY OF INDEPENDENCE
**Helen Argers**
*Avon*

LADY PAMELA
**Clare Darcy**
*NAL*

LADY SARA'S SCHEME
**Emily Hendrickson**
*NAL*

LADY WHO HATED
SHAKESPEARE
**Susan Carroll**
*Fawcett*

LONDON SEASON
**Joan Wolf**
*NAL*

LORD CLAYBORNE'S FANCY
**Laura Matthews**
*Warner*

LORD HARRY'S FOLLY
**Catherine Coulter**
*NAL*

LORD JOHN'S LADY
**Gayle Buck**
*NAL*

LORD OF DISHONOR
**Edith Layton**
*NAL*

LORD SATAN'S BRIDE
**Anne Stuart**
*Dell*

LORD STEPHEN'S LADY
**Janette Radcliffe**
*Dell*

LORD WRAYBOURNE'S
BETROTHED
**Jo Beverley**
*Walker*

LOVE'S A STAGE
**Laura London**
*Dell*

LURID LADY LOCKPORT
**Kasey Michaels**
*Avon*

LYDIA (LOVE IN TOWN)
**Clare Darcy**
*NAL*

MADALENA
**Sheila Walsh**
*NAL*

MARRIAGE OF
INCONVENIENCE
**Janet Louise Roberts**
*Dell*

MASKED DECEPTION
**Mary Balogh**
*NAL*

MATCH OF THE SEASON
**Susan Gordon**
*Walker*

MATTER OF DUTY
**Sandra Heath**
*NAL*

M'LADY RIDES FOR A FALL
**Marian Devon**
*Fawcett*

MIND OF HER OWN
**Anne MacNeill**
*NAL*

MINERVA'S MARQUESS
**Sheila Walsh**
*NAL*

MINUET
**Jennie Gallant**
*Fawcett*

MISS ARMSTEAD WEARS
BLACK GLOVES
**Marian Devon**
*Fawcett*

MISS CHARTLEY'S
GUIDED TOUR
**Carla Kelly**
*NAL*

MISS ROMNEY FLIES
TOO HIGH
**Marian Devon**
*Fawcett*

MISS RYDER'S MEMOIRS
**Laura Matthews**
*NAL*

MOONLIGHT MIST
**Laura London**
*Dell*

MY LADY MISCHIEF
**Janet Louise Roberts**
*Dell*

NABOB'S WIDOW
**Elsie Lee**
*Dell*

NOTORIOUS MARQUESS
**Marlene Suson**
Fawcett

PERFECT FIANCÉE
**Martha Powers**
*Fawcett*

PINK PARASOL
**Sheila Walsh**
*NAL*

PLAYFUL LADY PENELOPE
**Kasey Michaels**
*Avon*

PRIOR ATTACHMENT
**Dorothy Mack**
*NAL*

PROPER PROPOSAL
**Dawn Lindsey**
*NAL*

PROUD VISCOUNT
**Laura Matthews**
*NAL*

QUEEN OF HEARTS
**Megan Daniel**
*NAL*

RAKE'S PROTEGÉE
**Barbara Hazard**
*NAL*

RAMBUNCTIOUS
LADY ROYSTON
**Kasey Michaels**
*Avon*

RAVENWOOD'S LADY
**Amanda Scott**
*NAL*

REBEL BRIDE
**Catherine Coulter**
*NAL*

REBELLIOUS WARD
**Joan Wolf**
*NAL*

RED ROSE
**Mary Balogh**
*NAL*

RIGHTEOUS RAKEHELL
**Gayle Buck**
*NAL*

SANGUINET Series
**Patricia Veryan**
*Fawcett*

SAVAGE MISS SAXON
**Kasey Michaels**
*Avon*

SCANDAL BROTH
**Marian Devon**
*Fawcett*

SCANDAL IN BATH
**Samantha Holder**
*Warner*

SCANDAL-BOUND
**Anita Mills**
*NAL*

SCANDALOUS PUBLICATION
**Sandra Heath**
*NAL*

SECOND SEASON
**Elsie Lee**
*Dell*

SILVER NIGHTINGALE
**Sylvia Thorpe**
*Fawcett*

SINGULAR MISS
CARRINGTON
**Barbara Hazard**
*NAL*

SIR SHAM
**Marian Devon**
*Fawcett*

SPANISH MARRIAGE
**Madeleine Robins**
*Fawcett*

SPRING GAMBIT
**Claudette Williams**
*Fawcett*

SPY FOR LOVE
**Sara Orwig**
*Walker*

STEADFAST HEART
**Dorothy Mack**
*NAL*

SUITABLE MATCH
**Joy Freemen**
*NAL*

SUMMER CAMPAIGN
**Carla Kelly**
*NAL*

SURFEIT OF SUITORS
**Barbara Hazard**
*NAL*

TEMPORARY HUSBAND
**Barbara Allister**
*NAL*

TENACIOUS MISS
TAMERLAINE
**Kasey Michaels**
*Avon*

TROIKA BELLE
**Ira Morris**
*Fawcett*

TRYSTING PLACE
**Mary Balogh**
*NAL*

UNACCEPTABLE OFFER
**Mary Balogh**
*NAL*

**Camfield Place**
**Hatfield**
**England**

*To My Readers,*

*I send my love and best wishes to all of you.*

*I am so pleased that you have enjoyed my books all these years. Now that many of them are being made into films, I think you'll enjoy watching them too.*

*I hope my romances bring you beauty, joy and love throughout the rest of your life.*

*Affectionately,*

*Barbara Cartland*

Photo of Miss Cartland was taken at the 2nd Romantic Times Booklovers Convention in New York City, in 1983.

# Bookstores
# That Care

# A BOOKSELLER WHO CARES!

*Ann Milenovich (R), owner of two Book Rack stores in Denver, met up with many of her favorite authors at the RT Convention in Phoenix, in 1989. L to R: Kathryn Hockett, Kathryn Kramer, Nora Roberts.*

*Ann (L) with Anita Mills and Julie Garwood.*

# The BTC
# Network

N o one is quite sure how the BTC (Bookstores That Care) network came into being. Like Topsy, it just grew—and blossomed.

Since 1981, copies of *Romantic Times* have been shipped to enterprising bookstore owners directly through our shipping department. Occasionally, the *RT* staff added a newsletter in with these shipments, stuffed with late-breaking stories, and delicious tidbits of gossip. Sometimes, things were far too frantic around here to compose one, and after one of those times, bookseller Ann Milenovich wrote a note to our staff:

"We miss your personal letter with the shipments. A lot of us enjoy hearing the late news—*and* unprintable gossip!"

It finally struck us that we had this growing number of stores out there—and that we should set up more vigorous communication. After all, here was a group of entrepreneurs who cared as much about books as we did. As things expanded, we realized that this system was a wonderful conduit for spreading information, and we began shipping out promotional material and bookmarks along with the regular newsletter, and one thing lead to another.

Now it's hard to imagine *not* being in touch with this friendly bunch who love books and care about authors and readers. We have all appreciated watching our very personal network develop into a respectable and responsible force in paperback publishing.

And it's still growing! New stores join every day. Rewards are given out to readers, a.k.a. romantic sleuths, to find new stores for the network—they're having as much fun with the network as everyone else. And they *all* love their reward—a pile of new books!

The latest joint project between RT and the BTC is the establishment of **BOOKLOVERS DAY** the first Saturday of every November. To help celebrate the fun and pleasure of being a booklover, BTC bookstores hold parties across the nation. In some stores half a dozen or so avid booklovers get together, in other places up to fifty or even a hundred have been known to show up.

## *Suzanne Forster*

## Award-winning Author
## for
## Silhouette Books & Bantam Loveswept

**Dear readers & fellow romantics: Thank you for all your
wonderful letters—and for dreaming my dreams with me!
For a bookmark, send SASE to:**
Suzanne at 8 Summerwind Ct., N.B. CA 92663

---

**LORI HERTER has written for Candlelight,
Ecstasy, Silhouette, Now & Forever.**

**TO MY READERS: Thank you for your letters and support
over the past decade. Please watch for my new VAMPIRE/
Romance series coming soon from Berkley!**

**WRITE ME AT**
**1651 E. Fourth St, #150,
Santa Ana, CA 92701 (SASE)**

## *Lori Herter*

This is the day to celebrate the joy of books and of being fortunate enough to know a friendly, helpful bookstore. It's also fun to know that across the country, from 1 a.m. to 4 a.m., other booklovers will be celebrating, too.

A planned agenda and press kit to distribute to local media is available to all participating stores. It is suggested that booklovers of all genres speak to the gathering. Authors and readers, along with the owner/manager of the bookstore, will report on the state of books and even deliver amusing talks about reading and writing books.

Some owners, readers, and authors will host a brunch beforehand, from 11 a.m.-1 p.m., at a restaurant or community center near their bookstore, for a general meeting with speakers. Afterwards, everyone moves on to the bookstore for the drawing of door prizes, early Christmas book buying, autographing—and more party time!

In Florida, author Sydney Clary, a.k.a. Sarah Chance, has assigned authors in each county to "adopt a store" and set up appearances at their BTC. In Cincinnati, Linda Keller is helping to coordinate events at a large mall. A K-Mart Reader's Market district manager, Karen Ancell in Atlanta, has party plans for some thirteen of her stores!

Any bookstore that wishes to plan a party can receive helpful information about how to hold the event. *RT* will help to track down a local author to adopt a store.

There's not room in this section to list all the BTC stores, chain managers, and even librarians who care. But we continue to compile our listings, so newcomers are welcome to get in touch and be included for the next handbook or bookstore mailing!

Bookstores are wonderful haunts and should be cherished and preserved. Here's Our BTC Motto—❤

# BOOKLOVERS ARE EQUAL.

**N**o author is better than her readers or booksellers.

**N**o reader is better than her authors or booksellers.

**N**o bookseller is better than her readers or authors.

# WE FIGHT FOR WHAT'S WRITE.

# Listing
# By State

### Independents
### & Paperback Exchanges

# Bookstores That Care

## ♥ ALABAMA ♥

The Book Nook
  *Athens*
The Book Rack II
  *Florence*
Book Villa
  *Huntsville*
The Book Shelf
  *Huntsville*
Trade 'N Books
  *Montgomery*
Paperback Trade & Save
  *Tuscaloosa*

## ♥ ARIZONA ♥

Apacheland Book Co.
  *Apache Junction*
Linn's Books & Stuff
  *Mesa*
Little House of Books
  *Phoenix*
Second Time Around Books
  *Phoenix*

## ♥ ARKANSAS ♥

The Bookstop
  *Sherwood*
The Book Nook
  *Fort Smith*
Book Shelf
  *Siloam*

## ♥ CALIFORNIA ♥

The Book Rack
  *Arcadia*
Book Exchange
  *Azusa*
Bell Rose Bookstore
  *Bellflower*
Sunshine Books
  *Buena Park*
Paperback Emporium
  *Canyon Country*
Covina Book Store
  *Covina*
Bell Rose Bookstore
  *Downey*
Romance World
  *El Cajon*
Paperback Exchange
  *Eureka*
Book Barn
  *Folsom*
Book Exchange
  *Fontana*
Hubbard's Books
  *Fountain Valley*
The Book Mark
  *Fremont*
Bob E's Books
  *Hemet*
Book Exchange
  *Hemet*
The Book Nook
  *Lancaster*
The Book Rack
  *Lodi*
The Book Rack
  *Menlo Park*

A Book Garden
*Milpitas*
Paper Chase
*Milpitas*
Book Coral
*Mission Viejo*
Julie's Book Corner
*Modesto*
Genre Books
*Napa*
The Book Nook
*National City*
Jan's Paperbacks
*New Castle*
One For The Books
*Newhall*
Genny's Book Nook
*Newark*
Book Exchange
*Palm Springs*
Nancy's Paperback Exchange
*Paradise*
Village Bookstore
*Riverside*
Books 'N Things
*San Diego*
Yesterday's Paperbacks
*San Jose*
Paperbacks and More
*Santa Rosa*
The Bookworm
*Ukiah*
Linda's Used Books
*Visalia*
Ceil's N.C. Books
*Vista*
Bearly Used Books
*West Covina*
Discount Reader
*Westchester*

❤ COLORADO ❤

Book World
*Colorado Springs*
The Book Rack
*Colorado Springs*

The Book Rack
*Colorado Springs*
The Book Rack
*Denver*
The Book Rack
*Greeley*
The Book Rack
*Loveland*


❤ FLORIDA ❤

B & L Books
*Altamonte Springs*
The Book Stall
*Brandon*
Little Professor Book Center
*Cocoa*
The Book Rack
*Daytona Beach*
The Family Bookshop
*Deland*
Prospect News and Book
*Fort Lauderdale*
The Book Rack
*Fort Lauderdale*
The Book Rack
*Fort Walton Beach*
Jan's Book & Candle
*Holly Hill*
Top Shelf Inc.
*Inverness*
Book Bin
*Jacksonville*
The Book Nook
*Jacksonville*
Book Exchange
*Lake Placid*
The Bookworm
*Lake Worth*
Books of Paiges
*Miami*
Donna's Discount Books
*Miramar*
Paperbacks Ink
*Naranja*

The Book Rack
*Orlando*
Book Bin
*Orange Park*
Bee Ridge Books
*Sarasota*
Little Professor Book Center
*Satellite Beach*
Donna's Books
*Seffner*
The Book Fair
*Spring Hill*
Wilson's Bookstore
*St. Petersburg*
The Book Rack
*Stuart*
The Paperback Shop
*Tampa*
Maida's Bookstore
*Tampa*
Bobbe's Books
*Warrington*
Chapter I Bookstore
*W. Melbourne*

## ❤ GEORGIA ❤

Family Reading Service
*Albany*
The Booke Shoppe
*Albany*
A Book Nook
*Atlanta*
The Book Cellar
*Clarkesville*
Book Mark
*Columbus*
Books Etc.
*Conyers*
Kendall's Books
*Decatur*
The Book Mark
*Manchester*
Gwen's Paperbacks
*Snellville*

## ❤ HAWAII ❤

The Book Rack
*Honolulu*

## ❤ IDAHO ❤

The Bookworm
*Idaho Falls*

## ❤ ILLINOIS ❤

The Book Rack
*Buffalo Grove*
Exchange A Book
*Calumet City*
The Bookworm
*Decatur*
Treasure Trove Book Store
*E. Alton*
Reader's Heaven
*Elgin*
Polly's Paperback Exchange
*Fairview Heights*
Books & Company, Inc.
*Marion*
Book Market Paperback Sales
*Melrose Park*
Paperback Trading Co.
*Palos Heights*
Fran's Book Exchange
*Richton Park*
Scotland Yard Books
*Winnetka*

## ❤ INDIANA ❤

The Bookshelf
*Batesville*
The Bookstore
*Bloomington*
Carolyn's Bookstore
*Columbus*
The Book Exchange
*Fort Wayne*

The Bookworm
*Huntington*
Book Worlds
*Indianapolis*
The Book Rack
*Indianapolis*
The Paperback Shoppe
*Indianapolis*
The Book Rack
*Plainfield*

❤ IOWA ❤

Paperbacks Plus
*Dubuque*
The Book Exchange
*Waterloo*

❤ KANSAS ❤

Rainy Day Books
*Kansas City*
The Book Nook
*Wichita*

❤ KENTUCKY ❤

The Book Stop
*Erlanger*
Little Professor Bookstore
*Frankfort*
The Book Barn
*La Grange*
A Thousand and One Paperbacks
*Louisville*
Prescott Books
*Newport*

❤ LOUISIANA ❤

The Book Exchange II
*Baton Rouge*

The Book Mart
*Baton Rouge*
The Book Store
*Bogalusa*
Book Exchange #5
*Metairie*
Paperback Exchange
*Monroe*
The Book Rack
*Monroe*
The Book Mark
*Morgan City*
Donna's Bookstore
*West Monroe*

❤ MAINE ❤

Annie's Book Stop
*Auburn*

❤ MASSACHUSETTS ❤

The Book Exchange
*Ashland*
Annie's Book Stop
*Framingham*
Olde Methuen Bookshop
*Methuen*
The Paperback Exchange
*Milford*
Annie's Book Stop
*N. Dartmouth*
Annie's Book Stop
*Plainville*

❤ MARYLAND ❤

The Book Rack
*Cockeysville*
Greetings & Readings
*Towson*
The Paperback Exchange
*Westminster*

Annie's Book Stop
*Groton*

## ❤ MICHIGAN ❤

The Book Bank
*Allen Park*
Paperback Trade Inn
*Clawson*
Just Paperbacks
*Drayton Plains*
The Hill Shop
*Flint*
The Book Stop
*Highland*
Books Connection
*Livonia*
Non Stop Book Swap
*Marysville*
Village Paperback Exchange
*Plymouth*
Carol's Paperbacks Plus
*Pontiac*
The Book Stop
*Riverview*
The Book Exchange
*Royal Oak*
Phyl's Bookmark
*Saginaw*
Mister Jack's
*Stevensville*
Trenton Book Store
*Trenton*
Paperback Outlet II
*Utica*
Paperbacks and Things
*Westland*

## ❤ MINNESOTA

Trading Wins Paper Back Exchange
*Elk River*
Booked Solid
*Fridley*
Paperback Exchange
*Minneapolis*
Books Plus
*Osseo*

## ❤ MISSISSIPPI ❤

The Book Swap Shop
*Greenville*
The Book Rack
*Madison*
Pat's Book Barter
*McComb*
The Book Rack
*Tupelo*

## ❤ MISSOURI ❤

Paperbacks Etc.
*Ballwin*
White Oaks Books
*Blue Springs*
Annie's Book Stop
*Chesterfield*
Nancy's Trade-A-Book
*Columbia*
Rainy Day Books
*Independence*
Nancy's Trade-A-Book
*Jefferson City*
The Book Exchange
*Odessa*
The Armchair Adventurer
*St. Charles*
Bookmark, Inc.
*St. Charles*
The Book Store
*St. Louis*
Chapter One Books
*St. Louis*

## ❤ NEBRASKA ❤

Paperback Exchange
*Omaha*

## ❤ NEVADA ❤

The Book Round-Up
*Henderson*

Readers Delight Books
*Las Vegas*


💛 NEW HAMPSHIRE 💛

Fact & Fiction Books
*Exeter*
The Dartmouth Bookstore
*Hanover*
Annie's Book Stop
*Manchester*
Annie's Book Stop
*Nashua*
Carey's Book Store
*Plaistow*


💛 NEW JERSEY 💛

The Book Swapper
*Chester*
Linda's Book Exchange
*Cranford*
Paperback Trader
*Fairlawn*
Paperback Book Exchange
*Newton*
Paperback Reader Exchange
*Silverton*
The Book Trader
*Spotswood*
Book Swap
*Willingboro*


💛 NEW YORK 💛

The Bookshop
*Bayside*
Paperback Rider
*East Islip*
Jackson Heights Discount Books
*Jackson Heights*
The Book Loft
*New City*
Bookie's
*Patchogue*

Recycled Reading Shop
*Rhinebeck*
Book Thrift
*Rome*


💛 NORTH CAROLINA 💛

Luci's Book Nook
*Arden*
Book Trader
*Charlotte*
The Book Rack
*Gastonia*
The Book Exchange
*Hickory*
The Book Trader
*Kannapolis*
Books 'n Stuff
*Long Beach*
Browse About
*North Wilkesboro*
Book Exchange CenterInc.
*Sanford*


💛 NORTH DAKOTA 💛

The Book Fair
*Grand Forks*


💛 OHIO 💛

Nancy's Paperbacks
*Canton*
The Book Rack
*Cincinnati* (6 locations)
Paperback Exchange
*Columbus*
Wilkie News
*Dayton*
Book Mark II
*Dayton*
I Love Paperbacks
*Dayton*
Wright News & Books
*Dayton*

The Book Nook
  *Eaton*
Cover to Cover
  *Huber Heights*
Second-Hand Prose Books
  *Mentor*
The Paperback Place
  *Middleton*
Paperback Shack
  *Niles*
The Book Rack
  *North Olmstead*
Book Haven
  *Parma Heights*
Munchkin Book Shop
  *Swanton*
The Book Nook
  *Warren*
Toots Book Emporium
  *Westerville*
The Book Corner
  *Willoughby*


## ❤ OKLAHOMA ❤

The Book Rack
  *Edmond*
The Book Inn
  *Kingston*
The Book Rack
  *Midwest City*
The Book Nook
  *Oklahoma City*
The Book Rack
  *Oklahoma City*
The Book Rack II
  *Oklahoma City*
The Book Rack
  *Tulsa*


## ❤ OREGON ❤

Gresham Book Exchange
  *Gresham*
Clackamas Book Exchange
  *Milwaukie*

Laurie's Paperback Exchange
  *Oregon City*


## ❤ PENNSYLVANIA ❤

Books 'N More
  *Allentown*
Kline's Paperback Exchange
  *Butler*
Adamaszek's Book Nook
  *Corry*
Book Trade
  *Monaca*
Nancy's Fireside Book Exchange
  *McMurray*
The Book Rack
  *New Castle*
Books In A Barn
  *Nicholson*
Paperbacks Trade & Save
  *Pittsburgh*
The Book Rack
  *Sharon*
The Book Rack
  *Warren*
Paperback Trade
  *York*


## ❤ RHODE ISLAND ❤

Marie's Book Shoppe
  *Warwick*
Mary's Book Exchange
  *Warwick*


## ❤ SOUTH CAROLINA ❤

The Paperback Trader
  *Charleston*
Dee's Book Worm
  *Greenwood*
Book Exchange
  *Summerville*

## ❤ TENNESSEE ❤

The Book Mart
*Athens*
Book Stop Plus
*Barlett*
Book Trader
*Charlotte*
The Bookworm
*Hermitage*
The Book Exchange
*Hickory*
The Book Nook
*Jackson*
The Book Trader
*Kannapolis*
The Book Rack (2 locations)
*Memphis*
Village Book Store
*Memphis*
Book End
*Memphis*
The Book Case
*Memphis*
Book Shop Maybe?
*Nashville*

## ❤ TEXAS ❤

Donna's Book Stop
*Amarillo*
Magazine Book Exchange
*Amarillo*
Hastings Book & Records
*Amarillo*
The Book Rack
*Arlington*
The Book Exchange
*Austin*
The Book Rack
*Beaumont*
Judy's Paperback Books
*Brenham*
Carrollton Book Center
*Carrollton*

Bell's Books
*Dallas*
Pauline's Book Store
*Deer Park*
Simpson's Books
*Denison*
De Soto Book Store
*De Soto*
The Book Marker
*Fort Worth*
Books 'N Stuff
*Garland*
The Book Shelf
*Grand Prairie*
Book Shack
*Houston*
Paperback Trader
*Houston*
Paperback Exchange II
*Houston*
Dusty's Books
*Houston*
Katy Budget Books
*Houston*
Bender Square Books
*Humble*
The Bookshelf
*Lancaster*
Book Shelf
*Longview*
The Book Rack
*Lubbock*
Paperback Plus
*Mesquite*
The Book Rack
*North Richland Hills*
Re Run Books
*Pasadena*
GFI (Go For It) Books!
*Pearland*
The Book Rack
*Plano*
The Book Mark
*Richardson*
The Book Rack
*Sherman*
Paperback & Magazine Exchange
*Spring*

*Spring*
The Book Inn
*Tyler*
Second Chance Books
*Victoria*
The Book Rack
*Webster*
Reader's Paradise
*West Orange*


## ❤ UTAH ❤

The Book Attic
*Midvale*
Court's Book Exchange
*Spanish Fork*
Paperback Trader
*West Valley City*


## ❤ VIRGINIA ❤

Paperbacks Ink
*Newport News*


## ❤ WASHINGTON ❤

The Bookworm
*Kennewick*
Neppel Book Co.
*Moses Lake*
The Book Rack
*Oak Harbor*
J. & D. Bookswap

*Oak Harbor*
Paperback Plus
*Pt. Orchard*
Monohon's Paperbacks
*Tacoma*


## ❤ WISCONSIN ❤

The Book Store
*Appleton*
The Book Shop
*Green Bay*
The Book Nook
*Manitowoc*
Aardvark Bookstore
*Middleton*
The Book Store
*Sheboygan*
The Book Exchange
*Sturgeon Bay*
Pic-A-Bac
*Waukesha*
The Book Trader
*West Allis*


## ❤ WYOMING ❤

Book Nook
*Casper*
Ralph's Books & Cards
*Casper*
The Book Rack

---

## THE BOOKSTORES THAT CARE
welcome you to their
establishments to browse, buy, and discuss
every booklover's favorite subject—good books!
There are many more BTC stores in the United States,
but space in this handbook is limited.
More names will be included in the next RT Handbook.

# Directory
# for
# Traveling
# Booklovers

## ALABAMA

**Paperbacks Trade & Save—**
Cindy Agee
Bama Mall
2600 McFarland Blvd. E.
Tuscaloosa, AL 35405
205/758-3979—Near Birmingham
M-S,10-9/Sun,1-5
MC & Visa, 25% Romance
New & Used
*Loves photos, newsletters,*
*bookmarks (25-50), posters*

## CALIFORNIA

**Paper Chase Used Books—**
Marian Des Rochers
76 S. Dempsey Rd.
Milpitas, CA 95035
408/946-5944—Near San Jose
M-F,11-7/Sat,10-6
No CC, 35% Romance, Used
*Loves photos, newsletters,*
*bookmarks (20), posters*

**Paperbacks & More—**
Carolyn Stites & Minnie Coates
443 Stony Point Rd.
Santa Rosa, CA 95401
707/527-8214—Near San Francisco
M-F,10-6/Sat,9:30-5:30
No CC, 40% Romance, Used
*Loves photos, newsletters,*
*bookmarks (50-60), posters*

> You can send bookmarks &
> publicity material to these
> stores and hundreds of
> others with RT's shipments
> of magazines each month.

**Bearly Used Books—**
Michelle Thorne
1013 South Glendora Ave.
West Covina, CA 91790
818/338-1939—Near LA
M-F,11-6/Sat,10-6/Sun,12-5
No CC, 45% Romance
New & Used
*Loves bookmarks (75), posters*

**Jan's Paperbacks—**
Janice Lucas
1205 Grass Valley Hwy.
Auburn, CA 95603
and
4877 Granite Dr.
Rocklin, CA 95677
916/885-3170 & 624-4363
Near Sacramento
M-F,10-5/Sat,10-4/Sun,12-4
No CC, 33% Romance
New & Used
*Loves bookmarks (6), posters*

**Books 'N Things—**
Hedy Ladek
7089 Navajo Rd.
San Diego, CA 92119
619/462-4200
M-F,10-6/Sat,9:30-5:30
No CC, 25% Romance
New & Used
*Loves bookmarks (25), posters*

**The Book Rack—**
Charlotte Brewer
1373 Lakewood Mall
Lodi, CA 95242
and
6285 Pacific Ave.
Stockton, CA 95207
209/368-6947 & 477-0735
Near Sacramento
M-S,10-7/Sun,1-5
MC & Visa, 60% Romance
New & Used
*Loves bookmarks (50), posters*

**Book Barn—**
Charlotte Wager
335 A E. Bidwell St.
Folsom, CA 95630
916/983-7006—Near Sacramento
M-S,10-5
No CC, 60% Romance
New & Used
*Loves boomarks (25-50), posters*

**Paperback Emporium—**
Janie Kopecky
18918 Soledad Canyon Rd.
Canyon Country, CA 91351
805/251-4508—Near LA
T-F,10-5:30/Sat,10-5
No CC, 33% Romance, Used
*Loves photos, newsletters,*
*bookmarks (25), posters*

**Hubbard's Books—**
9475 Heil Ave.
Fountain Valley, CA 92708
No CC, 35% Romance, Used
*Loves bookmarks (25)*

**Book Corral—**
Barbara Koneski
25571 Jeronimo Rd. #9
Mission Viejo, CA 92691
714/855-8054—Near LA
M-F,10-5/Sat,10-6/Sun,12-5
No CC, 33% Romance
New & Used
*Loves bookmarks (25), posters*

**Bob E's Books—**
Bob Ella Evans & Michell Kenny
475B W. Stetson
Hemet, CA 92343
714/652-9021—2 hrs. E. of LA
M-S,9:30-5
No CC, 50% Romance, Used
*Loves bookmarks (35), posters*

**FLORIDA**

**Bobbe's Books—**
Bobbe Kochinski
611 New Warrington Rd.
Pensacola, FL 32506
904/455-4424—1 hr. from Mobile
M-S,10-5
No CC, 20% Romance
New & Used
*Loves photos, newsletters,*
*bookmarks (25), posters*

**The Paperback Shop—**
Nita Suarez
1824 W. Waters Ave.
Tampa, FL 33604
813/932-9082
M-S,9-5
No CC, 50% Romance
New & Used
*Loves bookmarks (100), posters*

***Bobbe Kochinski of Pensacola, Florida, loves romances.***

*Melva Bailey of The Book Rack in Daytona Beach has added a second store to her site.*

**The Book Rack—**
Melva Bailey
1132-C Beville Rd.
Daytona Beach, FL 32014
904/258-7816
M-S,9:30-5:30
No CC, 50% Romance
New & Used
*Loves bookmarks (50), posters*

**Paperbacks Ink—**
Rosemary Van Allen
27435 S. Dixie Hwy.
Naranja, FL 33032
305/248-9868—Near Miami
M-S,10-8/Sun,12-5
MC, Visa, AE, 50% Romance New & Used
*Loves newsletters, bookmarks (40)*

**Family Bookshop—**
Judy Murray
1301 N. Woodland Blvd.
Deland, FL 32720
904/736-6501—Near Daytona
M-S,10-6
No CC, 20% Romance
New & Used
*Loves newsletters, posters*

**Bee Ridge Books—**
Dot Youngblood & Fran Allgaier
4104 Bee Ridge Road
Sarasota, FL 34233
813/377-8998—Near Tampa
M-S,9:30-5
No CC, 60% Romance
New & Used
*Loves bookmarks (15), posters*

**The Book Stall—**
Claire Jones & Helen Gergulis
606 Oakfield Dr.
Brandon, FL 33511
813/685-8402—Near Tampa
M-F,9:30-6/Sat,9:30-5:30
No CC, 65% Romance
New & Used
*Loves bookmarks (20), posters*

**Book Exchange—**
Vicky Spires
206B Interlake Blvd.
Lake Placid, FL 33852
813/465-7774—Near Tampa
M-F,9-5/Sat,9-1
No CC, 60% Romance
New & Used
*Loves bookmarks (12), posters*

**Wilson's Bookstore—**
Jeff Morris
2394 9th St. N.
St. Petersburg, FL 33704
813/896-3700
M-F,9:30-6/Sat,9:30-4:30
Visa, MC, 40% Romance
New & Used
*Loves bookmarks (25), posters*

**B & L Books—**
Janice Joyce
(New location beginning Oct.,'89)
State Rd. 434, Jamestown Blvd.
Altamonte Springs, FL 32714
407/682-0090
M-S,10-5
No CC, 60% Romance
New & Used
*Loves newsletters,
bookmarks (20), posters*

**The Book Rack—**
Virginia and Fred Darnell
2703 E. Commercial Blvd.
Fort Lauderdale, FL 33308
305/771-4310
M-S,9-6/Sun,12-5
No CC, 40% Romance
New & Used
*Loves  bookmarks (25), posters*

*In Joliet, Illinois, readers head
for The Book Market Paperback
Sales & Trading Center, owned
by Jan Staley.*

**GEORGIA**

**A Book Nook—**
Joseph Nunan & Steven Leaf
3342 Clairmont Rd.
Atlanta, GA 30329
404/633-1328—Near Atlanta
M-S,9-10:30/Sun,10-10
No CC, 20% Romance
New & Used
*Loves bookmarks (75), posters*

**IDAHO**

**Bookworm—**
K. J. Gordon
1515 Northgate Mile
Idaho Falls, ID 83401
208/522-1162
M-F,10-9/Sat,10-7/Sun,12-5
No CC,70% Romance
New & Used
*Loves bookmarks (100), posters*

**ILLINOIS**

**The Book Market Paperback
Sales & Trading Center—**
Jan & Gary Staley
1157 W. Jefferson
Joliet, IL  60435
815/744-4240—Near Joliet
M-W,F,10-6/Sat,10-5
MC, Visa, 60% Romance
New & Used
*Loves bookmarks (125), posters*

**Sandpiper Books—**
Ronald Budovec
185 E. Lake St.
Bloomingdale, IL 60108
312/ 980-3199—Near Chicago
M-F,10-6/Sat,10-5
Visa, MC, 50% Romance
New & Used
*Loves photos, newsletters,*
*bookmarks (100-200), posters*


**The Book Rack—**
Lillian Pitlik & Diana Barred
213 W. Dundee
Buffalo Grove, IL 60089
312/537-6633—Near Chicago
M-F,10:30-6/Sat,10:30-6
No CC, 40% Romance
New & Used
*Loves photos, newsletters,*
*bookmarks (12-24), posters*


**Book Market Paperback Sales**
**& Trading Center—**
Bill & Virginia Linzmeier
11138 W. Grand Ave.
Melrose Park, IL 60164
312/455-4456—Near Chicago
T-F,10-6/Sat,10-5
No CC, 60% Romance
New & Used
*Loves photos, newsletters,*
*bookmarks (10-25), posters*

**Paperback Peddler—**
Richard Christian
975 Aurora Ave.
Aurora, IL 60505
312/897-6622—Near Chicago
M-F,10-6/Sat,10-5/Sun,12-4
Visa, MC, 50% Romance
New & Used
*Loves bookmarks (50), posters*


**The Book Mark—**
Mary Harrison & Lora Grogan
Rend Lake Plaza
West City, IL 62812
618/439-4525—Near St. Louis
M-S,9-9 /Sun,12-6
Visa, MC, 50% Romance, New
*Loves newsletters,*
*bookmarks (50), posters*


**The Paperback Trading Co.—**
Ruth & Larry Kuhn, Jean Gnap
6531 W. 127 St.
Palos Heights, IL 60463
312/371-2540—Near Chicago
M-S,10-6/Sun,12-4
 and
8825 So. Ridgeland
Oak Lawn, IL 60453
312/598-8442—Near Chicago
M-S,10-5:30
No CC, 40% Romance
New & Used
*Loves bookmarks (36), posters*

*Virginia*
*Linzmeier*
*has every-*
*thing for the*
*romance*
*reader in her*
*Melrose*
*Park, Illinois,*
*Book Market.*

## INDIANA

**The Paperback Shoppe—**
Ray & Jenny Walton
6800 Pendleton Pike
Indianapolis, IN 46226
317/547-3959
M-S,10-6/Sun,12:30-4:30
No CC, 30% Romance
New & Used
*Loves bookmarks (50), posters*

**The Book Store—**
Mary Holmes
1042 W. 17th St.
Bloomington, IN 47401
812/336-4697—Near Indianapolis
M-F,9:30-5:30/Sat,10-5
No CC, 60% Romance
New & Used
*Loves bookmarks (20), posters*

**Book World—**
James Terrell
2206 E. 10th St.
Anderson, IN 46012
312/642-0776
M-S,10-5/Sun,12-4
  and

7775 E. Washington St.
Indianpolis, IN 46219
317/359-0099
M-S,10-5/Sun,10-5
No CC, 40% Romance
New & Used
*Loves bookmarks (20), posters*

**Carolyn's Bookstore —**
Carolyn Stouder
3116 20th St.
Columbus, IN 47201
812/372-7823
M-S,10:30-5:30/closed W
No CC, 75% Romance
New & Used
*Loves bookmarks (100), posters*

## IOWA

**Book Exchange—**
Kathy Newlon
325 E. 4th St.
Waterloo, IA 50703
319/291-2163
M-F,10-4/Sat,10-12
No CC, 60% Romance
New & Used
*Loves bookmarks (100), posters*

*Cars line up at Helen Gipson's store —she keeps the Baton Rouge, Louisiana, romance readers happy at her haven for serious collectors.*

(L to R) *Chiri Shelley, manager, and Georgette Fraser, owner, of The Book Rack in Cockeysville, Maryland.*

## LOUISIANA

**The Book Mart—**
Helen Gipson
13519 Hooper Rd.
Baton Rouge, LA 70818
504/261-8017—Nr. New Orleans
M-S,9:30-6
MC, Visa, 70% Romance
New & Used
*Loves bookmarks (20), posters*

## MARYLAND

**The Book Rack—**
Georgette Fraser
12 Scott Adam Rd.
Cockeysville, MD
301/667-6897—Near Baltimore
M-F,10-5/Sat,9:30-5
No CC, 40% Romance
New & Used
*Loves bookmarks (50), posters*

## MASSACHUSETTS

**Annie's Book Stop—**
Eleanor Arnold
9 Manmar Drive,
Plainville, MA 02762
508/695-2396—Near Providence
M-S,10-6/Sun,10-2
No CC, 45% Romance, Used
*Loves bookmarks (20), posters*

**Paperback Exchange—**
Maggie Easler
136 Main St., Milford, MA 01757
508/473-0642—Nr. Framingham
T-F,9-5:30/Sat,9-2
No CC, 45% Romance, Used
*Loves bookmarks (50), posters*

**Annie's Book Stop—**
Dale Cole
Nobscot Shopping Center
883 Edgell Road
Framingham, MA 01701

*Dale Cole owns Annie's Book Stop in Framingham, Massachu-setts— a great haven for readers.*

*Kerene Seratzki's wonderful store, Booked Solid, in friendly Fridley, Minnesota, has rows and rows of romances.*

508/877-1891—Near Boston
M-F,10-6/Sat,9-5/Sun,12-5
Visa, MC, 30% Romance
New & Used
*Loves bookmarks (75), posters*

## MICHIGAN

**Just Paperbacks—**
Mary Wright
4500 Dixie Hwy.
Drayton Plains, MI 48020
313/673-1859—Near Detroit
M-F,9:30-5:30/Sat,10-4
Visa, MC, AE, 70% Romance
New & Used
*Loves bookmarks (100), posters*

**Paperbacks & Things—**
Joan Adis
8044 Wayne Rd.
Westland, MI 48185
313/522-8018—Near Livonia & Dearborn
M-S,9:30-8:30/Sun,12-5
No CC, 60% Romance
New & Used
*Loves bookmarks (50), posters*

## MINNESOTA

**Booked Solid—**
Kerene Seratzki
6578 University Ave., N.E.
Fridley, MN 55432
612/574-9218—Near Minneapolis
M-F, 11-8/Sat, 10-5
No CC, 75% Romance
New & Used
*Loves bookmarks (50), posters*

**Paperback Exchange—**
Diane Kitterman
2227 W. 50th
Minneapolis, MN 55419
612/929-8801
M-F,10-5:30/Sat,10-4
No CC, 30% Romance, Used
*Loves bookmarks (5), posters*

**Books Plus—**
Bonnie & Don Niles
213 Central Ave.
Osseo, MN 55369
612/424-4122—Near Minneapolis
M-F,9:30-5:30/Sat,9-5
Visa, MC, 45% Romance
New & Used
*Loves bookmarks (50), posters*

*Nancy Zlotek, owner of Annie's Book Stop in Nashua, New Hampshire, welcomes all readers on their travels.*

## MISSOURI

**Rainy Day Books—**
W.K. Jennings
4201 H. So. Noland Rd.
Independence, MO 64055
816/373-9169—Near Kansas City
M-F,9-8/Sat,9-6/Sun,12-5
MC, Visa, 45% Romance
New & Used
*Loves newsletters,
bookmarks(50), posters*

**Annie's Book Stop—**
Dee Dee Ahearn
13457 Alive At Woodsmill
Chesterfield, MO 63017
314/878-2688—Near St. Louis
M-F,10-6/Sat,10-5/Sun,12-5

No CC, 33% Romance
New & Used
*Loves newsletters,
bookmarks (10), posters*

**Nancy's Trade-A-Book—**
Nancy Heidbreder
2219A Missouri Blvd.
Jefferson City, MO 65109
and
2716 Paris Rd. #6
Columbia, MO 65202
314/634-2987 & 474-2677
M-F,9-6/Sat,9-5/Sun,12-5
No CC, 50% Romance
New & Used
*Loves photos, newsletters,
bookmarks (25), posters*

*You'll find romances galore at Rebecca Ilfeld's Annie's Book Stop in Manchester, New Hampshire.*

*Helen Haney's Paperback Readers' Exchange, Inc., Spotswood, NJ, is a mecca for romance fans.*

## NEBRASKA

**Paperback Exchange—**
Gay Winchester & Julie Thompson
4601 S. 50th Street #102
Omaha, NE 68117
402/734-7733—Near Omaha
M-F,10-5/Sat,10-4/Sun,12-4
No CC, 50% Romance, Used
*Loves bookmarks(12), posters*

## NEW HAMPSHIRE

**Annie's Book Stop—**
Nancy Zlotek
493 Amherst St.
Nashua, NH 03063
603/882-9178—Near Boston
M-F,10-6/Sat,10-5/Sun,1-5
No CC, 40% Romance
New & Used
*Loves bookmarks (25), posters*

**Annie's Book Stop—**
Rebecca Ilfeld
264 Mammoth Rd.
Manchester, NH 03103

603/622-5526—Near Boston
M-Sun,10-6
No CC, 50% Romance
New & Used
*Loves photos, newsletters, bookmarks (50), posters*

## NEW JERSEY

**The Book Trader—**
Eve Cameron, Linda Stoddard
1789 Hooper Ave.
Silverton, NJ 08753
201/255-4960—bet. NY & Phila.
M-S,9:30-5
No CC, 35% Romance, Used
*Loves bookmarks (50), posters*

**Paperback Readers' Exchange—**
Helen Haney
529 Main St. & Devoe Ave.
Spotswood , NJ 08884
201/251-6205—Near East Brunswick
T-S,10-5/Sun,12-4
No CC, 35% Romance
New & Used
*Loves  bookmarks (10), posters*

**Paperback Exchange—**
Judith W. Fairman
287 Newton-Sparta Rd.
Newton, NJ 07860
201/579-2225—Near Morristown
M-S,9:30-5/Sun,1-4
No CC, 50% Romance, Used
*Loves bookmarks (100), posters*

## NEW YORK

**Jackson Heights Discount Books**
Ava Grubman
77-15 37th Ave.
Jackson Heights, NY 11372
718/426-0202—Near Manhattan
M-S,9-9/Sun,11:30-6:30
Visa, MC, 30% Romance
New & Used
*Loves bookmarks (10)*

**The Book Loft—**
Maryann Herbison
2-A Laurel Rd.
New City, NY 10956
914/638-1192—Near Manhattan
M-S,10-5
No CC, 40% Romance, Used
*Loves photos, newsletters,
bookmarks (10), posters*

## OHIO

**The Book Corner—**
Janey Owens
4825 Robin Hood Dr.
Willoughby, OH 44094
216/942-0071—Near Cleveland
M-S,11-7
No CC, 25% Romance
New & Used
*Loves bookmarks (25), posters*

**Second-Hand Prose—**
Mary Bee Hummer & Jan Steffens
8791 Mentor Ave.
Mentor, OH 44060
216/255-9587—Near Cleveland
M-S,10-6
No CC, 45% Romance
New & Used
*Loves bookmarks (50), posters*

**I Love Paperbacks—**
Shirley Hempel
5985 Old Troy Pike
Huber Heights, OH 45424
513/236-4995—Near Dayton
M-S,10-7:30
Visa, MC, 70% Romance, Used
*Loves bookmarks (25), posters*

*I Love
Paperbacks
in Huber
Heights,
Ohio,
belongs
to Shirley
Hempel,
a longtime
romance fan.*

Nancy Christiana, owner, and Lee Boyles at the cozy Nancy's Fireside Book Exchange in McMurray, Pennsylvania.

**Book Haven—**
Charlotte Zimmerman
6513 Pearl Rd.
Parma Heights, OH 44130
216/842-2699—Near Cleveland
M-F,10-9/Sat,9-5
Visa, MC, 40% Romance
New & Used
*Loves photos, newsletters,*
*bookmarks (50), posters*

**Book Mark II Book Store—**
Lorna T. Haney
200 Valley St.
Dayton, OH 45404
513/222-9612—Near Cincinnati
T-S,9-5
No CC, 33% Romance, Used
*Loves bookmarks (25), posters*

## OKLAHOMA

**The Book Rack—**
Juanima L. McFarland
Garnett Plaza Shopping
11311 E. 31st St.
Tulsa, OK 74146
918/663-2701
M-S/10-5
MC, Visa, 40% Romance
New & Used
*Loves bookmarks (20), posters*

## OREGON

**Clackamas Book Exchange—**
Iona & Bob Lockwood
7000 S.E. Thiessen Rd.
Milwaukie, OR 97267
503/659-2559 —Near Portland
M-F,10-6/Sat,10-4
No CC, 50% Romance, Used
*Loves photos, newsletters,*
*bookmarks (20-25), posters*

## PENNSYLVANIA

**Nancy's Fireside Book Exchange—**
Nancy Christiana
226 E. McMurray Rd.
McMurray, PA 15317
412/941-8186—Near Pittsburgh
T-S,10-5
No CC, 75% Romance
New & Used
*Loves bookmarks (12), posters*

*Katy Budget Books in Houston has enough titles to keep every Texas romance booklover happy!*

**The Book Rack—**
Fred & Mary Bobby
114 W. State St.
Sharon, PA 16146
412/342-2066—Near Pittsburgh
M-S,10-5
No CC, 75% Romance
New & Used
*Loves bookmarks (20), posters*

**Book Trade—**
Christopher Dessler
1008 3rd Ave.
New Brighton, PA 15066
412/847-3282—Near Pittsburgh
M-S,10-5
No CC, 70% Romance
New & Used
*Loves photos, newsletters, bookmarks (lots!), posters*

**The Book Rack—**
Judy Pacelli
41 N. Mercer St.
New Castle, PA 16101
412/656-1779—Near Pittsburgh
M-S,10-5
No CC, 50% Romance
New & Used
*Loves newsletters & posters*

**Books 'N More—**
Gwendolyn Allen & Victoria Zsilavecz
1409 N. Cedar Crest Blvd.
Allentown, PA 18104
215/435-4444—Near Philadelphia
M-F,9-8/Sat,9-5
MC, Visa, 60% Romance
New & Used
*Loves bookmarks (12), posters*

**The Paperback Trade—**
Venetia Mann
(in the Schoolhouse Outlet Center)
165 South Richland Ave.
York, PA 17404
717/843-2947
M-S,10-5
No CC, 40% Romance, Used
*Loves posters*

**Book Trade—**
Elaine M. Dessler
1263 Brodhead Rd.
Monaca, PA 15061
412/775-2665—Near Pittsburgh
M-F,10-8/Sat,10-5
No CC, 70% Romance
New & Used
*Loves newsletters & posters*

## RHODE ISLAND

**Marie's Book Shoppe—**
Marie Ricci
202 Warwick Mall
Warwick , RI 02893
401/732-2212—Near Cranston
M-F,10-6/Sat,10-6/Sun,12-5
No CC, 75% Romance
New & Used
*Loves photos, newsletters,*
*bookmarks (25), posters*

## SOUTH CAROLINA

**The Paperback Trader—**
Jane Gaskin
1836 Ashley River Rd.
Charleston, SC 29407
803/556-5383
M-S,9-7/Sun,12-5
No CC, 50% Romance
New & Used
*Loves bookmarks (50), posters*

**Book Exchange—**
Sharon Monheit
Heritage Square, Hwy. 78
Summerville, SC 29483
803/875-2562—Near Charleston

M-S,10-8/Sun, 1-6
No CC, 65% Romance
New & Used
*Loves photos, newsletters,*
*bookmarks (lots!), posters*

## TENNESSEE

**Book Case—**
Marion Diehl, Nina Hamilton & A'nl Isom
617 N. White Station Rd.
Memphis, TN 38122
901/685-8768
M-S,10-5:30
No CC, 25% Romance
New & Used
*Loves photos, newsletters,*
*bookmarks (50), posters*

**Book Worm—**
Pam Young
4812 Lebanon Rd.
Hermitage, TN 37076
615/889-8099—Near Nashville
T-S,9-6
No CC, 60% Romance
New & Used
*Loves newsletters,*
*bookmarks (20-25), posters*

*Sandra Shipman, of The Book Inn, Tyler, Texas, knows how to satisfy her romance readers.*

**Village Book Store—**
Barbara Hunter
3127 Mendenhall Rd. So.
Memphis, TN 38115
901/362-6502
M-S,10-5/Sun,1-5
Visa, MC, AE, 80% Romance
New & Used
*Loves photos, newsletters,*
*bookmarks (15), posters*

**Book Mart—**
Wanda Worley
207 East Madison
Athens, TN 37303
615/745-1859—Between Knox-
ville & Chattanooga
M-S,10-9/Sun,1-6
No CC, 80% Romance
New & Used
*Loves photos, newsletters,*
*bookmarks (25), posters*


**TEXAS**

**Katy Budget Books—**
Tamra Doré
19726 Saums at Fry Rd.

(Below) *Seated: Ann Wren, at*
*her Book Rack in Arlington,*
*Texas. Standing, L to R: Betty*
*Andrews, Michelle Pairsh,*
*Jana Wren.*

Houston, TX 77084
713/578-7770—Near Houston
M-F,10-7/Sat,10-6/Sun,12-5
Visa & MC, 35% Romance
New & Used
*Loves photos, newsletters,*
*bookmarks (25), posters*

**Book Rack—**
Ann Wren
5210 Rufe Snow,
N. Richland Hills, TX 76180
817/656-5565—Near Fort Worth/Dallas
M-F,10-6/Sat,10-5:30
No CC, 30% Romance
New & Used
*Loves photos, newsletters,*
*bookmarks (25), posters*

**Book Rack—**
Ann Wren
2304 W. Park Row
Arlington, TX 76013
817/274-1717—Near Fort Worth/Dallas
M-F,10-6/Sat,10-5:30
No CC, 25% Romance
New & Used
*Loves photos, newsletters,*
*bookmarks (25), posters*

**The Book Inn—**
Sandra Shipman
Front-Beckham Center
520-A East Front St.
Tyler, TX 75702

(Above) *Delia Lee and Tina*
*Austin, at Ann Wren's Book*
*Rack in N. Richland Hills, Texas.*

*Pam Hayes' Bookmark, a hotbed for romance readers, is located in Richardson, Texas.*

214/593-6391—Near Dallas
M-S,9-5
No CC, 70% Romance
New & Used
*Loves photos, newsletters, bookmarks (35), posters*

**Pauline's Book Store—**
Pauline E. Ross
1617 Center
Deer Park, TX 77536
713/479-7300—Near Houston
M-S,10-6
No CC, 65% Romance
New & Used
*Loves photos, newsletters, bookmarks (20), posters*

**ReRun Books—**
Jack Sherrell
123 W. Southmore
Pasadena, TX 77502
713/477-5554—Near Houston
M-S,9-6:30,
Visa & MC, 33% Romance, Used
*Loves photos, newsletters, bookmarks (12), posters*

**Book Mark—**
Pam Hayes
34 Arapaho Village
Richardson, TX 75080
214/690-8123—Near Dallas
M-S,10-5:30
No CC, 50% Romance
New & Used
*Loves newsletters, posters*

**The Book Shelf—**
Jenny Jones
902 W. Hwy. 303, Suite 109
Grand Prairie, TX 75051-3922
214/660-1346—Near Dallas
M-S,10-6
No CC
*Loves photos, newsletters, bookmark (25), posters*

**Book Mark—**
Pam Hayes
34 Arapaho Village
Richardson, Texas 75080
214/690-8123
M-Sat, 10-5:30
No CC, 50% Romance
New & Used
*Loves newsletters, posters*

*Frances Blaisdell has fun and sells lots of romances at her Paperback Trader in West Valley City, Utah.*

**Book Marker Book Store—**
Paula Oates
5421 Stanley Keller Rd.
Fort Worth, TX 76117
817/281-4313
M-S,10-5:30
No CC, 65% Romance
New & Used
*Loves photos, newsletters, bookmarks (20), posters*

**Reader's Paradise—**
Leigh Mott & Linda Guidry
2830 Western Ave.
W. Orange, TX 77630
409/882-0746—Near Houston
M-S,10-6
No CC, 80% Romance
New & Used
*Loves photos, newsletters, bookmarks (2), posters*

**Carrollton Book Center—**
Jim Duster
536 Carrollton Pk. S/C
Carrollton, TX 75006
214/418-7888—Near Dallas
M-S,10-6
AE, MC, Visa, 20% Romance
New & Used
*Loves photos, newsletters, bookmarks (20), posters*

**The Book Rack—**
Carole Williams
141 W. Spring Creek Pkwy. #413
Plano,TX 75023
214/517-5234—Near Dallas
M-F,10-6:30/Sat,10-5:30
No CC, 33% Romance
New & Used
*Loves newsletters, bookmarks (50), posters*

**The Book Rack—**
Ellen Sevier
16924 Hwy. 3
Park Plaza II
Webster, TX 77598
713/332-9249—Near Houston
M-F,10-5:30/Sat,10-4
No CC, 50% Romance
New & Used
*Loves photos, newsletters, bookmarks (20), posters*

**GFI (Go For It!) Books—**
Norman Schaffner
3419 E. Broadway
Pearland, TX 77581
713/485-6189—Near Houston
M-F,11-7/Sat,11-5
Visa & MC, 60% Romance
New & Used
*Loves newsletters, bookmarks (20), posters*

**Books 'N Stuff—**
Dolores Bell
2917 South Fifth St.
Garland, TX 75041
214/271-3418—Near Dallas
M-S, 9-5
MC & Visa, 60% Romance
New & Used
*Loves bookmarks (20), posters*


## UTAH


**Paperback Trader—**
Frances Blaisdell
3526 South Market St.
West Valley City, UT 84119
801/966-8156—Near Salt Lake City
M-S,10-6
No CC, 30% Romance
New & Used
*Loves bookmarks (25), posters*


**Court's Book Exchange—**
Hazel Court
430 N. Freedom Blvd.
Provo, UT 84601
  and
44 N. Main
Spanish Fork, UT 84660
801/377-1747 & 798-9013
M-S,11-7/M-S,12-6
No CC, 75% Romance
New & Used
*Loves bookmarks (10), posters*


**The Book Attic—**
Jean Landers
121 W. Center St.
Midvale, UT 84047
801/562-2086—Near Salt Lake City
M-S,10-6
No CC, 40% Romance, Used
*Loves bookmarks (40), posters*


## WISCONSIN

**The Book Store—**
Janice E. Dooley
1032 Lincoln Ave.
Sheboygan, WI 53081
414/452-6383—Near Milwaukee
M-F, 9:30-5/Sat,10-4
No CC, 30% Romance
New & Used
*Loves posters*


**The Book Shop—**
Corrine Maxwell & Peggy Onate
603 So. Military
Green Bay, WI 54303
414/498-0008—Near Milwaukee
(winter) M-F,9-8/Sat,9-5/Sun,12-4
(summer) M-F,9-9/Sat,9-4
MC & Visa, 50% Romance
New & Used
*Loves bookmarks (100), posters*


**The Book Trader—**
Marilyn Wicinski
7829 W. Greenfield Ave.
Milwaukee, WI 53214
  and
6254 N. Port Washington Rd.
Milwaukee, WI 53217
  and
3172 S. 27 St.
Milwaukee, WI 53215
414/259-1451
M-F,10-6/Sat,10-4
Visa & MC, 50% Romance
New & Used
*Loves bookmarks (30), posters*


**The Book Store—**
Susan Dobbe
333 W. Northland Ave.
Appleton, WI 54911
414/734-8908—Near Milwaukee
M-S,9:30-9
No CC, 75% Romance
New & Used
*Loves bookmarks (100), posters*

## WASHINGTON

**J & D Book Swap—**
Jan Dearborn & Doris Daniel
9035 "B" 90th Ave. N.W.
Oak Harbor, WA 98277
206/675-8884—Near Seattle
M-S,10-6
MC & Visa, 50% Romance
New & Used
*Loves bookmarks (25), posters*

**Monohon's Paperback Exchange—**
J. Monohon
1314-F East 72 St.
Tocoma, WA 98404
206/537-8971—Near Seattle
M-F,10-8/Sat,10-6/Sun,12-5

Visa & MC, 20% Romance
New & Used
*Loves bookmarks (10)*

## WYOMING

**Book Nook—**
Shirley Peterson
918 E. 2nd St.
Casper, WY 82601
307/237-2211—middle of Wyoming! 200 miles from Denver
M-S,10-5
No CC, 30% Romance, Used
*Loves newsletters,
bookmarks (10), posters*

# Booklovers Day

## The First Saturday in November

*Go to your favorite Bookstore That Cares and Celebrate that You Love Books*

*Meet your local authors and fellow readers.*

**If you want to join the authors who are adopting stores and help plan a party, contact Romantic Times.**

# BOOK RACK

## Thousands of Used Paper Back Books

*Licensed Shops to serve you in these locations. Most cities have multiple shops.*

**ALABAMA**
Anniston
Auburn
(2) Birmingham
Florence
Gadsden
Mobile
Saraland
Tuscaloosa

**ARKANSAS**
Blytheville
Little Rock
North Little Rock

**CALIFORNIA**
Arcadia
Glendale
Lodi
Menlo Park
San Jose
Stockton
Ventura
Pismo Beach

**COLORADO**
(2) Aurora
Colorado Springs
Denver
Fort Collins
Greely
Lakewood
Loveland

**CONNECTICUT**
Glastonbury
Tolland

**FLORIDA**
Coral Springs
Daytona Beach
Deerfield Beach
Dunedin
(2) Fort Lauderdale
Fort Pierce
Fort Walton Beach
Hollywood
Jacksonville
Key West
Lake Worth
Largo
North Miami
Ocala
Orange Park
Orlando
Ormond Beach
(2) Pensacola
Port Richey
Stuart
Tampa

**GEORGIA**
Macon
Rome
Valdosta
Warner Robbins

**ILLINOIS**
Bloomington
Champaign
Chicago
Geneva
Lansing
Naperville
Peoria
Western Springs

**INDIANA**
Bloomington
(2) Fort Wayne
Granger
(5) Indianapolis

**IOWA**
Bettendorf

**KENTUCKY**
Bowling Green
Elizabethtown
Florence
Hopkinsville
Murry
Owensboro
Paducah
Russellville

**LOUISIANA**
(2) Baton Rouge
Bossier City

Denham Springs
Gretna
Houma
La Fayette
New Orleans
Shreveport
Slidell

**MASSACHUSETTS**
Dracut
Lexington
South Yarmouth
Springfield
West Springfield

**MICHIGAN**
Muskegon
Sawyer

**MISSISSIPPI**
Gulfport
Hattiesburg
(3) Jackson
Laurel
Madison
Pearl
South Haven
Starkville
Tupelo
Waynesboro

**MISSOURI**
Cape Girardeau
Saint Louis

**NEVADA**
BOOKSHELF-
Las Vegas

**NORTH CAROLINA**
Charlotte
Gastonia
Greensboro
Winston Salem

**OHIO**
(6) Cincinnati
North Olmsted
Parma Heights
Maple Heights
Youngstown

**OKLAHOMA**
Bartlesville
Edmond
Midwest City
(3) Oklahoma City
Tulsa

**PENNSYLVANIA**
(2) Allentown
New Castle
Pittsburgh
Sharon
Warren

**RHODE ISLAND**
Smithfield

**SOUTH CAROLINA**
Surfside Beach

**TENNESSEE**
(3) Chattanooga
Clarksville
Cleveland
Collierville
Dyersburg
Greenville

Jackson
Johnson City
Kingsport
Knoxville
Maryville
(4) Memphis
Murfreesboro
Nashville
Oakridge

**TEXAS**
Arlington
Beaumont
El Paso
Houston
Irving
Lake Jackson
Lubbock
Plano
Richland Hills
Sherman

**VIRGINIA**
Alexandria
(2) Richmond

**WASHINGTON**
Oak Harbor

**WYOMING**
Cheyenne
Casper

**CANADA**
Dartmouth,
Nova Scotia

**HAWAII**
Honolulu

*If you are interested in owning a Book Rack, contact*
*Fred Darnell at the Home Office:*

# Book Rack Management

**2703 East Commercial Blvd.**
**Fort Lauderdale, Florida 33308**
**305/771-4310**

# Chain Store Managers Who Care

**ARIZONA**
B. Dalton —Scott Leroy
*(Siesta Mall)—Mesa*
B. Dalton—Su Harambe
*(Tri-City Mall)—Mesa*
B. Dalton—Maria Ruiz
*(Metro Center)—Phoenix*
Waldenbooks & More—Melinda
*(Fontaine Square)—Phoenix*

**CALIFORNIA**
Crown—Beverly Lyon
*La Cresenta*
Waldenbooks —L.J. Short
*Mountain View*
Waldenbooks—Ann
*San Bernadino*
Waldenbooks —Diane Wilkinson
*Santa Ana*

**COLORADO**
Waldenbooks—Connie Rinehold
*Aurora*

**FLORIDA**
Brentano's —Wes Broom
*Boca Raton*
Waldenbooks—Doug
*Coral Springs*
Waldenbooks—Mort Sadler
*Hallandale*
Waldenbooks —Debbie Barr
*Kissimmee*
B. Dalton—Susan Bain
*(Culter Ridge Mall)—Miami*

Waldenbooks —Laurel Roberts
*West Palm Beach*
Reader's Market —Lisa Mouton
*Orlando*

**GEORGIA**
Reader's Market—Karen Ancell
*Atlanta*

**ILLINOIS**
Waldenbooks —Jack/Dan/Terry
*Chicago*

**INDIANA**
Waldenbooks—Janet Melton
*(Honey Creek Sq.)—Terre Haute*

**IOWA**
Waldenbooks—*Sioux City*

**LOUISIANA**
Waldenbooks—Brad
*Bossier City*

**MASSACHUSETTS**
Reader's Market—Teresa Silvia
& Rose Ring—*Warwick*

**MICHIGAN**
Waldenbooks—Jayme
*Kalamazoo*

**NORTH CAROLINA**
Waldenbooks—Terry Bizens
*(Eastland)—Charlotte*


**OREGON**
Waldenbooks—Katie Barber
*Tigard*


**PENNSYLVANIA**
Waldenbooks—Gail Link
*Media*
Waldenbooks—Judy Trovato
*Monroeville*
B. Dalton—Ellen Parkinson
*Willow Grove*


**TENNESSEE**
Waldenbooks—Kenneth Green
*Chattanooga*

**TEXAS**
B. Dalton—Judith Amsley
*Dallas*
Waldenbooks—Becky
*Odessa*


**VIRGINIA**
Waldenbooks—Jane Brumback
*Fredericksburg*


**WASHINGTON**
B. Dalton—Angela Butterworth
*(Facteria Square Mall)*
*Bellevue*
B. Dalton—Char Daniels
*Bellevue*
B. Dalton—Shirleen Bold
*Spokane*

---

*D*ue to space, this section for chain stores is very brief. There are **many more** Managers Who Care and as they contact us, we will include them in the next handbook, THE STORY CONTINUES.

*Romantic Times* and *Rave Reiews* magazines are distributed by Kable and IPD to thousands of Waldenbooks, B. Dalton, Reader's Market, Little Professor, and Coles of Canada bookstores.

These chains have their own distribution system, which does not include handling the bookmarks and promotional materials that readers enjoy. However, if a chain store employee has a strong romance following and wants to receive materials, all he or she need do is write or call *RT*'s office. Ask for JERRY, who is in charge of bookstore sales and writes the sizzling BTC newsletter each month.

### ☎ 718/ 237-1097

# Annie's Book Stop

## We're nation-wide for booklovers

**ARIZONA**
Phoenix

**CALIFORNIA**
Pacific Grove
San Francisco
Vallejo

**COLORADO**
Englewood

**CONNECTICUT**
Avon
Torrington
Willimantic

**FLORIDA**
Melbourne
Naples
New Port Richey
Palm Harbor

**IOWA**
Council Bluffs

**ILLINOIS**
Vernon Hills

**MASSACHUSETTS**
Acton
Andover
Ashland
Auburn
Belmont
Beverly
Brockton
Chelmsford
Cochituate
Dedham
East Falmouth
Framingham
Franklin
Groton
Hanson
Haverhill
Kingston
Lexington
Malden
Marlborough
Miilford
Natick
North Dartmouth
Orleans
Plainville
Quincy
Raynham
Rowley
Salem
Sharon
South Weymouth

Swansea
Uxbridge
Wakefield
Waltham
West Boylston
West Yarmouth
Westborough
Westfield
Westwood
Williamstown

**MAINE**
Auburn
Freeport
Kittery
North Windham
Portland
Wells
Wiscasset

**MICHIGAN**
West Bloomfield

**MINNESOTA**
Bloomington

**MISSOURI**
Chesterfield
Florissant
St. Louis

| NORTH CAROLINA | NEW JERSEY | TEXAS |
|---|---|---|
| Asheville | Hillsborough | Arlington |
| | Pompton Lakes | |
| | Sussex | |
| **NEW HAMPSHIRE** | | **VIRGINIA** |
| Concord | **NEW YORK** | Fredericksburg |
| Hampton | East Northport | |
| Keene | Hudson | |
| Laconia | Kingston | **VERMONT** |
| Manchester | Saratoga Springs | Rutland |
| Nashua | Schenectady | |
| North Conway | | |
| Peterborough | **RHODE ISLAND** | **WISCONSIN** |
| Rochester | East Providence | Hudson |
| | North Kingstown | |

If you're interested in opening an Annie's Book Stop, contact:
15 Lackey Street, Westborough, MA 01581• (616) 366-9547

# Discover half-priced paperbacks at Annie's

- ❤ Browse through dozens of categories,
  from bestsellers to rare finds!

- ❤ Trade your own gently read paperbacks for credit!

- ❤ Curl up with a good book in our comfortable
  surroundings while your kids explore our
  ultra-special, extensive and exciting new
  children's book nook!

- ❤ You have never visited a book store like it!

# Corresponding
# With
# Authors

## Jasmine Cresswell aka Jasmine Craig

*Author of 34 novels of contemporary romance, romantic suspense, Regencies, and mainstream historicals published by Harlequin Intrigue, Silhouette, Fawcett, and Berkley/Jove/Charter.*

CHASE THE PAST-*Harlequin Intrigue*
DEVIL'S ENVOY-*Berkley/Jove*
EMPIRE OF THE HEART-*Charter*
FREE FALL-*Harlequin Intrigue*
CHARADES-*Harlequin Intrigue-October 1989*

## Emily Carmichael

*Author of five historical romances published by Warner Books.*

DEVIL'S DARLING-*Warner*
AUTUMNFIRE-*Warner*
SURRENDER-*Warner*
TOUCH OF FIRE-*Warner-5/89*
VISIONS OF THE HEART-*Warner-10/90*

## Leona Karr aka Lee Karr

*Author of romantic suspense, gothic, and historical fiction published by Avon Books, NAL/Signet, Leisure Books, Harlequin Intrigue, and Zebra.*

TREASURE HUNT-*Harlequin Intrigue-8/89*
DARK CRIES AT GRAY OAKS-*Zebra-8/89*
BEYOND THE TEXAS RAINBOW-*Zebra-11/89*
CASTLE OF CRUSHED SHAMROCKS-*Zebra-12/89*
FORBIDDEN DREAMS-*Zebra-4/90*

## Maggie Osborne aka Margaret St. George

*Author of 15 novels of historical fiction and contemporary romance published by NAL/Signet, William Morrow, and Harlequin American.*

CHASE THE HEART-*William Morrow*
PORTRAIT IN PASSION-*NAL/Signet*
ALEXA-*NAL/Signet Historical*
YANKEE PRINCESS-*NAL/Ssgnet*
WHERE THERE'S SMOKE-*Harlequin American*
CASTLES AND FAIRYTALES-*Harlequin American*
DEAR SANTA-*Harlequin American-12/89*

# It's Fun to Network
# with Authors

here has always been casual exchanges between readers and authors, and some great friendships have been formed through the years. But now a new phenomenon is taking place—networking between authors and readers—and snowballing into something special.

**Bookmarks:** Many readers are enjoying a hobby that goes back to the Victorian days—collecting bookmarks. Booksellers find that bookmarks stimulate sales and draw the interest of readers to a variety of books. If anything, a catchy bookmark makes an author's name more visible. When there are over 100 romances a month, every bit of promotion helps—especially when the author is new on the scene.

Brenda Joyce, Eileen Nauman, and Shirl Henke have come up with spectacular "hunk" bookmarks (as the readers named them). In Shirl's case, the model is her husband.

As several booksellers said: "Women customers like to take home the bookmark of Jim Henke to show their husbands. After all, the real man is what one lives with! It makes the husbands feel less competitive with all those heroes on the covers."

Brenda Joyce started a trend with her "hunk" bookmarks. She believes that the ideal hero is in the reader's imagination, so she doesn't ever show his face on her bookmarks.

Eileen Nauman, on the other hand, writes military romances, and prefers a man "in and out" of a uniform on her colorful bookmarks. Her model is always about to slip off his jacket!

For a closer look, all three bookmarks are on the back cover of this Handbook, or you can write away and request a sample.

**Helping the Cause:** Another new trend in the romance novel world is the growing camraderie among the readers. Many are acting in pairs, or alone, as "Little Literary Sisters" for some of their favorite authors.

Theresa DiBenedetto, who was once an "LLS" before she got published, has assisted in developing a "Sister" program. A reader can help out by reminding wholesalers and booksellers to order her "sister's book," and assisting an author when she comes through town on a book tour.

Theresa has prepared a form/questionnaire (see Directory, page 324) and she will gladly send it to any interested reader with SASE.

After all, a reader may become an author someday, too, and

## CONVENTION MEMORIES
## Phoenix, 1989

*(Right) One of the memorable nights was a visit to Rawhide, an old west town complete with Indian carvings, hayride, steak fry, and singing under the stars.*
*Laughing it up— (L) Libbi Goodman, literary agent with writer Janis Hudson.*

*(Below, L to R) Enjoying the night of nights—Ron Hickman, Florida distributor, with Carol Stacy and Jerry Johnson of Romantic Times.*

wouldn't it be nice to have "Little Literary Sisters" around the country making sure a new book has been placed prominently on the shelves?

Being a romance author is a very unique and satisfying profession. Some authors make a pleasant living, while others graduate into superstardom and command over $100,000 a year income or more.

In other professional groups, members are reputed to be snobs, recluses, or unpleasantly temperamental individuals. Romance writers are different. Warm and friendly, they have their own code of honor, and those few who don't live up to it are instantly awarded the title of PD (for prima donna) until they are rehabilitated!

Romance writers, readers, and booksellers are special. They believe and practice equality and friendship.

What makes a romance author special is this motto:

*"It Is Not Ourselves, But Our Responsibilities We take Seriously."*

A romance author is willing to share her knowledge and experience with aspiring writers, because she realizes how difficult and frustrating it can be to get published.

A romance author prizes her booksellers and wholesellers, and tries always to see that her writing, her cover, and book promotion is of the highest standards.

A romance author respects her fellow published authors and is not threatened by another's deserved success.

A romance author answers her fan mail to the best of her ability.

Romance writers appreciate mail. A special group of authors are included in this handbook, because they enjoy comments and suggestions, and enjoy knowing that their books bring hours of pleasure to readers. Unfortunately, they can't afford tremendous postage bills and the services of secretaries, but if you included a SASE, it would be most appreciated.

Without readers, as they well know, there wouldn't be published writers!

Authors will be adopting stores across the country for the celebration of BOOKLOVERS DAY, each November, on the first Saturday. Through the authors' directory, a reader or bookseller can learn if a favorite author lives in her state and can invite her to the local event.

Throughout this Handbook, you will find photos from conventions in the past. All readers are invited to attend and authors and the staff of RT look forward to welcoming them. Our group loves to party!

To make the romance novel world flourish, we all have to cooperate. Remember the slogan: We Fight For What's Write!♥

# Author Index

❤ ❤ ❤ ❤ ❤ ❤ ❤ ❤ ❤

**Check with *Romantic-Times*, each issue, for additional addresses.**

# Chicago Romance Writers

*Sharing And Celebrating Their Work And Successes.*

Shy as a youngster, **Maureen Kurr** chose to write stories instead of telling them. As an adult, she felt guilty accepting money for her first novel she would have continued writing whether or not money was involved. To date, her third book published by Leisure, *Deceptive Heart,* is her favorite, although the one she's working on is proving to be as much fun.

**Leslie Lynn** and **Lynn Leslie** are pseudonyms for sisters-in-law Elaine Sima and Sherrill Bodine. Their first book, *Buried Shadows* was published by Lynx in November 1988. Fawcett will publish two Regencies in 1989. The tentative title of the first is *The Rake's Redemption. Street of Dreams* will be a Harlequin Intrigue, release date to be announced.

Published under her own name, **Jan Millelia** also writes as **Jan Mathews** and as **Jan Michaels**. Her January Intimate Moments, *Once Forgotten* and February Second Chance at Love, *The Rialto Affair,* were both special to her. She and three other writers authored Harlequin American's Rocky Mountain Magic Series. *Ghost Dancing* will be a late 1989 release.

**Patricia Pinianski** writes alone for Harlequin Intrigue and Superromance as **Patricia Rosemoor**, and with partner Linda Sweeney as **Lynn Patrick**. She was Roseanne McKenna for her first sale, winner of the 1983 RWA Golden Heart Award for Best Young Adult Manuscript. Her next Intrigues will be May and September 1989 releases—*Do Unto Others* and *Ticket to Nowhere*.

**Martha Jean Powers**, who also writes as **Jean Paxton**, was drawn to Regencies by a love of history and a sense of humor. So far, her fifth, *The Gray Fox Wagers*, is her favorite.

Linda Sweeney collaborates with Patricia Pinianski as **Lynn Patrick**. Together, they published eight romances for Dell and are now writing for Harlequin Superromance. Their latest book, *Good Vibrations*, is a February 1989 release. Linda also teaches writing both at the community college level and through the Writer's Digest School.

Jeanne Triner and Kale Clements write together as **Jeanne Kaye Triner** and **Caylin Jennings**. Jeanne and Kaye literally met over the back fence while Jeanne was working on *By Any Other Name*, her first Harlequin Superromance, and their friendship soon turned into a partnership.

# Connie
# Rinehold

*Contemporary and Historical*
*Romance*

## SILKEN
## THREADS

Harlequin Superromance
October 1989

*970 Lansing St.*
*Aurora, CO 80010*

# Beverly
# Allen

*writing as*
## Beverly Hunt

# KEEPER OF THE DAWN

*science fiction   fantasy   adventure   romance*
*Crown  Publishers*
970 Lansing St   Aurora, CO  80010

Historical
Romances
by

# MADELINE BAKER

Winner of the 1988 Romantic
Times Reviewer's Choice Award
for Best Indian Romance Series*

Reckless Heart* ............................................ (1985)
Love in the Wind ......................................... (1986)
Reckless Love* .............................................. (1987)
Love Forevermore ........................................ (1988)
Reckless Desire* ........................................... (1988)
Renegade Heart ........................................... (1989)

*Coming in 1989/90*

First Love, Wild Love     September 1989
Lacey's Way                         March 1990

I love to hear from my readers. Please feel free to
write me in care of Leisure Books, 276 Fifth Avenue,
New York, NY 10001.

Personal reply guaranteed!
SASE appreciated.

# Kathryn Kramer

a.k.a.
Katherine Vickery
and Lynn Kramer

Reviewer's
Choice Award Winner
1986 & 1988

UNDER GYPSY SKIES
FLAME OF DESIRE

## Kathryn Kramer

Love's Blazing Ecstasy—1985
(NAL/Signet)

Flame From The Sea—1987
(Berkley/Charter)

Desire's Masquerade—1987
(Dell)

Under Gypsy Skies—1988
(Dell)

Destiny And Desire—1988
(Berkley/Charter)

Desire's Deception—1989
(Berkley/Jove)

*Treasure Of The Heart—1990
(Dell)

Lady Rogue—1990
(Dell)

## Katherine Vickery

Flame Of Desire—1986
(NAL/Onyx)

Tame The Wild Wind—1988
(NAL/Onyx)

*Flame Across The
Highlands—1990
(Pocket)

*Desire Of The Heart—1991
(Pocket)

## Projects in the works:

Midsummer Night's Desire
*Legacy Of Love
Sail The Sea Of Desire
*Softly Whispers My Heart
*The Heart's Honor

A special thank you to my mother, Marcia Hockett, for her invaluable help; to my editors whose advice and expertise has helped me to grow as an author; to Kathryn Falk and Kathe Robin who will never know how much they inspire me; and to my readers, whose support and letters are so very appreciated. Thank you.

*Tentative titles, subject to change

# Kathryn Hockett

**a.k.a.**
Marcia Hockett
(and Historical Researcher
for Katherine Vickery)

Romance
Mother of the Year
Award
**Romantic Times 1988**

*Rapture's Delight*—1988
(Zebra)

*Angel of Passion*—1989
(Zebra)

*\*Renegade*—1989
(Zebra)

*\*Surrender
the Moonlight*—1990
(Zebra)

**Marcia (Kathryn) Hockett** began her career by aiding her daughter, Kathryn Kramer, in doing research for her historical romances. Recently, however, another dimension has been added and Kathryn Hockett has begun a writing career of her own. Future projects include co-authoring a saga with her daughter and writing more of the romances Kathryn loves—Westerns. Future sites for stories include Arizona, Nevada, Montana, Texas and Oklahoma.

**[SASE appreciated]**
**1046 8th Street**
**Boulder, Colorado 80302**

**Marcia Hockett
&
Kathy Kramer**

# Victoria London

# Seductive Scoundrel

Zebra June 1989

"Victoria London has a special gift for writing lively historical espionage novels laced with fascinating details, adventures and steamy sensuality."

Romantic Times

### Ecstasy's Embers
Zebra February 1985
Reviewer's Choice Award

**Passion's Pirate**
Zebra March 1986

**Destiny's Desire**
Zebra June 1987

P.O. Box 1   Bay Station   Brooklyn, NY 11235

314

# LEE MAGNER

Dear Readers,
   I was born in Bloomington, Indiana, and raised in Wilmington, Delaware, graduated from Indiana University (B.A. in Spanish) and Bryn Mawr College (M.S.S.).
   After working in a variety of fields, I pursued my youthful ambition of becoming a writer. I'm married, have a young son named KT, and when I'm not reading or writing, I'm chauffering my son to his activities and sewing scout badges like many other parents. I hope you enjoy my books as much as I enjoy writing them.

---

## Dell Candelight Ecstasy and Supremes

BEGUILING PRETENDER ('87)          ❤ THE GAMBLER'S GAME ('86)

NIGHT OF THE MATADOR ('87)         TORCH SONG ('86)

HIDDEN CHARMS ('85)                TENDER REFUGE ('85)

---

## Silhouette Intimate Moments

MASTER OF THE HUNT ('89)           SUTTER'S WIFE ('90)

MUSTANG MAN ('88)                  MISTRESS OF FOXGROVE ('89)

❤ *RT Reviewer's Choice Award for Best Ecstasy of 1986*

*I enjoy hearing from you.*
For bookmark & newsletter, send SASE:
Lee Magner, P.O. Box 16212, Alexandria, VA 22302

315

# *Bobbi Smith*

# Award Winning Author
## of
# Zebra Historicals

## 1988 Golden Certificate Award

| | |
|---|---|
| *Rapture's Rage* | *Desert Heart* |
| *Forbidden Fires* | *Captive Pride* |
| *Wanton Splendor* | *Texas Splendor* |
| *Rapture's Tempest* | *Pirate's Promise* |
| *Arizona Temptress* | *Island Fire* |

*Arizona Caress, July '89*
*Silken Bondage, Early '90*
(tentative title)

I love to hear from my readers (SASE Helps):
**Bobbi Smith,** P.O. Box 6117, St. Charles, MO 63302-6117

# MARION SCHULTZ

### Author of Mystery & Romance

**THE GIRL WITHIN**
Fawcett, Aug. '83, July '87

**MYSTERIOUS SUMMER**
Scholastic, Sept. '83

**THE MAKE-BELIEVE BOYFRIEND**
Fawcett, May '85

**THE MASTER OF BRENDAN'S ISLE**
(writing as Marion Clarke)
Zebra, Aug. '85

**WHO NEEDS GLAMOUR, ANYWAY?**
Fawcett, June '88

**TRACY HARMON: LOVE SPECIALIST**
Fawcett, Early '89

**HOTLINE TO TERROR**
Fawcett, Early '89

**GOING HOLLYWOOD**
Fawcett, Late '88

*I'm a grandmother who lives in California and writes mainly young adult romance. I would love to answer your letters if you send them (SASE) in care of Fawcett Books, 201 E. 50, New York City, 10022.*

# KATHLEEN DRYMON

*Zebra Historical Romances*

Kimberly's Kiss 1987
Destiny's Splendor 1989
Velvet Savage 1989

*a.k.a. Kathleen McCall*

Ivory Rose 1988
Windswept Heart 1988

"I love to hear from my readers!"
Please send SASE TO:
P. O. Box 2371
Arcadia, FL. 33821

# BARBARA DAWSON SMITH

**NO REGRETS,** Silhouette, '85
**DEFIANT EMBRACE,** Zebra, '85
**DEFIANT SURRENDER,** Zebra, '87
**STOLEN HEART,** Avon, '88
**SILVER SPLENDOR,** Avon, Aug. '89
**DREAMSPINNER,** Avon, Feb. '90

Readers,
I love to hear from
you. If you'd like a
bookmark or news
about upcoming
titles, please send
a SASE.

Barbara Dawson Smith
P.O. Box 70331
Houston, TX 77270-0331

321

322

## Louisa Rawlings

I adore writing historical romances set primarily in France and I meticulously research them, attempting to capture the sociological and psychological realities, as well as the historical accuracy of their times for my discerning readers.

I have ravishing covers and amusing bookmarks! Please send a SASE (and your favorite jokes, if possible—I collect them) to:

Louisa Rawlings
P.O. Box 422 Cooper Station
New York, NY 10276

# DIRECTORY
## for Getting In Touch With MORE of Your Favorite Authors
### Please include a SASE (self-addressed-stamped-legal-size-envelope)

**Blaine Anderson**—I'm a new author, *Love's Sweet Captive* (Popular Library, 1989), and I love to write historicals!—%Popular Library, 666 Fifth Ave., NYC 10103.

**Rebecca Brandewyne**—Best wishes to all of you. We've come a long way together!—% Warner, 666 Fifth Ave., NY, NY 10103.

**Jude Deveraux**—Thank you for all your support through the years. I love writing for you.—%Pocket Books (Jude's Bookmarks), 1230 Sixth Ave., NY, NY 10020.

**Theresa DiBenedetto**—Author of *Wildflower* and future historicals for Berkley Publishing Group.—P.O. Box 743, Hallandale, FL 33009.

**Sara Edwards**—Husband and wife team, *Crystal Rapture* and *Fire and Sand*. Satin Ribbon bookmark available.—P.O. Box 2166, Bremerton, WA 98310.

**Carol Finch**—Gina Robins and I (both Zebra authors) say hello!—RT. 1, Box 260, Union City, OK 73090.

**Rebecca George**—Author of *A Wild Desire,* and *Call Home the Heart.* Reviewer's Choice Award for 1988.—29 Harcourt Dr., Greenville, SC 29601.

**Sharon Gillenwater**—Author of *Unwilling Heart* and *Highland Whispers.* " Thank you, readers! I'd love to hear from you."—P.O. Box 8053, Federal Way, WA 98003.

**Jennifer Green, a.k.a. Jeanne Grant**—I thoroughly enjoy writing romances, and I appreciate hearing from you.—%Silhouette, 300 E. 42, NYC 10017.

**Pat Hagan**—Love to hear from my readers! For newsletter of what's happening to my Coltrane family.— P.O. Box 1245, Black Mt., NC 28711.

**Catherine Hart**—I live in Ohio, but enjoying receiving letters at my publisher.—%Leisure Books, 276 Fifth Ave., NY, NY 10001.

**Joan Mary Hart**—The response to my Silhouette, *Stranger at the Wedding,* was wonderful. I enjoy receiving requests for my bookmark and newsletter.— P.O. Box 6363, Laguna Niguel, CA 92677.

**Dee Hendrickson, a.k.a. Emily Hendricksen**—I create hand-painted bookmarks, in keeping with my Regency novels!—252 Fairview, Incline Village, NV 89451.

**Shirl Henke** (see bookmark on back cover of this book)—I chose my own hero for a model. Write away for "Jim Henke, Shirl's Sweet Inspiration for Moon Flower."—P.O. Box 72, Adrian, MI 49221.

**Tom Huff a.k.a. Jennifer Wilde**—I love to hear from my fans. —Write to Ballantine. (Jenny's bookmark), 201 E. 50th, NY, NY 10022.

**Brenda Joyce** (see bookmark on back cover)—With each historical romance, I print a special "Hunk" bookmark, as the readers call them. No head, just a sexy body! I live in Europe, but write to me % *Romantic Times.*

**Donna Julian**—Look for my first book, Pre*tty Poison* (Lynx).—P.O. Box 6062, St. Charles, M0 03302.

**Laura Kinsale**—Greetings to all my loyal readers. Thank you for helping me get my break-out book in October, 1989.—Write %Avon, 105 Madison Ave., NY, NY 10016.

**Johanna Lindsey**—I enjoy your comments. I live in Hawaii, but my mail is forwarded immediately from my publisher.—%Avon, 103 Madison, NY, NY 10016.

**Mary Kay McComas**—Author of Loveswept's OBSESSION prizes her readers. Bookmarks available.—P.O. Box 1499, Front Royal, VA 22630.

**Nelle McFather**—Hi, readers. Hope you enjoy my books as much as I enjoy writing them. Newsletter available.—Rt. 1, Box 351, Waycross, GA 31501.

**Judith McNaught**—I'm always delighted to hear from readers. If you have any comments or questions, my address is— P.O. Box 795491-Box RR, Dallas, TX 75379.

**Mary Martin**—Zebra historical romance author with next book coming out from Lynx.—3817 Lemay Ferry, #121, St. Louis, MO 63125.

**Anita Mills**—This Regency and historical author has special postcard made up for her books. A 15 cent stamp appreciated!—P.O. Box 7574, Overland Park, KS 66207.

**Peggy Moreland**—My stories come from my heart. If they have touched yours, please let me know! Bookmark available.—P.O. Box 2231, Edmond, OK 73013.

**Helen Myers**—Author of *Confidentially Yours* and *Kiss Me Kate* (A Silhouette Desire Man of the Month, Spring, 1980)—RT 2, Box 820-C, Winnsboro, TX 75494.

**Amanda O'Dell**—*Wanton Surrender* was a Zebra Heartfire Release. More are on the way. Bookmark/Newsletter available.—P.O. Box 27064, Pittsburgh, PA 15235.

**Miriam Pace**—I enjoy hearing from readers. Send SASE for tip sheets on fiction writing techniques—11079 Mars Pl., Mira Loma, CA 91752.

**Diana Palmer**—You're all great and I love you!—P.O. Box 844, Cornelia, GA 30531

**Doris Parmett**—LOVESWEPT author of *Diamond in the Rough, Sassy,* and *Heart-throb.* Newsletter and bookmark.—P.O. Box 554, New Providence, NJ 07974.

**Michalann Perry**—Newsletter and a bookmark straight from the heart of Texas!—P.O. Box 1291, Rowlett TX, 75088

**Paula Detmer Riggs**—I write for you, the reader. Please let me know if you enjoy my work! Bookmarks available.—P.O. Box 12306 La Jolla, CA 92037.

**Eugenia Riley**—Bookmark to readers for SASE, promotional materials to booksellers available— P.O. Box 840526, Houston, TX 77284-0526.

**Karen Robards**—I live in Kentucky, but my mail is immediately forwarded from my publisher—%Avon, 103 Madison Ave, NY, NY 10016.

**Doreen Roberts**—Would love to hear from you! Send SASE for bookmark and newsletter.—P.O. Box 219097, Portland, OR 97225.

**Nora Roberts**—Bookmarks available each season with my forthcoming releases. I appreciate your letters.—%Jesco, 17 James St., Bloomfield, NJ 07003.

**Lucia St. Clair Robson**—After writing western novels, I'm turning to the Orient for my next release. Hope you enjoy it!—P.O. Box 327, Arnold, MD 21012.

**Nan Ryan**—Get ready for more sizzling adventures. I'm moving around the country, presently in Georgia. Publisher will find me.—%Dell, 666 Fifth Ave., NY, NY 10103.

**Bertrice Small**—Do I have bookmarks! Gorgeous ones depicting my covers. *The Kadin* now available in hardcover (see p. 346.)—P.O. Box 765, Southold, NY 11971.

**SOUTHWEST WRITERS—Kathryn Davenport, Martha Hix, Karla Hocker, Emma Merritt, Constance O'Banyon** and **Evelyn Rogers**— cordially invite you to write for our free newsletter. Some bookmarks available. —P.O. Box 160674, San Antonio, TX 78280.

**Flora Speer**—Please send SASE for bookmarks and newsletter. I always enjoy hearing from my readers.—P.O. Box 347, West Hartford, CT 06107.

**Lisa Ann Verge** (a.k.a. Lisann St. Pierre)—I love to hear from my readers! For newsletter/bookmarks, do write.—P.O. Box 454, New York, NY 10028.

**Donna Winters**—Greetings from the author of *Great Lakes Romances.* Send large SASE for newsletter/autographed bookmark—P.O. Box 177, Caledonia, MI 49316.

**Eleanor Woods**—I always enjoy receiving mail from my readers. Bookmarks are available.—P.O. Box 385, Hattiesburg, MS 39401.

# Sources

**BOOKLOVERS CONVENTION —Phoenix, 1989**

TOP: *(L to R) Fred Darnell of the Book Rack chain, Ruth Langan, Virginia Darnell (Founder of the Book Rack), Nora Roberts.*
LEFT: *Scott Leroy, B. Dalton manager, with (front to back) Catherine Palmer, Michalann Perry, Judith Steel.*
RIGHT: *Edwin Buckhalter, publisher of Severn House.*
LOWER RIGHT: *(L to R) Marylyle Rogers, Sarah Edwards with Gerald Ratcliff, producer of the BOOKRAK catalog.*

# A Good Source
# is Hard
# to Find

$\mathcal{E}$ very romance reader and writer needs good sources today, so we worked conscientiously to compile the rest of this handbook with your needs in mind.

Feel confident that you are dealing with considerate and responsible people when you write to any of our sources. But be sure to send them your "wants" and a SASE when you write away for out-of-print titles.

By this time you are probably aware that a SASE stands for a self-addressed, stamped envelope (legal size is best). It is suggested that you include one for all the people you are addressing, including authors (except for Kathleen Woodiwiss, who, since the 1970s has not bothered to answer her fan mail because she doesn't have help!).

If you are interested in submitting a romance for publication, or have suggestions or complaints, we have listed the leading romance publishers' addresses.

Be aware that editors move like rabbits, so if you do not have the name of the current romance editor, address your request to the "romance editor."

One of the best ways to get information about writing and promoting romantic fiction, and the romance industry, plus have fun with kindred spirits, is to attend the annual Romantic Times Booklovers Convention. Everyone is welcome, husbands, too!

In 1990, the event will take place in San Antonio, and in 1991, New York City, to celebrate the 10th anniversary of *RT*. The ABA (American Book Association trade show) will also be held in Manhattan that week, so attendees will get a full menu of books, books, and more books.♥

## Romance Jargon

**AKA**
  Also known as
**Harl.**
  Abbreviation for Harlequin
**M & B**
  Mills & Boon of England

**SASE**
  Self-addressed, stamped envelope (legal size)
**SCAL**
  Berkley's Second Chance at Love series

332

333

336

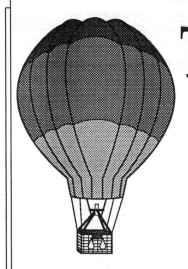

# CONVENTION MEMORIES
Phoenix, 1989

*Some of the Pocket authors winning awards at the Book-lovers Convention in Phoenix. (Front row, L to R) Mallory Dorn Hart, Kimberley Cates, Jude Deveraux, Ruth Langan. (Back): their proud editor, Linda Marrow.*

# Romance Publishers

*I*f you wish to explore the possibility of submitting a manuscript to any romance publisher, it is best to send a "query letter" that briefly describes the plot and characters of your novel, the length, the category, and your writing background. If an editor is interested, she will write back and ask to see the manuscript. Address query to "Romance Editor" and include a SASE for reply.

**Avon**
105 Madison Avenue
New York, NY 10016

**Ballantine**
201 E. 50th Street
NY, NY 10022

**Bantam**
666 Fifth Ave.
New York, NY 10103

**Berkley**
200 Madison Ave.
NY, NY 10016

**Dell**
666 Fifth Ave.
New York, NY 10103

**♥ Harlequin/Silhouette**
300 E. 42nd St.
New York, NY 10017

**♥ Leisure**
276 Fifth Ave.
NY, NY 10001

**NAL**
1633 Broadway
NY, NY 10016

**Pocket**
1230 Sixth Ave.
NY, NY 10020

**St. Martin's**
175 Fifth Ave.
NY, NY 10010

**Warner**
666 Fifth Ave.
NY, NY 10103

**Zebra/Pinnacle**
475 Park Ave. So.
NY, NY 10016

♥ Indicates that tip sheets are always available with SASE.
Call the Hot-Line, ☎ **718/237-1097**, when you have
questions about finding an editor, an agent, or if you need advice.

# Recommended Romance Agents
### and a few
### of their clients

**Edward J. Acton**
928 Broadway
NY, NY 10010
*(Bertrice Small, Jennifer Wilde)*

**Meredith Bernstein**
2112 Broadway
NY, NY 10023
*(Maura Seger, Mallory Dorn Hart)*

**Elaine Davie**
Village Gate Square
274 N. Goodman St.
Rochester, NY 14607
*(Marcia Evanick, Dean Barrett)*

**Libbi Goodman**
P.O. Box 47786
Phoenix, AZ 85068-7786
*(looking for mainstream
women's fiction)*

**Adele Leone**
26 Nantucket Place
Scarsdale, NY 10583
*(Janelle Taylor, Phoebe Conn)*

**Barbara Lowenstein**
121 W. 27
NY, NY 10001
*(Marion Chesney, Miriam Minger)*

**Denise Marcil**
316 W. 51st St.
NY, NY 10024
*(Mary Kay McComas, Laura Parker)*

**Evan Marshall**
228 Watchung
UpperMontclair, NJ 07043
*(Joan Hohl, Megan Daniel)*

**Alice Orr**
Kearns & Orr
686 Lexington Ave., #504
NY, NY 10022
*(new agency)*

**Jane Rotrosen**
318 E. 51st. St.
NY, NY 10022
*(Iris Johansen, Tom and Sharon
Curtis)*

**Pat Teal**
2036 Vista Del Rosa
Fullerton, CA 92631
*(Jill Marie Landis, Laura Taylor)*

**Maureen Walters**
Curtis Brown Agency
10 Astor Place
NY, NY 10003
*(Eileen Nauman, Sydney Clary)*

☛ ✉ **Send a query letter and a SASE to an agent.
Some of the above may charge nominal reading fees.**

# Book
# Promotion
# Tips

Over 100 romantic novels are being published each month, and an author is wise to plan marketing strategy for her book at least five months before it is published. Here's what to consider—

**Cover:** An author should confer with her editor if she has a strong feeling about the look/color/historical details.

**Positioning:** The prime spot is called "lead" title—at top of order form for distributors and book buyers. Fight for this, if possible!

**Promotion:** Advertising and promotional materials can be guaranteed if written into an author's contract. Otherwise, take your chances!

**Bookmarks:** This colorful promotional item is highly visible, effective, and inexpensive for publicizing an author's name and title.

**Excerpts:** Booksellers appreciate reading the opening chapter or a scene, or more (depending on author's budget), particularly when the novel is by a brand new author.

**Letters to Distributors/Wholesalers:** Authors should be in touch with their state wholesalers, who are partial to local writers. Personal letters to wholesalers nation-wide is another consideration. This can be done with *RT*'s monthly mailings to over 600 wholesalers.

**Reviews:** *Romantic Times* reviews all romance novels. Authors or editors should send galleys or manuscripts 2-3 months ahead of publication. Pre-publication quotes are useful on covers & promo materials.

**Advertising:** *Romantic Times* has rates available for black and white ads (full, half, and third of a page ) color (front, back and inside covers). Ads should be reserved 4-6 months before publication. *RT* makes up ads or they can be sent in camera ready.

**Promotional Services:** One of the reliable services for creating bookmarks, flyers, and ads is LIAISONS. (See opposite page.)
Another is JESCO, owned by Joan Schulhafer, 17 James Street, Bloomfield, NJ 07003, who can also handle TV, newspaper, and magazine publicity as well as author tours and promotion materials.

**Bookstores:** Authors can send out 25-100 bookmarks, and/or flyers, excerpts, etc., to over 500 avid romance bookstores known as Bookstores That Care in *RT*'s monthly magazine shipments.

# Hardcovers
# from
# Severn House

**BRANDEWYNE, REBECCA**
Upon a Moon-Dark-Moor

**CANHAM, MARSHA**
Blood of Roses

**CARTLAND, BARBARA**
Escape
Game of Love
Love on the Wind
Love Casts Out Fear
Royal Punishment

**COFFMAN, VIRGINIA**
Jeweled Darkness (Gothic)
Richest Girl in the World
(Contemp.)

**DEVERAUX, JUDE**
Enchanted Land

**JERINA, CAROL**
Embrace An Angel

**LEY, ALICE CHETWYND**
Masquerade of Vengeance
(Regency)

**LINDSEY, JOHANNA**
Captive Bride
Fires of Winter
Paradise Wild
Pirate's Love

**MARTEN, JACQUELINE**
Dream Walker
*(Unique new-age romance)*
Glory in the Flower

**MCBAIN, LAURIE**
Moonstruck Madness

**MCNAUGHT, JUDITH**
Whitney, My Love
Once and Always

**MILLER, LINDA LAEL**
Wanton Angel
Moonfire

**RYAN, NAN**
Outlaw's Kiss

**SHAW, LINDA**
Songbird

**SMALL, BERTRICE**
The Kadin

**SPENCER, LAVYRLE**
Sweet Memories

346

# Reference Books

**Burack, Sylvia**
*The Writer's Handbook:* 100 chapters of writing tips by famous authors & editors, plus 2200 markets. ($27.00)

**Crawford, Diane**
*Recipes for Romance:* 110 Romance writers share their recipes and comments. (Trade, $9.00)

**Falk, Kathryn**
*How To Write a Romance and Get It Published*
(New Revised Edition, available Feb., 1990, $5.95)

**Kenner, John**
*1001 Ways to Market a Book* (Trade, $15)

**Kidwell, Catherine**
*I Couldn't Put It Down:* How to Write Fiction in 10 Easy Lessons. (Trade, $8.00)

**Laudermilk, Sharon & Hamlin, Teresa**
*The Regency Companion:* A guide to the historical period for Regency readers.

**Lee, Linda**
*How To Write & Sell Romance Novels*: A step-by-step guide. (Trade, $10)

**McCormack, Thomas**
*The Fiction Editor:* A Book for Writers, Teachers, Publishers, Editors, and Anyone Else Devoted to Fiction. Scholarly, essential book that's provocative and stimulating for novelists. (Hardcover, $13)

**Shatzkin, Leonard**
*In Cold Type:* A revealing in-depth look behind the scenes of the publishing industry—a must read! (Hardcover, $18)

**Wibberly, Mary**
*To Writers With Love:* Methods and ideas for writing series romances by famous Harlequin author. (Trade, $9)

Add $2 per book for p/h. Make check payable to
*Romantic Times.*
Send to: **Romantic Times, 163 Joralemon St.,
Brooklyn Heights, NY 11201**

# Romantic
# Times

**"The Bible of Romantic Fiction..."**— USA Today

*S*tarted in 1981, *Romantic Times* reviews and rates over 100 romantic novels every issue—historicals, series, Regency, romantic supense, long contemporaries—and profiles authors, spotlights romance bookstores, and publishes letters and comments from readers.

*Romantic Times* goes to readers by home subscription, and is also sold at chain book stores, independents, and through hundreds of new and used bookstores across the country.

Bookstores That Care can order wholesale quantities (minimum of 6), and will receive a counter display, poster and monthly bookstore newsletter, along with over 100 booksmarks, posters, and other promotional materials. **Published bi-monthly, $2.75 per copy.**

**Subscription Rates:**
One Year, 6 issues, $15 (4th class), 2 Years, $25 (4th class)
One Year, 6 issues, $22 (1st class) 2 Years, $44 (1st class)
Canadian: One Year $25 (check made out to U.S. funds by bank)
Other countries, please send for rates.

# Rave
# Reviews

hen readers wanted coverage on other genres of fiction, *Romantic Times* started another book review magazine in 1987. *Rave Reviews* is divided into the various popular fiction genres—**mainstream contemporaries, historicals, mysteries, thrillers, sf/fantasy, horror,** as well as **romances.**

Reviewers are assigned to read all the new books and then they choose the best for review. A certain number of hardcovers (ones destined for the bestseller lists) are also included.

When an author is a famous name with a book that will be everywhere in sight, and it's a mediocre book—you'll see the exceptional bash. With so many good books being published, it doesn't seem worthwhile to take up space on bad reads just for the sake of it! Especially with the prices of books soaring.

The *Rave* staff profiles many established new authors as well as exciting new names on the scene. Editor Marc Cerasini, a leading expert on the horror and occult genres, has organized a great team.

*Rave Reviews* goes to chain bookstores and independents, as well as home subscribers. **Published bi-monthly, $2.75 per copy**

**Subscription Rates:**
   One Year, 6 issues, $15 (4th class), 2 Years, $25 (4th class)
   One Year, 6 issues, $22 (1st class) 2 Years, $44 (1st class)
   Canadian: One Year $25 (check made out to U.S. funds by bank)
   Other countries, please send for rates.

**MAKE CHECK PAYABLE TO ROMANTIC TIMES**

Special Issue                Issue #25

Writing the Regency Novel

# Fiction
# Writers

*R*eaders of *How To Write a Romance and Get It Published*
wrote in requesting more information about the writing and
marketing of romance novel. As a result, *Fiction Writers*
magazine came into existence in 1985.

It is devoted to the aspiring as well as the published writers, and
prints the latest news from editors, agents, and authors alike, as well
as articles on writing techniques, and author promotions.

Back issues are still available for some of the "genre editions."

**The Regency Edition:** a fact-filled issue of profiles, lists of publishers, and research books.

**The Western Edition:** everything you wanted to know to start
writing a western novel.

**Promoting a Novel: (1 and 2):** Two separate issues focusing on the
understanding of promotion and publicizing romance novels.

**Young Adult Romances:** Edited by YA author Cindi Savage,
contains full market information too. (Available Aug, 1989)

**Published quarterly,** *Fiction Writers* magazine is sold only
through home subscriptions at this time.

1 Year, 4 issues $20 (4th class) 2 Years, 8 issues $40
1 Year, 4 issues $24 (First class) 2Years, 8 issues $48
Back Issues, $5 each (Add $1 if you wish 1st class postage)

Make check payable to *Romantic Times*:
Send to **Fiction Writers, 163 Joralemon St., Brk, NY 11201**

# Manuscript Evaluation
# &
# *How To Write a Romance*
# Home Study Course

*M*any writers are unable to get professional criticism for their work because they do not belong to a critique group or live near a city where creative writing is taught. As a result of receiving unexplained rejection letters, many new writers feel hopeless and helpless.

Do not fret. Help is near, and it's not that expensive. Susan Perry, at *RT*, heads our Manuscript Evaluation service. She will see that your manuscript gets constructive criticism **and** you receive explicit directions for improving your work.

Over the years, this service has developed an expert staff—mainly New York editors who work free-lance, or are at home for a few years raising young children. They provide guidance to appropriate agents and editors, if the manuscript is publishable.

Send a SASE for the **MANUSCRIPT EVALUATION** brochure which outlines the guidelines. You can find expert help with a **query letter, outline, first chapter, partial manuscript,** or the **complete version.**

For severals years we've received requests for a personal **Home Study Romance Course.** There are many aspiring writers who don't have the slightest idea of how to plan, organize, and execute a romance novel, but they believe they have talent worthy of developing. Beginners can now "get started" through a special lesson plan and communicate (via the mail) with an expert teacher chosen by the *RT* staff.

If the ideas and characters are running around in your head, but you are not focusing (and sticking to) one plot and set of characters, an instructor could be an enormous help.

Send a SASE for the home-study (with a personal instructor) course— **How To Write a Romance.** You can choose from several categories: Historical, Series, or Regency.

## CONVENTION MEMORIES
### Phoenix, 1989

*The LIAISONS team for author promotions at the 7th annual Booklovers Convention in Phoenix. (L to R) Beverly Hunt, Sam Rinehold, Connie Rinehold.*

*(L to R) Annie and Gypsy, editors of PAPERBACK PREVIEWS, the monthly tabloid for ordering current books by mail.*

*Gerald Ratcliff (L), compiler of the BOOKRAK catalog, a great source for the reader, with Bertrice Small (holding her new hardcover edition of* The Kadin) *and Tom Huff a.k.a. Jennifer Wilde.*